Has Liberalism Failed Women?

This page intentionally left blank

Has Liberalism Failed Women?

Assuring Equal Representation in
Europe and the United States

Jytte Klausen and Charles S. Maier, eds.

palgrave

HAS LIBERALISM FAILED WOMEN?
© Jytte Klausen and Charles S. Maier, 2001
Softcover reprint of the hardcover 1st edition 2001 978-0-333-94680-0
All rights reserved. No part of this book may be used or reproduced in any manner whatsoever without written permission except in the case of brief quotations embodied in critical articles or reviews.

First published 2001 by
PALGRAVE
175 Fifth Avenue, New York, N.Y. 10010 and
Houndmills, Basingstoke, Hampshire RG21 6XS.
Companies and representatives throughout the world

PALGRAVE is the new global publishing imprint of St. Martin's Press LLC Scholarly and Reference Division and Palgrave Publishers Ltd (formerly Macmillan Press Ltd).

ISBN 978-1-349-42641-6   ISBN 978-0-230-10750-2 (eBook)
DOI 10.1057/9780230107502

Library of Congress Cataloging-in-Publication Data
Has liberalism failed women? : assuring equal representation in Europe and the United
States / Jytte Klausen and Charles S. Maier, eds.
  p. cm.
Includes bibliographical references and index.

  1. Women in politics—Europe. 2. Women in politics—United States. 3. Political participation—Europe. 4. Political participation—United States. 5. Sex discrimination against women—Europe. 6. Sex discrimination against women—United States. I. Klausen, Jytte. II. Maier, Charles S.

HQ1236.5.E85 H37   2001
305.42'094—dc21

2001021828

Library of Congress Cataloging-in-Publication Data available from the British Library.

A catalogue record for this book is available from the British Library.

Design by Letra Libre, Inc.

First edition: June 2001
10 9 8 7 6 5 4 3 2 1

Contents

Acknowledgments vii

PART I
THEORETICAL PERSPECTIVES

Chapter 1   Introduction   3
Charles S. Maier and Jytte Klausen

Chapter 2   The Descriptive Political Representation of Gender: An Anti-Essentialist Argument   19
Jane Mansbridge

Chapter 3   The Politics of Parity: Can Legal Intervention Neutralize the Gender Divide?   39
Claus Offe

Chapter 4   The French Parity Movement   55
Françoise Gaspard

PART II
PARITY AS AN ELECTORAL ISSUE

Chapter 5   Constitutionalizing Equal Access: High Hopes, Dashed Hopes?   69
Isabelle Giraud and Jane Jenson

Chapter 6   Breaking the Barriers: Positive Discrimination Policies for Women   89
Pippa Norris

Chapter 7   Women and the Third Way: Collaboration and Conflict   111
Anna Coote

Chapter 8   Changing the Rules of the Game: The Role of Law and the Effects of Party Reforms on Gender Parity in Germany   123
Christiane Lemke

PART III
POLICY PROCESSES

Chapter 9	From Equal Pay to Parity Democracy: The Rocky Ride of Women's Policy in the European Union *Agnès Hubert*	143
Chapter 10	Quotas, Parity, and the Discursive Dangers of Difference *Hege Skjeie*	165
Chapter 11	Constitutional Reform and Gender Mandates *Jutta Limbach*	177

PART IV
CAUTIONARY TALES

Chapter 12	The Distinctive Barriers to Gender Equality *Rogers M. Smith*	185
Chapter 13	Representation and the Electoral Interests of Women and African Americans: A Convergence at Last? *Carol Swain*	201
Chapter 14	When Women Voted for the Right: Lessons for Today from the Conservative Gender Gap *Jytte Klausen*	209

Contributors	229
Index	235

Acknowledgments

We are grateful to the Program for the Study of Germany and Europe at the Minda de Gunzburg Center for European Studies, Harvard University and the Center for German and European Studies, Brandeis University, for funding for the conference on which this book is based, with additional support from the European Union Center at the Center for European Studies, Harvard University. We also want to thank Lisa Eschenbach, who was responsible for organizing the conference, for her indefatigable cheer and efficiency. Mark Baker and Melissa Bass assisted in the preparation of the manuscript. We are indebted to both for their help in fixing prose and style.

This page intentionally left blank

Part I

Theoretical Perspectives

This page intentionally left blank

Chapter One

Introduction:
New Perspectives on the Use
of Parity Mandates and Quotas to
Guarantee Equality between Men and Women

Charles S. Maier and Jytte Klausen

This book presents to English-speaking readers a concept for assuring group representation—one based on gender, however, not race or ethnicity—advocated by many in Europe, but generally rejected out of hand in the United States. Contributors discuss the theory and experience of mandating quotas for the presence of women candidates for national office, whether by compelling electoral procedures that will return a fixed number to elective office or by requiring parties to nominate a minimal percentage. The rough analogue in the United States has been "affirmative action," which has been applied prevailingly to educational admissions, employment opportunity, job contracts, and only indirectly to voting. Quotas for guaranteed representation provide one among several possible measures available to boost the presence of underrepresented groups in public office. Even before the courts began to dismantle affirmative action as constitutionally suspect, advocates of affirmative action in the United States often separated the procedures they supported from the imposition of fixed quotas.

Proposals to change the way we elect our representatives often stimulate acute controversy. When Lani Guinier suggested changes to the U.S. electoral system that would guarantee minority representation, she was pilloried in most discussions and President Clinton withdrew her from consideration for national office.[1] The opposition her views evoked arose from several sources: American liberal reluctance to believe that specific categories of humanity should have the right to have their specificity guaranteed a numerically assured outcome of representatives; a general unwillingness to mandate equality (or proportionality) of outcomes rather than alleged equality of opportunity; concern over the multiplicity of categories and groups that might claim a specific quota of representation; and, so some advocates might charge, a persistent racism that denies the special historical burdens of African Americans. Others found it particularly problematic that Guinier would see a cause for public concern when whites vote for white representatives, but not when blacks vote for blacks.[2]

In Europe, however, quotas for female representation have not evoked the same shocked outcry, even when opponents have vigorously challenged their wisdom or their compatibility with classical individualist liberalism. In the United States, affirmative action has been employed to address racial and gender inequalities, but in the European context the focus has, for reasons that merit discussion, been primarily on correcting the numerical imbalance between men and women in political organizations, governments, and public institutions. There have been little public outcry, no manifestations of mass protests either for or against, and the changes that are taking place have been debated mostly by intellectuals and couched in the subdued language of legal theory and constitutionalism. From the boldest French proposals to assure an equal representation of men and women comes the term *parité* or "parity," which is what the editors have adopted as a shorthand for the range of legally, indeed constitutionally mandated systems for assuring quotas of female representation. In fact, though, the essays discuss a broader menu of alternatives. This introduction seeks to place in the context of institutional experience and the longer theories of representation what is at stake. The editors present these studies for the purpose of discussion, not advocacy. Jytte Klausen took the initiative in organizing the April 1999 conference on "Gender Parity and the Liberal Tradition: Proposals and Debates in Europe and the United States" held at the Minda de Gunzburg Center for European Studies at Harvard University, a gathering that brought together enthusiastic reporters of recent experience, skeptical discussants, and those remained undecided. As the Director of the Center for European Studies, Charles Maier served as co-convener.

The debate centered on several broad issues: the first was the capacity of liberalism or liberal democracy, conceived as an ideology postulating the political rights and participation of formally equal individuals, to accommodate the feminist demands for quotas of representatives. A second theme that emerged was the impact on feminism of working within liberal-democratic political institutions, as it became "mainstreamed" and underwent the transformation that afflicts all successful reform movements. Finally, the papers examined the political and institutional consequences that might emerge from parity legislation. A full picture of the consequences of the legislative changes already attained cannot yet be made, and no definitive answers exist. The broad strokes of constitutional language do not become operative on their own, but require subordinate legislation, rules, and regulations before they can be translated into practical policy. Despite the simplicity of the demand for parity representation, the policies designed to sustain it are often technically complicated and raise complex issues. It is axiomatic that in policymaking, the means create their own politics. It may turn out that the quest for parity representation is fraught with pitfalls of the kind associated with "unintended consequences," including the creation of a new policy elite that will develop a bureaucratic interest in maintaining particular policies.

This introduction summarizes first some of the challenges for liberal theories of representation, then the institutional context in which the parity movement has arisen. So too the essays in this book have been grouped to take up questions of theory and then diverse experiences. The discussion of feminist theory and parity arguments here do not intend to recapitulate the longstanding and familiar controversies over equality and difference. Most contributors and the editors take for granted that women legitimately stress their "difference" as well as their inherent claims to political equality and that legislation can legitimately recognize and address relevant differences, as it has ever since workplace protection laws of the last century. To arrive at substantively equal claims and privileges in a political community, legislators and constitutional drafters have recognized inherent vulnerabilities or historical disabilities. But whose vulnerabilities, whose disabilities receive particular attention? On what grounds? How are they to be redressed? When do claims of difference become grounds for affirmative action or other compensatory mandates? And, as feminist theorists would add, should not claims of difference constitute claims for representation even if no vulnerability or disability is involved? To which those uneasy with such claims ask: at what limiting point does the recognition of difference undercut the claims for equality on the part of those who qualify for no recognition of difference?

Parity and Representation

Classical liberal democratic theory was preoccupied enough with issues of extending equality that it rarely discussed difference. Feminist claimants in the French Revolution deployed ideas of difference as well as equality—those whom Joan Scott refers to as pressing the "paradox" of both—but they did not win either. Interestingly enough, conservative theorists remained more open to the claims of difference and collective attributes. Edmund Burke argued for Ireland and India; John C. Calhoun, America's brilliant but antidemocratic theorist, urged that group rights be protected by requiring a "concurrent majority" be required for legislation. But the group he sought to protect comprised slaveholders in the South.[3] Even Mill, who eloquently argued for women's suffrage, did not envisage women as forming a collective subject that would organize under the proportional representation he advocated; they would participate as a class of voters and citizens in general. Mill recognized that legislators represented "interests," and only through collective deliberation might legislation become disinterested. He would, one can imagine, have had little problem with suggesting that while women might not have constituted an interest in the nineteenth century, interest was when interest claimed.[4] As Judith Butler has argued, agency is created at the site of political struggle; it is not necessarily preexistent.[5]

These issues remain difficult, but equally challenging is the meaning of representation. The overarching question to which both editors have continually returned is what is involved in political "representation." Representation was a necessity once political units became too large to allow for every citizen's participation in an assembly. The right to speak for citizens had to be vested in a small number of legislators. But what did it take to speak for a larger number? Early notions of "virtual representation"—that the good and disinterested representative could speak in general for constituents barred from voting for him—came under attack in the aftermath of the American and French revolutionary eras, even if suffrage exclusions yielded very slowly. And specific exclusions on the basis of race, gender, colonial subjection, resident alien status, illiteracy, relative poverty, lack of fixed abode, youth, insanity, and criminal conviction remained in place and indeed some still do. But the franchise constitutes only the first step in achieving representation. If women and racially excluded voters ultimately got the vote, should they also achieve a minimal number of their own to speak for them?

Entitlement to spokespersons by one scheme or another does not necessarily resolve the problem of representation. Parity arguments suggest that representative systems require a substantial quotient of women among the representatives. Several possible reasons can be appealed to, each of them eminently worth serious debate. The first refers to the needs of the group represented; it presupposes that "speaking for" requires not just judgment or sympathy but a sharing of attributes. The citizens' dignity and worth as a woman or a minority member requires having a legislator with the same inherent attributes. Perhaps because only a woman finally will know what a women's needs are—but perhaps because modern democracy values the replication of gender and racial characteristics among the ranks of those who have power.

This implies that the legitimate role of political representation is not just, or maybe not even primarily deliberation—as Mill believed it was and as advocates of discursive rationality suggest today—but some sort of physical or visible epitomization of the public. This is a claim that may become widely accepted, above all when so much of public debate involves visual media. Still, it seems to us of a less initial persuasiveness than claims made on the basis of equality, citizenship, and the need for voice in deliberative procedures. There is no inherent reason that the replication of difference cannot be agreed on as at least one prerequisite for representative government—but it does not follow from any simple extension of Enlightenment premises. It is a debate that has yet to be confronted fully and openly in the United States.

Parity arguments can be based on a more general assumption, namely that the quality of democracy as a whole—its value for men as well as women—is diminished if a significant group does not have its own members among the representatives. If this premise is accepted, then the persistently low numbers of elected women should be redressed for the sake of all of us.

A third argument would involve claims of civic education: ever since Tocqueville and Mill, the process of choosing representatives and of political discussion in general has been viewed as transforming self-regarding individuals into citizens with a more expansive set of values. Parity outcomes might contribute decisively to the civic awareness of women or all of us.

Of course, each claim can be debated. If parity is demanded, which groups are to be excluded from asking for a quota of parliamentary making such a plea? One ready answer is that parity is a response not merely to strikingly low relative presence of women among officials, but to established histories of legal discrimination and prejudice. Parity helps make up for earlier injustice. Like affirmative action it can be defended as, in effect, a sort of historical reparation.

The European Context and Transatlantic Lessons

In Europe today, parity schemes have been partially accepted without any fundamental objections being raised. On June 1, 1999, the series of amendments to the treaty foundation of the European Union (EU) agreed to by the governments of the member states in the Treaty of Amsterdam from 1997 became law. (Some member states have yet to ratify the changes.) Among many other things, the treaty transformed an old article forbidding discrimination on the basis of nationality—an essential lever for the breaking down of protectionism in what started out as a free trade agreement—into a basic rights charter, as the *Charter of Fundamental Rights of the*

European Union.[6] In addition to the old prohibition, the treaty foundation for the European Union now also prohibits discrimination on the basis of "sex, race or ethnicity, religion or belief, disability, age or sexual orientation."[7] Other amendments defined the constitutional obligations with respect to women further by requiring that, "the Community shall aim to eliminate inequalities, and to promote equality, between men and women." The European Commission, the executive arm of the union, was charged with the task of actively combating discrimination and the European Court of Justice (ECJ) given judicial oversight.

The treaty changes cap similar developments in the member states. In June and July 1999, French legislators voted to change the French constitution to say that "the law favors equal access by men and women to electoral mandates and elective functions."[8] The amendment eliminated existing judicial objections against affirmative action policy based on the constitution prior to the change and paved the way for a new law that requires all political parties to have 50 percent of all electoral candidates be women. The parties will loose campaign funding, which in France is provided exclusively by the state, if they do not comply. Legal developments in Germany have followed a similar path. The Basic Law from 1949 stipulated that men and women should have equal rights. The original gender neutral language became the focus of criticism after the Constitutional Court held state level affirmative action plans that awarded women priority over men in public sector hirings unconstitutional with the argument that they violated men's rights to be judged on merit. A proposal to change the constitution gained support in the wake of the decision and in 1994 the Basic Law (the German constitution) was changed to allow for proactive policies promoting equality. The constitution now stipulates that, "the state shall promote the realization of equal rights for men and women and strive to abolish existing disadvantages." The Constitutional Court subsequently relinquished its objections against affirmative action plans and, in 1997, upheld another plan scheme that had been brought before the court.

These three cases are by no means isolated events but rather the tip of the iceberg. In countries with less strenuous traditions for constitutional constraint and court review—notably Great Britain and the Scandinavian countries—the focus has for a decade or more been on amending public sector procedures, party rule books, and trade union constitutions to guaranteeing equal access and representation for women. Considered as a whole, the reform efforts reflect a significant change in strategy on the part of women's organizations and feminists. The movement's success—both in terms of the broad scope of legislative changes and increased recruitment of women into elected offices—is best described as a movement. Indeed, as is characteristic of movements, the demands and the narratives used to justify them vary from country to country even as the initiators have looked abroad for inspiration and support for their demands. The present book may well be the first attempt to discuss the reforms under one cover and as instances of a coherent challenge to liberal constitutionalism.

The European embrace of affirmative action policies is one more example of the importance of transatlanticism as an intellectual current. Will Europeans face some of the same issues that have arisen in the United States in connection with the evolution of affirmative action from anti-discrimination legislation to the more controversial use of racial group preferences prescribing parameters for the distribution of certain benefits or positions of influence? Some immediate difference can be observed that puts the European experiment on different tracks. The beneficiaries have been women alone. Most quotas have, this far at least, been voluntarily adopted by political organizations and applied primarily to internal organizational affairs. Although quotas for preferential hiring of women in the public sector exist, no similar attempt has been made to plan access to other distributive goods, public contracts or higher education, for example, as in the United States. Affirmative action policies have not—at least not yet (see the chapter by Agnès Hubert)—imposed significant restraint or administrative burdens on private actors. This may change, however, as the EU regulatory framework on gender equality develops. It has been proposed, for example, that one way to promote gender equality may be to require public authorities and private industry to submit "gender impact statements" (similar to those now prepared to assess environmental impact) prior to the initiation of certain new policies or projects.

The U.S. civil rights movement gave birth to two important levers for racial and gender equality—affirmative action and the failed campaign for an equal rights amendment, known as the ERA, to the U.S. Constitution—which serve as both a source of inspiration and a cautionary lesson for the parity movement. The ERA, had it passed, would have prohibited "the abridgment or denial of equal rights by federal or state law on the grounds of sex." Passed by both houses of the U.S. Congress, the amendment died when the deadline for ratification by the states expired in 1982. At the end of the campaign, the fight for the ERA was widely regarded as having helped the Right and hurt the Left, giving birth to a "new Right" that helped elect Ronald Reagan as president in 1980.[9] It is not clear if the parity movement has the potential similarly to stimulate a political backlash capable of undoing the movement and its gains. The French parity movement has stimulated strong opposition but, as Françoise Gaspard writes in the chapter that follows, mostly among intellectuals rather than among conservative women's groups, many of which instead have come out in favor.

The task of drawing lessons is complicated by the fact that it is not clear what the lessons may be. Current controversies in the United States regarding affirmative action regard the means for achieving racial equality more than the goal. The question arises if any inherent differences exist between voluntarily adopted equality mandates, in use in Great Britain and Germany, or the constitutional mandates now imposed by the French constitution and perhaps also by the European Union. Since the reach and the practical implications of the new treaty language is not yet clear, we can only speculate about the trajectory that EU gender equality regulation may take. Generally speaking, new EU capacities are established through a protracted interaction process between the European Court of Justice, the European Commission, and member-state governments. Were gender equity to become a matter of EU competence, it is reasonable to anticipate that the means of implementation will assume the usual character of directive, rules, and statements of objectives, which it is then up to the member states to enforce. The prospect of seeing gender equality join the already very long list of EU regulatory policies is not a pretty one. It is axiomatic in political science that the means of policy are not neutral to the end. It may be the case that the specific ways in which parity mandates are adopted by organizations and imposed on national legal frameworks matter more for the politics of gender equality than the debate has this far acknowledged.

Consequences of Parity

Do the legal changes implied by the new means for achieving political equality between men and women challenge the practice and theory of twentieth-century liberal constitutionalism? The answer provided by advocates of the use of quotas—and as Françoise Gaspard acknowledges in the chapter that follows, parity obviously implies a quota, even if it one that simply furnish men and women with numerically proportional representation—is both yes and no. They point to statistical evidence that, if left to the "hidden hand" of the political system as it has functioned for the better part of the century, women will not get a fair share of political power. They also point out that contemporary liberalism already tolerates rules that by virtue of their historical origin and context have tended to guarantee a specific outcome. The difference, it is argued (see the chapter written by Hege Skjeie) is simply that in place of the covert preference for men perpetuated by gender neutrality, the new rules ensure that women are fairly included. In summary, yes, parity is a criticism of liberalism because liberal designs have failed to produce the equality between the sexes that application of a gender-blind constitution should have been expected to bring about. And no, parity is not incompatible with liberalism because gender equality mandates are not a big change within the already commodious framework of liberal practice, which has periodically sought to overcome entrenched inequalities, whether of access to health care, education, and life chances in general.

But are parity provisions a means or an end? To cite Mill again, "the whole of history consists of the slow process by which [barriers of sex, class, and social position] have since been wearing away."[10] The problem was that Mill assumed—as have liberal thinkers since—that gender-neutral constitutionalism would be sufficient to provide for the elimination of male privilege, which he regarded as a function of legal inequality. Cultural and social inequality confounded nineteenth-century liberalism. Parity can be defended as a means of chipping away at more of those inequalities that arise from gender. But the arguments on its behalf are often drawn from the disparity of men and women in the legislators, not the policy outcomes that might derive from that disparity. It was left to the political process—and to economic development—to determine the exact degree of equality and the areas of public and private life in which equality was important. The anticipated link between formal rights and change in the gender balance of legislatures has been slow to materialize.[11] In 1945, women occupied only 3 percent of the seats in the lower houses of national parliaments in 26 Western countries. Three decades later, slow progress brought the number up to less than 12 percent. Even today, women hold only on average 13.4 percent of the seats in the lower houses (or single houses) in European countries (not just the EU member-states). The average encompasses 12.9 percent women in the U.S. House of Representatives and 38.9 percent of the seats in the Nordic countries, both figures historical highs.[12] With a few and recent exceptions—which are without exception examples of the efficiency of quotas—gross political inequality persisted for five to seven decades of full voting rights.[13] These statistics provided ammunition for the movement to change laws on two scores. The lack of any real progress on women's access to political offices suggested on the one hand that stasis could be broken only by means of rule changes, while on the other hand the successful use of quotas by Scandinavian political parties showed that changing the rules worked.

Skeptics have questioned the use of parity mandates because they may lead to the creation of a dualist political system based on sex. One concern is that if women are perceived as being elected on the basis of quotas and having not "earned" their seat, they may exert only a diminished political influence. Thus far this seems an unfounded worry. The new recruits have blended into party organizations much in need of new hands and energy. But other objections also arise in light of the potential results of parity quotas. Men with seniority and experience might be replaced by inexperienced women. If too few qualified women were interested in political careers, parties might be compelled to fill the "quota" seats with unqualified candidates. Having to run against the skewed odds imposed by quotas might discourage good male candidates from running for office. If for example, fifteen men and five women compete for ten places on the party election ticket (in Europe parties control the ticket), the five women would be granted seats without competition, but only one out of three men would be selected.

It will take time before the actual effects of quotas are felt, but judged on the basis of the Scandinavian countries in which quotas have been in use for some time, the constraints of electoral politics and party competition quickly dull any adverse edge. Quotas act, in effect, as a one-time term limit on male incumbents. Once women have been elected to take the place of a man, the life of the party goes on without unduly handicapping male participants. Voters do not vote for candidates for reasons of sex alone, and once women have been elected, the incumbency factor works to their favor. When it comes to issues, women do not form a bloc, and one of the effects of quotas has actually been to make disagreements between female representatives more visible.

The displacement of men has been more apparent in some arenas of representation than in others, for example, in the case of party leadership councils where trade union representatives sometimes were the first casualties. (Because unions always have relied heavily on seniority as a norm for the allocation of representative office, union leaders are often elderly men even today when the gender composition of union memberships has changed radically.) The other side of the coin is that quotas have promoted elite circulation and opened up new population groups for recruitment by parties. In part because the evidence is not yet in, discussions of the effect of quotas often assume the character of opponents and supporters looking at the same evidence and one side declaring the glass half-empty and other announcing it half-full. In actuality, we are mostly confined to theorizing about the political calculus of gender mandating because we know too little.

Quotas, State Intervention, and the Left's New Agenda

Quotas are not just a formal constitutional or political innovation. They also represent a form of social planning because they aim to guarantee equality of results, not just facilitate equality of opportunity as do more fluid policies (see the chapter by Jane Mansbridge). The parity debate thus has continuities with earlier controversies over political efforts to assure greater substantive economic equality, as during the Great Depression of the 1930s, and social reforms thereafter. Like economic planners, the parity movement advocates are impatient with the results produced by unfettered market outcomes and want to plan for equality of results by using the rule-making capacity of states to fix it. However, as in the past, those resisting appeal to the deviation from the formal rules, not the potential results.

Curiously, the parity thrust for gender equality has been met with no comparable resistance as emerged against earlier social and economic reforms, whether for national schemes of insurance, high progressive taxation, or rights for trade unions. Indeed, quotas for the representation of women—be they 30 or 50 percent—have been voluntarily adopted by the organizations that employ them and have been regarded as a means for reaching larger strategic objectives. Nonetheless, there have been challenges to earlier affirmative action schemes on the basis of provisions for gender equality, and parity plans sometimes represent responses to earlier defeats. The demise of what amounted to a "safe seats for women only" policy briefly employed by the British Labour Party is a case in point. As part of the party's decade-long reform effort to overcome the legacy of political exile during the Thatcher years, women activists persuaded the party to accept a series of all-women shortlists in safe-seat by-elections. The strategy guaranteed the election of a number of new women members of parliament, but in 1996, two disgruntled men persuaded an industrial tribunal to consider the all-women shortlists in violation of the Sex Discrimination Act. The tribunal held with the men, and the experiment was stopped. Both the German Constitutional Court and the French *Conseil d'Etat* rejected affirmative action plans with the argument that they discriminated against men. It was decisions like these that made feminists abandon the gender-neutral language that dominated post-1945 equality legislation and argue for gender-specific legislation.

The feminist turn toward parity ideas has coincided with the emergence of a "new constitutionalism" on the part of European left-wing parties. Casting around for a reformist agenda that compensated for the dismantling of statist economic policies, the "Third Way" of Tony Blair and Lionel Jospin has looked to changes in legal institutions as a lever for progressive equality. Basic rights, devolution, and an enhanced role for courts and judges in determining what is fair and what is not fair does not require increased taxation or market regulation, but still allows left-wing parties to cast themselves as radical reformers. The constitutionalist approach to gender equality also exploited the weakening of national political institutions that has been a byproduct of European integration. The process of integration encouraged the shift to a regulatory approach in place of the redistributive policy template that dominated in an earlier era's attack on inequality. Since the EU does not and cannot engage in redistribution, except between regions, it follows that the policy means available are restricted to regulatory action and court action leveraged through the ECJ. Certainly some critical aspects of gender inequality could still be addressed by redistributive means if policymakers were to decide that redistribution is once more possible. It is nevertheless also the case that redress for inequality between the sexes requires substantively different types of policies than did class inequality.

The curious disability of the new state-form that the European Union represents compared to the twentieth-century model of national parliamentary democracy based on strong parties and interests groups further encourages the development of a new civic form of claim-making. Reform in the European Union is based on the assertion of "rights" through courts, promoted by public interest groups armed with lawyers competent to argue cases before the court, and EU-based actors eager to establish vertical networks of extra-electoral representation that bypasses national governments. The implicit adoption of a more American mode of claim-making and interest representation based on the definition of civic rights is both serendipitous and deliberate. Budgetary austerity and fiscal conservatism are obviously important contextual variables that have worked to encourage a shift in political strategies from redistributive claims to the assertion of rights with indeterminate price tags.

It is ironic that European activists have seen the advantages of a legally oriented affirmative action approach in a period when United States courts and commentators have shown increased uneasiness with such remedies to persistent inequality of outcomes. Still, it seems unlikely that the last word has been spoken in America or in Europe. Group consciousness in politics—whether in the pressing of collective historical claims, the demand for a share of public commemoration, or the strategic calculations of candidates for office—remains as high as it ever been in the United States, and is becoming ever more salient in European polities. Debates on gender quotas arise naturally in such a discursive milieu. And even if particular remedies are rejected, the discussion will serve us well in thinking through the premises of the rights regime our polities already have in place. It is in that spirit that we present this book.

A Note on Organization and Contributors

A few of the contributors have been important actors in promoting reform. Jutta Limbach is the first woman to become chief justice of the German Constitutional Court and has played an important role in the reformulation of German legal thought on equality issues. Françoise Gaspard, a former mayor and member of the French National Assembly, was one of the authors (together with Claude Sevan-Schreiber and Anne Le Gall) of the book that launched the parity movement, *Au Pouvoir, Citoyennes! Liberté, Égalité, Parité,* from 1992. As an advisor to the Forward Studies Unit in the European Commission, Agnés Hubert as helped build EU policies on gender equality. Their contributions detail the legal reasoning or lay out the philosophy and strategies of the movement.

Some contributors reflected on the distribution of costs and benefits of the "new constitutionalism" across different social and political actors, from parties and unions to courts, as well as between the two sexes, while others tried to predict the results of the outcomes. Claus Offe, as well as Isabelle Giraud and Jane Jenson, see reasons to be concerned that the constitutionalist approach to equality will divert attention from the paramount importance of social issues. Based on the German and Norwegian examples respectively and focusing more on questions of political representation and participation than social questions, Christiane Lemke and Hege Skjeie instead find reasons to be optimistic about the gains made by means of rule changes. Pippa Norris and Anna Coote stress how the recruitment of women to the political parties, the British Labour Party in particular, has helped save a party system in deep crisis. By pinpointing some of the reasons—often serendipitous rather than principled ones—that reform became possible, Norris and Coote also suggest that the reforms may owe less to feminism than to the Left's desire to find a road back to political power after the collapse of the "Golden Age" welfare state. Jytte Klausen cautions that the constitutional approach works to eliminate partisan gains from gender equality reforms and the politics of reform is far more contingent than often anticipated by advocates. Both ERA and U.S. affirmative action policies loom large as a comparative backdrop that can be used to suggest lessons or parallels to the current European initiatives, particularly in the chapters by Jane Mansbridge and Rogers Smith. Conversely, Carol Swain takes the European experience as a source of inspiration for considering the possibilities for a new approach to affirmative action in the United States.

Notes

1. Lani Guinier, *The Tyranny of the Majority. Fundamental Fairness in Representative Democracy* (New York: Free Press, 1994).
2. Lani Guinier, "No Two Seats: The Elusive Quest for Political Equality," *Virginia Law Review* 77 (November): 1456.

3. Joan Wallach Scott, *Only Paradoxes to Offer: French Feminists and the Rights of Man* (Cambridge, MA: Harvard University Press, 1996). Analogous issues arose in the treatment of ethnic or national minorities in the context of the nation-state. Even the Wilsonian premises of the Paris Peace Conference—that granting nation-state status to peoples earlier denied was a first principle of liberal internationalism—endeavored to secure the position of the minorities within the new states. Unhappy experience led to a more general equality-only premise to the United Nations Convention on Human Rights in l947, but in recent years the pendulum has swung back to the protection of group rights, and cultural and sometimes political autonomy.

4. John Stuart Mill, *Representative Government* in *Utilitarianism, Liberty, Representative Government* (London and New York: Everyman Edition, 1960), pp. 240–41, 248–75. For a robust defense of women's suffrage that combines arguments from equality with women's particular needs, as "being physically weaker, they are more dependent on law and society for protection," see pp. 290–92. Mill's concepts would have allowed a women's party to capture roughly half a legislature, but presumably once women had the franchise, no need for such a party would exist.

5. Judith Butler, "Contingent Foundations," in Butler, Seyla Benhabib, Drucilla Cornell, and Nancy Fraser, *Feminist Contentions: A Philosophical Exchange* (New York and London: Routledge, 1995), pp. 47–51. Butler provocatively asked, "Who is the feminist 'We'?" and argued that every collective agent is subject to redefinition, contestation, and overhaul, even (and perhaps not fully consistently) as somehow it—the category of women—subsists.

6. The Charter contains 52 articles, each of which is backed up by a more or less developed net of EU and national rules, resolutions, and legislation, as well as court rulings with the European Court of Justice claiming ultimate authority. See

    http://www.europarl.eu.int/charter/en/default.htm

7. Now Article 13, previously Article 6a. Article 2 of the Consolidated Treaty places "equality between men and women" as an objective for the community on par with, for example, "high level of employment" and "a high degree of competitiveness and convergence." Article 3.2. states that "the Community shall aim to eliminate inequalities, and to promote equality, between men and women."

8. *Journal Officiel* (157) July 9, 1999. The vote marks the conclusion of a process that began when the Constitutional Council voided a 1982 law creating numerical quotas giving women 30 percent of the slots on ballots in municipal elections.

9. Jane J. Mansbridge, *Why We Lost the ERA* (Chicago: Chicago University Press, 1986).

10. John Stuart Mill, *The Subjection of Women* (Indianapolis: Hackett, 1988), p. 46.

11. Women acquired suffrage in most Western democracies within a decade of male suffrage. The exceptions were France, where women could not vote until 1944, and Switzerland, where they were not allowed to vote in national elections until 1971.
12. http://www.ipu.org/wmn-e/world.htm
13. Andrew Reynolds, "Women in the Legislatures and Executives of the World: Knocking at the Highest Glass Ceiling," *World Politics* 51:4 (1999):547–572 (esp. p. 557).

This page intentionally left blank

Chapter Two

The Descriptive Political
Representation of Gender:
An Anti-Essentialist Argument

Jane Mansbridge

This analysis has two prongs. First, I argue that democratic representation should facilitate the two functions of deliberation and aggregation. Second, I argue that representative arrangement should be subject to the processes of strict scrutiny and affirmative action in the context of historical patterns of domination and subordination.

The logic runs as follows: 1) On the issues that affect the polity, democratic deliberation and aggregation are most legitimate when political interests are represented in the decision-making assembly in proportion to their representation among the population. Democratic deliberation is best performed by "descriptive" representatives (for example, women representing women) in the particular historical contexts of (a) a history of communicative distrust and (b) uncrystallized interests. 2) When a polity has experienced a history of group domination and subordination, proportional descriptive representation of the subordinate group is unlikely to arise naturally without some form of affirmative action. When historical patterns of domination and subordination can be identified, therefore, they require conscious redress.[1]

The analysis is anti-essentialist because it relies for its key arguments on historical, contingent processes. Its arguments for strict scrutiny and affirmative action rely on historical processes of domination and subordination. Its arguments for descriptive representation rely on the historical processes of communicative distrust and uncrystallized interests.

Because part of this argument relates to "democratic legitimacy," I must note at the outset that "legitimate democracy" in my analysis is a regulative ideal. That is, it is an ideal that no actual democracy can ever reach in full. It is an ideal toward which democracies should strive, knowing that they can never attain that ideal in its perfect form. For full legitimacy, the *deliberative* function would require perfect information and communication in an "ideal speech situation" in which power is absent.[2] For full legitimacy, the *aggregative* function, appropriate for instances of irresolvable conflict, would require equal power from each participant. These conditions are not achievable. Thus, in this analysis, democracies never attain full normative legitimacy. Rather, democracies approach normative legitimacy to the degree that their processes approach the conditions of legitimacy. "Good enough" democracy is all we can hope for, along with democracy that, recognizing the costs of change, tries to make strides toward greater legitimacy.[3]

The Deliberative and Aggregative Functions of Democracy

Representative assemblies have, crudely speaking, two functions—deliberation and aggregation. In the deliberative function, the goal should be to represent all perspectives that can contribute information and insight. In the aggregative function, the goal should be to represent in proportion to their numbers in the population those interests that come in conflict on the issue at hand. These two functions of deliberation and aggregation thus generate principles of representation that indicate what interests ought to be represented on each political issue.

In its deliberative mode, representative democracy aims at understanding which policies are good for the polity as a whole, which policies are good for a representative's constituents, and when the interests of various groups within the polity and constituency conflict. It also aims at transforming interests and creating commonality when that commonality can be genuinely good for all. This deliberative function, which aims at understanding, demands that ideally a representative body should include every perspective that might generate information or insight relevant to the understanding that leads to a decision.

Understanding the deliberative function of representative democracy allows us to identify which—of the many and varied perspectives and interests that each individual has—ought to be represented in the decision-making arena, and when. The answer is relatively obvious: the perspectives and interests of particular individuals should be represented in collective deliberation when those perspectives and interests are relevant to a collective decision.

In many cases, the perspectives and interests relevant to a collective decision can be represented by individuals who do not themselves have those perspectives and interests but who are otherwise qualified to represent them. Specific forms of training (such as training in the law), specific forms of experience (such as experience in a legislature), and even the very distance someone may have from an issue by not having a personal interest or perspective on it—any of these may make someone a better representative of another's interests than the other would be him or herself. Good representation in these cases does not require personal involvement. Effective principal-agent mechanisms ensure, or at least increase the probability of, good representation.

In other cases, however, the relevant interests and perspectives are best represented by individuals who bear those interests and perspectives in their own persons and see them through the lens of their own experience. Representative deliberation is enhanced by such "descriptive" representation in at least two contexts—a history of communicative distrust and moments of uncrystallized interests.

Communicative Distrust

The quality of the mutual communication between representative and constituent varies from group to group and from era to era. Historical circumstances can interfere with adequate communication between members of one group and members of another, particularly if one group is historically dominant and the other historically subordinate. A history of dominance and subordination typically breeds inattention, even arrogance, on the part of the dominant group and distrust on the part of the subordinate group.

In such conditions of impaired communication, including impairment caused by inattention and distrust, the shared experience imperfectly captured by descriptive representation facilitates vertical communication between representatives and constituents. Representatives and voters who share some version of a set of common experiences and the outward signs of having lived through those experiences can often read one another's signals relatively easily and engage in relatively accurate forms of shorthand communication. Representatives and voters who, in addition, share membership in a subordinate group can also forge bonds of trust based on that shared experience of subordination.[4]

In the United States, for example, African American constituents in districts represented by an African American legislator are more likely to contact their representatives than African American constituents in districts represented by a European American legislator. As one black congressman commented, "Black constituents feel comfortable with me and see that I feel comfortable with them." Historically subordinate groups differ from one another in this dimension. Women constituents in districts represented by a woman are *not* more likely to contact their representatives than women constituents in districts represented by a man. Although problems in communication between men and women exist, the size of the male/female gaps in communication is probably smaller than the size of gaps in communication created by race, nationality, or class.[5]

For voters in the United States, many vital interests are represented through what I call "surrogate" representation—representation by legislators elected from other districts.[6] Surrogate representatives need not be descriptive representatives. But descriptive representation often plays its most useful role in the surrogate process, as representatives who are themselves members of a subordinate group help circumvent the barriers to communication between dominant and subordinate groups. In the United States, black representatives are likely to be contacted by blacks "throughout the region," not just in their own districts. The district administrator for Mickey Leland, a black Texas Democrat, told Carol Swain: "What people don't understand is that Mickey Leland must be the [black] Congressman for the entire Southwest." When activists in the struggle for an Equal Rights Amendment to the constitution did not trust the advice of the senator with whom they were working, their distrust stemmed in part from the fact that the senator and his major staffer were both men. With the staffer reportedly dismissing the activists as "hysterical women," the barriers to communication were large.[7]

When there is a strong history of communicative distrust—as there is in the United States between African Americans and European Americans and to a lesser degree between women and men—descriptive representation greatly facilitates the communication between constituent and representative, representative and constituent. This enhanced vertical communication improves the larger deliberative democratic process.

Uncrystallized Interests

In certain historical moments, citizen interests on particular issues are relatively "uncrystallized." Those issues have not been on the political agenda long, candidates have not taken public positions on them, and political parties are not organized around them. In Central Europe immediately after the transition to democracy, for example, many political interests were relatively uncrystallized, as hundreds of new political parties struggled to define themselves on the issue map. (One Polish party called itself the "Party X," using a consciously contentless signifier; another defined itself, with almost as little content, as "slightly West of center.") When interests are uncrystallized in this way, the best way to have one's most important substantive interests represented is often to choose a representative whose descriptive characteristics match one's own on the issues one expects to emerge. Then, as issues arise unpredictably, a voter can expect the representative to react more or less the way the voter would have done, on the basis of descriptive similarity.

Even in political systems in which many issues, such as those involving economic class, are relatively crystallized, other issues, such as those involving gender, are surfacing and evolving rapidly on the political agenda. When this is the case, individuals for whom these relatively uncrystallized interests are extremely important may get their best substantive representation from a descriptive representative.[8]

The original geographic representation of voters in the United States was undoubtedly intended in part to capture this form of descriptive representation. Today, party and campaign promises provide more important predictors of a representative's future actions than the part of the country in which the representative grew up. Yet even today a voter might well want to select a descriptive representative for accurate representation on issues that are not well covered by these predictors. When a representative's behavior is not easily predicted by party and promises, a voter may be best served by a representative who in his or her own person and experience embodies the characteristic perspectives and interests associated with the voter's geographical territory, socioeconomic class, ethnicity, gender, sexual orientation, or other trait.

The importance of descriptive representation in contexts of uncrystallized interests derives largely from the deliberative function of representation. In the horizontal communication among deliberating legislators, a descriptive representative can draw on elements of experiences shared with constituents both to explore the uncharted ramifications of newly presented issues and to speak on emerging issues with a voice carrying the authority of experience. Transformations in ideas and even in self often derive from interactions with a descriptive representative of another group who can speak from experience.[9]

Representative deliberations do not absolutely require the participation of representatives with relevant perspectives in proportion to the incidence of those perspectives in the population. In theory, deliberation seems to require only a single representative, or a "threshold" presence, in order to add the appropriate insight, experience, or perspective to the collective understanding.[10] Getting the relevant facts and perspectives into the deliberation should be what counts, not how many people advance these facts, insights, and perspectives. In practice, however, groups that are subordinate in a historical system of domination and subordination often need the full representation that proportionality allows in order to achieve deliberative synergy, critical mass, dispersion of influence, and a range of views within the group.

First, deliberation is often synergistic. More representatives usually produce more, and sometimes better, information and insight. This is as true for dominant as for subordinate groups. Subordinate groups, however, have a further need to explore among themselves new ideas that counter the prevailing wisdom. Representative deliberation takes place not only in the assembly but also in small groups, including relatively like-minded groups. Such smaller deliberations allow representatives to change their preferences and their understandings of their groups' interests. Groups whose members will be affected by a decision might therefore legitimately demand, even under deliberative criteria, as many representatives as reflect their numbers in the population, in order to give their experiences and perspectives the full value of their collective insight.

Second, representatives of subordinate groups may need a critical mass to become willing to enunciate minority positions. Minority status can be silencing, but allies help each member break the silence. The representatives may also need a critical mass to convince others—particularly members of dominant groups—that the perspectives or insights they are advancing are widely shared, genuinely felt, and deeply held within their group.

Third, governing bodies usually include a variety of committees and subcommittees in whose deliberative spaces the most important features of policy are often hammered out. Having sufficient numbers of representatives to disperse into the relevant policy areas allows members of the subordinate group to influence decisions wherever those decisions would be improved by their perspectives.

Finally and most importantly, because the content and range of any deliberation is often unpredictable, a variety of representatives is usually needed to represent the varied inflections and internal oppositions that together constitute the complex and internally contested perspectives, opinions, and interests characteristic of any group. This range of views is not easily represented by only a few individuals. On this analysis, African Americans in the United States were far more richly represented deliberatively by a Congress that included William Gray III (a black member of Congress who did not support the Congressional Black Caucus's alternative budget because he was chairman of the Budget Committee in the House) and George Crockett (a black member of Congress who condemned the State Department for refusing to grant Yasir Arafat an entry visa and who supported the legalization of marijuana) than by a Congress that included only one of these two.[11]

No matter how purely deliberative the assembly, therefore, reasons of synergy, critical mass, and internal diversity give each relevant perspective a legitimate claim on as many representatives on that body as is justified by its proportion in the population. The claim for proportionality is reinforced by the fact that in practice almost all democratic assemblies are aggregative as well as deliberative, and achieving the full normative legitimacy of the aggregative function requires that the members of the representative body cast votes for each affected conflicting interest in proportion to the numbers of such interest-bearers in the population.[12]

The Aggregative Function

In its aggregative mode, representative democracy aims at producing some form of relatively legitimate decision in the context of fundamentally conflicting interests. In this aggregative function, the representative assembly should, in moments of conflict, ideally represent the interests of every group whose interests conflict with those of others, in proportion to the numbers of that group in the population. Proportionality with equally weighted votes in the legislature for interests that conflict in the issues before the legislature is the representative equivalent of the aggregative ideal in direct democracy of one person/one vote.

Aggregation does not benefit from descriptive representation as much as does deliberation. Once the citizens have deliberated among themselves and elected their representatives, once representatives and constituents have deliberated together on the issues up for decision, and once the representatives have deliberated fully among themselves, the deliberative process should ideally have clarified and transformed interests sufficiently to make possible either consensus on a solution that is good for all, or, in the more likely event that such a solution has not been crafted, a vote in which prior deliberation has clarified the conflict.[13] In both the vertical communication between representative and constituents and the horizontal communication among representatives, a representative's having had the experiences of a member of an affected group and being able to speak with a voice from that group can improve the quality of the deliberation. But the act of casting a vote in the process of aggregation could, strictly speaking, be done by a machine. This act requires no match between the experiences or personal characteristics of the representatives and the constituents.

Proportional representation of interests, by contrast, is crucial at the aggregative moment. In combination with either cross-cutting interests or power-sharing, and with strong protections for minority rights, the proportional representation of interests can allow a democracy to approach democratic legitimacy in aggregation. Yet just as no actual democratic deliberation ever meets the demands of full information and an ideal speech situation, so no actual aggregation can achieve the political equality necessary for fully legitimate aggregation. Democracies must make do not only with "good enough" deliberation, but also with "good enough" aggregation.

Generating Criteria for Representation from the Aggregative and Deliberative Functions

The deliberative and aggregative functions of democracy provide a clear answer, at least in theory, to the question, "What interests should be represented?" Earlier theorists do not seem to have grasped this point.

In 1981, for example, James Morone and Theodore Marmor criticized congressional legislation that required citizens on advisory boards to be "broadly representative of the social economic, linguistic and racial populations of the area" by asking rhetorically what demographic characteristics ought to be represented:

Common sense rebels against representing left-handers or redheads. What of Lithuanians? Italians? Jews? The uneducated? Mirror views provide few guidelines for selecting which social characteristics merit representation.[14]

Other commentators similarly assumed that no principled guidelines could be enunciated to suggest what groups ought to be represented or when, and what groups ought to be represented on a "mirror," or "descriptive," basis. Bernard Grofman wrote that "One difficulty with the mirror view is that it is not clear what characteristics of the electorate need to be mirrored to insure a fair sample." Hannah Pitkin, Rian Voet, and Amy Gutmann, and Dennis Thompson all came to the same conclusion. This criticism has so often been thought to be simply unanswerable that its mere statement has been taken as dispositive.[15]

Yet, as suggested earlier, the criterion of *relevant perspectives and interests* in deliberation and the criterion of *conflicting interests* in aggregation provide reasonable answers to the question of what groups ought to be represented and when. The contexts of *historical distrust* and *uncrystallized interests* provide partial answers to the question of which groups ought to be represented *descriptively* and when.

The question of which perspectives are relevant to a decision and which interests conflict (and how closely an issue approaches either common or conflicting interests) will, of course, often be contested. So will the question of when groups have a history of communicative distrust and interests are relatively uncrystallized. But the uncertainty generated by a contest over how to put a principle into practice differs greatly from the uncertainty generated by not having a relevant principle at all. As we have seen, many previous theorists have suggested incorrectly that the root problem is that no principles are available at all for selecting which interests and perspectives should be represented.

Patterns of Domination and Subordination

In the absence of bias in a system, one might expect the descriptive characteristics of elected representatives to mirror more or less exactly the characteristics of the citizenry. Legitimate forms of bias, however, enter in several ways. Certain descriptive characteristics in the population are associated with a lessened ability to play effectively the role of representative. If experience is helpful in the representative task, older people can legitimately be disproportionately represented in the legislature, producing a corresponding bias against the young in the deliberation. If familiarity with the law is helpful, lawyers can legitimately be disproportionately represented, producing a corresponding bias for that profession.

More controversially but I think defensibly, the deliberative process among the citizenry in elections to a legislature ought also to select against those opinions that are either highly impractical or antithetical to the public good. As a consequence, in an appropriately functioning deliberative system, the most useful ideas should appear in the legislature in greater proportions than their prevalence in the citizenry, and the most evil ideas in lower proportions. The deliberative process should thus serve to promote good ideas and weed out bad not only among the citizens but also in the elections to the legislature. This form of bias too is democratically legitimate.

Many forms of bias in the legislature are, however, democratically illegitimate. That is, they have no root in any legitimate democratic function. Here I will focus on those forms of bias that derive from existing patterns of domination and subordination. When such patterns exist, efforts to correct imbalances in political representation should be based in recognizing both the historical roots of domination and the proximate causes of existing political inequalities.

All human societies as we know them embody patterns of domination and subordination. By a pattern of domination and subordination I mean a pattern in social organization in which members of one group create and reinforce inequalities between themselves and members of another group through the exercise of power—that is, the threat of sanction and the use of force. The exercise of power may be conscious and intentional, as in the institution of slavery. Yet it need not require individual intent, as in some cases of gender inequality. Members of a group with the power to make a decision that affects others may, without conscious intent, simply ignore the interests or perspectives of members of a group with less power. They may do no more than choose and enforce a course of action that is in their interests with little recognition of the ill effects of that choice on others. The pattern requires no more than that the members of a more powerful group take the interests of the less powerful less into account than their own. When harm or disadvantage is imposed this way systematically over time because the members of one group in general have more power than the members of another, the process creates, and then reinforces, a pattern of domination and subordination.

In the arena of gender, most societies have developed elaborate systems of domination and subordination. The basis for categorization into the dominant or subordinate group is, moreover, almost entirely ascriptive. Women and men perceive themselves as "born with" the traits that place them in one or another category. The traits are not, of course, fully ascriptive. Individuals today can to some degree choose to change their gender. Societies can also change the way they allocate individuals to the categories of male and female, making the markers of gender more or less fluid and more or less socially irrelevant. Yet where societies have developed entrenched patterns of domination and subordination based on a category such as gender, they are far more likely to emphasize the relevant markers than to deemphasize them.

When these patterns of domination and subordination have a long historical record, it would be surprising if they did not affect patterns of political representation. Voters are usually less likely to elect representatives who bear the markers of a subordinate group, and members of subordinate groups are usually less likely to have access to the education, connections, and funding that facilitate running for office. They are also less likely to see themselves as future representatives.

As Virginia Sapiro argued in 1981, the increased descriptive representation of women in many legislatures had undermined the perception that politics is a "male domain." Similarly, the growing number of black elected officials in the South of the United States from 1960 to 1970 dramatically changed that region's political culture, creating a new norm of blacks as political participants. So too for interlocking patterns of subordination. When female elected representatives are almost all white, and black representatives are almost all men, the pattern sends an implicit message that black women do not wield political power.[16]

This is a historically specific and contextual dynamic. Normatively, making a claim for descriptive representation on these grounds requires historical grounding for the factual contention that the social meaning of membership in a given descriptive group incorporates a legacy of second-class citizenship. Such a claim could point, for confirmation, to a history of being legally deprived of the vote. The claim of a past history of domination resulting in lower than proportionate descriptive representation should trigger strict scrutiny of the historical and proximate causes of discrimination and, if the claim is sustained, affirmative action of some sort to produce greater proportional representation.

Avoiding Essentialism

The most significant problem with efforts to promote descriptive representation derives from the tendency of both the political movements promoting these forms of representation and the resulting political measures to generate or intensify, intentionally or not, essentialist understandings of membership in the group. Political organizing is greatly facilitated by such essentialist understandings, as every nationalist movement can attest. Work in psychology on "minimal group formation" suggests how easy it is to activate in-group bias, which may have some unconscious essentialist base. The process of concept formation also reveals how dominant conceptualizations marginalize subordinate ones within human thought processes. Most of us cannot think "table" without unconsciously conjuring up a four-legged, brown piece of furniture, thereby marginalizing in our considerations the many tables with more or fewer legs and different colors. The problem of simple categorization becomes much worse when, as is often the case in human affairs, one group is socially dominant and becomes the norm, setting expectations and structuring institutions so that those who do not conform to that norm are perceived as deviant or lesser beings, perceive themselves as deviant, and cannot function as well in the structures designed for the members of the dominant group.[17]

Even political groups based on descriptive identity that challenge the hegemony of the dominant group cannot escape this internal dynamic. Feminist organizations in the United States that appeal to "sisterhood" have often portrayed that sisterhood primarily in terms that reflected the concerns of the dominant (white middle-class) groups in the movement. Black feminist writers who have challenged that dominance within feminism have themselves portrayed black women as having a singular "Afrocentric standpoint." Although human cognitive processes prevent our eliminating this tendency to assume homogeneity within a group, we can fight that tendency by cultivating avenues of dissent, opposition, and difference within organizations, struggling to appreciate contradictions within a larger perceptual standpoint, and using the plural rather than the singular in writing.[18]

The advocacy of descriptive representation can emphasize the worst features of essentialism. When an extreme descriptivist writes, "it is impossible for men to represent women," that statement implies the corollary, that it is impossible for women to represent men.[19] It also implies that any woman representative represents all women (and all women equally), regardless of the women's political beliefs, race, ethnicity, or other differences.

Essentialism thus requires active opposition. Countering essentialism in politics requires not only a conscious and continually renewed awareness of the affective and cognitive traps that human psychology sets for us in these matters, but also political rationales that stress contingent and non-essentialist explanations for our actions. Efforts to provide proportional descriptive representation for women, African Americans, black South Africans, or lesbians and gays must stress the historically contingent factors that have created the less powerful positions that members of these groups presently occupy. This task is not difficult, for these historical factors usually have blatant objective markers. In most cases specific historical laws have denied civil rights to members of these groups. In other cases, prejudice traceable through many concrete historical practices has produced a similar end.

Different political remedies for redressing underrepresentation also have more or less essentialist implications. There are good reasons for choosing, when possible, more fluid remedies, and grounding them explicitly in historical rationales. "Microcosmic" forms of representation, based on some version of the lot, are best kept advisory and experimental for a good while, as they currently are. "Selective" forms such as quotas are also best kept experimental. Permanent quotas are both static and highly essentializing. They imply, for example, that any "woman" can stand for all "women," any "black" for all "blacks." They do not respond well to constituents' many-sided and cross-cutting interests.

Drawing political boundaries to produce majority-minority districts is also both relatively static and essentializing. Cumulative voting in at-large districts is far more fluid, as it allows individuals to choose whether they want to cast all their votes for a descriptive representative or divide their votes among different representatives, each of whom can represent one or another facet of the voters' interests. Such systems, however, have their own costs in party collusion to produce non-competing candidates and the consequent voter demobilization.[20]

Systems of proportional representation with party lists have well-known costs, but are still a relatively flexible way to introduce selective descriptive representation, as the parties can change the descriptive composition of those lists easily in each election.[21] Experimental decisions by political parties to make a certain percentage of candidates descriptively representative of an underrepresented group are far preferable to quotas imbedded in law or constitutions, for ad hoc arrangements can be flexible over time.

Less obtrusive, although also undoubtedly less immediately successful, are other "enabling devices," such as schools for potential candidates and reforms aimed at reducing the barriers to representation, such as those studied by the Canadian Royal Commission on Electoral Reform: "caps on nomination campaign expenses; public funding of nomination campaign expenses.... the establishing of formal search committees within each party to help identify and nominate potential candidates from disadvantaged groups; financial incentives to parties that nominate or elect members of disadvantaged groups; and so on."[22] High-quality daycare at the workplace of elected officials or vouchers for such daycare might reduce the barriers to political entry for parents of young children. Scholarships to law schools for members of historically disadvantaged and proportionally underrepresented groups would reduce another major barrier to entry. Forgiveness of student loans for members of these groups who go into public office or public service would serve the same end. This last approach aims at identifying and then reducing the specific structural

---

Least Fluid

1. Quotas in constitutions
2. Quotas in law
3. Quotas in party constitutions
4. Majority minority districts
5. Quotas as party decisions
6. Proportional representation and/or cumulative voting
7. "Enabling devices"
    a. schools and funding for potential candidates
    b. caps on nomination campaign expenses
    c. public funding of nomination campaign expenses
    d. establishing formal search committees within each party to help identify and nominate potential candidates from disadvantaged groups
    e. high-quality public daycare for elected officials
    f. scholarships to law schools and public policy schools for members of historically disadvantaged and proportionally underrepresented groups

Most Fluid

Figure 2.1

barriers to formal political activity that serve to reduce the percentages in office of particular disadvantaged groups.[23] (See Figure 2.1)

From this perspective, the recent French movement for "parity" for women in the French representative assemblies presents a conundrum. The movement explicitly positions itself as non-essentialist. It employs the language of "universality."[24] It thus explicitly rejects the argument I make from historical contingency. It also thus distinguishes women from all other underrepresented groups. In the analysis of this movement, women are not a class, social category, or community. They are not a "minority." They are "everywhere."[25]

The claim for parity is not based on the universalistic idea that if the barriers to women's participation were removed, women would "naturally" take 50 percent of the seats in the legislature. Reasoning from removing barriers could generate a claim for 53 percent of the seats in the French legislature (proportionate to current population). Instead the parity movement argues for 50 percent "and no more" on the grounds that women are "half" the human race.[26] Reasoning from removing barriers would apply to groups other than women, a move the parity movement wants to deny.

The French arguments for parity, in my view, cannot be sustained analytically without extending the argument to other groups that are analytically parallel. The category of age is "everywhere," but the parity movement does not make the different age groups candidates for explicit descriptive representation. Differences in sexual orientation are also "everywhere," but the parity movement does not admit sexual orientation as a candidate for explicit descriptive representation.

The practical reasons for wanting to distinguish women from all other groups are obvious. By doing so the parity movement counters the argument that insuring women 50 percent representation will open the door to other claims. It also counters the argument from French universalism, with its cherished difference from the group-oriented politics of the United States and other countries.[27] To accomplish this distinguishing task, however, French proponents of parity must argue that being a "woman" merits representation in the same way that being "human" does. The category "human," while perhaps hard to defend, rests on a long line of reasoning based on the creation and maintenance of equal respect and concern within the human race. I have not seen a line of reasoning that establishes the category "woman" on a similar footing.

Rather, to save a parity argument that applies only to women and no other group, one must rely on some deep structural and perhaps essentialist binary (such as yin and yang, the female and the male principle). Without such an essentialist gloss, I do not see which characteristics of the category "woman" merit cross-contextual, transhistorical representation.[28]

My own view is that at this historical moment the case for reforms designed to produce 50 percent female representation in the French assembly is strong on historically contingent, non-essentialist grounds. Communicative distrust between men and women is still palpable.[29] Many uncrystallized issues regarding gender are currently emerging for legislative decision. Women's historically subordinate political status is marked by having won the vote only in the first half of the twentieth century. I see no intellectual reason to make a deeper claim.

Notes

1. This paper draws on Jane Mansbridge, "Should Blacks Represent Blacks and Women Represent Women? A Contingent 'Yes'," *Journal of Politics* 63 (1999): 628–57 (with the permission of The University of Texas Press).
2. Jürgen Habermas, *Communication and the Evolution of Society,* trans. Thomas McCarthy (Boston: Beacon Press, 1979).
3. Jane Mansbridge, "Using Power/Fighting Power: The Polity," *Democracy and Difference,* ed. Seyla Benhabib (Princeton: Princeton University Press, 1995).
4. For the history of blacks' justified mistrust of whites in the United States, see Melissa Williams, *Voice, Trust, and Memory: Marginalized Groups and the Failings of Liberal Representation* (Princeton: Princeton University Press, 1998), ch. 5.
5. For African American constituent contact, see Claudine S. Gay, "The Impact of Black Congressional Representation on the Behavior of Constituents," presented at the annual meeting of the Midwest Political Science Association, 1996. For member of Congress comment, see Carol M. Swain, *Black Faces, Black Interests: The Representation of African Americans in Congress* (Cambridge, MA: Harvard University Press, 1993), 219. For women's contact, Elizabeth Haynes, "Women and Legislative Communication" (typescript) (Cambridge: Harvard University, 1997). For gender gaps in communication when implicitly comparing gender and ethnicity, see Deborah Tannen, *Gender and Discourse* (New York: Oxford University Press, 1994), 73 and 188. Psychologists have now begun routinely to include in their studies measures of size of difference as well as statistical significance, thanks to Janet Shibley Hyde, "Meta-Analysis and the Psychology of Gender Differences," *Signs* 16:1 (1990): 5–73 and others. Tannen and other linguists have not yet adopted this useful strategy. Yet even in psychology it is not yet standard to compare the size of gender differences to the size of other common differences—an omission that contributes to the common magnification of gender differences (see Jane Mansbridge, "Feminism and Democratic Community," *Democratic Community: NOMOS XXXV,* eds. John W. Chapman and Ian Shapiro [New York: New York University Press, 1993]).

6. "Surrogate representation," as defined in Jane Mansbridge, "The Many Faces of Representation," 1998 Working Paper, John F. Kennedy School of Government, Harvard University, resembles in many ways what Burke called "virtual representation" (Edmund Burke, "Letter to Sir Hercules Langriche," *The Works of the Right Honorable Edmund Burke,* vol. 4 (Boston: Little Brown, [1792] 1871, 293), but differs in including the aggregative as well as the deliberative function of democracy, material interests, and preferences as well as morally right answers, and negotiation among self-interested groups as well as the good of the nation as a whole. On Burke, see Hanna Fenichel Pitkin, *The Concept of Representation* (Berkeley: University of California Press, [1967] 1972), 169–175. Burke's stress led him not to address questions of proportionality, whereas for surrogate representation, proportionality is crucial.
7. On Leland, see Swain, *Black Faces, Black Interests,* 218. On the miscommunication between Senator Birch Bayh and the ERA advocates, see Jane Mansbridge, *Why We Lost the ERA* (Chicago: University of Chicago Press, 1986). On the responsibility for communicating with gay "constituents" throughout the nation felt by one of the few openly gay memebers of the U.S. House of Representatives, see Mansbridge "Should Black," 648.
8. Two of Anne Phillips's four "key arguments" for descriptive representation can be seen as variants of the argument from uncrystallized interests. Both "the need to tackle those exclusions that are inherent in the party-packaging of political ideas" and "the importance of a politics of transformation in opening up the full range of policy options" (Anne Phillips, *The Politics of Presence* (Oxford: Oxford University Press, 1995), 25; see also 43–45, 50, 70, 151ff) are particularly strong when political ideas are uncrystallized. Phillips's analysis of transformative politics is far fuller than I have the space to report here.
9. See Williams, *Voice, Trust, and Memory* on authentic voice and Phillips, *Politics of Presence* on transformations. Representative Barney Frank (personal communication) reports that a past history of interaction in the legislature allows anti-gay legislators to see him as an individual with many dimensions and makes it easier for them to take seriously his perspective on anti-gay legislation.
10. See Hanna Fenichel Pitkin, *Concept of Representation,* 84; Jane Mansbridge, "Living with Conflict: Representation in the Theory of Adversary Democracy," *Ethics* 91:1 (1981): 466–76, 469; Will Kymlicka, *Multicultural Citizenship* (Oxford: Oxford University Press, 1995), 146–47; Phillips, *Politics of Presence,* 47, 67ff.
11. See Swain, *Black Faces, Black Interests,* 41, 49–71 for Gray and Crockett, and *passim* for the diversity in opinions and styles within the spectrum of African American representation in Congress in the 1980s and early 1990s. See Iris Marion Young, "Deferring Group Representation," *Ethnicity and Group Rights: NOMOS XXXIX,* eds. Ian Shapiro and Will Kymlicka (New York: New York University Press, 1997) for the concept of diversity of

opinion within a single "perspective." For both deliberative and aggregative purposes, the full diversity within any larger perspective or interest should ideally be represented in proportion to numbers in the population, subject to the critical deliberative limitations of 1) threshold representation when a useful perspective would otherwise not be represented at all in a proportional distribution (Kymlicka, *Multicultural Citizenship,* 147) and 2) the winnowing out and reduction in salience of relatively harmful and useless ideas.

12. For a fuller exposition of the requirements of deliberative and aggregative democracy, see Jane Mansbridge, *Beyond Adversary Democracy* (Chicago: University of Chicago Press, [1980] 1983); "Using Power/Fighting Power: The Polity" in Seyla Benhabib, ed., *Democracy and Difference* (Princeton: Princeton University Press, 1995); "Living with Conflict"; and "Many Faces of Representation."

13. Although the political issues that the media report are usually contentious (and some theorists even define "politics" as requiring conflict), outcomes that are genuinely good for all are not impossible, even in large national-scale political systems. In the U.S. Congress, in which heterogeneity of interests makes genuine unanimity least likely, many decisions are made by genuine unanimity. Politicians are happiest when they can find ways of doing good that will gain them credit all round and make no enemies. That a policy is good for all, of course, does not make it equally good for all.

14. James A. Morone and Theodore R. Marmor, "Representing Consumer Institutions: The Case of American Health Planning," *Ethics* 91 (1981), 431 and 437, quoting the National Health Planning and Resources Development Act of l974, which called for consumers of health care to sit on the boards of more than two hundred Health Systems Agencies.

15. Bernard Grofman, "Should Representatatives Be Typical of their Constituents?" *Representation and Redistricting Issues,* ed. Bernard Grofman et al. (Lexington, MA: D. C. Heath, 1982), 98; Pitkin, *Concept of Representation,* 87–88; Rian Voet, "Gender Representation and Quotas," *Acta Politica* 4 (1992), 395; Amy Gutmann and Dennis Thompson, *Democracy and Disagreement* (Cambridge, MA: Harvard University Press, 1996), 154.

16. Virginia Sapiro, "When Are Interests Interesting?" *American Political Science Review* 75:3 (1981): 712 (see also Phillips, *The Politics of Presence,* 39, 79ff); on black officials, see Mack Jones, "Black Office-Holding and Political Development in the Rural South," *Review of Black Political Economy* 6:4 (l976): 406; (trial transcript from "Whitfield v. Democratic Party," cited in Lani Guinier, *The Tyranny of the Majority: Fundamental Fairness in Representative Democracy* (New York: Free Press, 1994), 54 (also 34, 36).

17. For minimal group experiments, see Marilynn Brewer, "In-group bias in the minimal intergroup situation: A cognitive-motivational analysis," *Psychological Bulletin* 86 (1979): 307–324; for concept formation, see Katharine

T. Bartlett, "Feminist legal methods," *Harvard Law Review* 103 (1990): 829–88, 848.

18. For the U.S. feminist movement, see Elizabeth Spelman, *Inessential Woman: Problems of Exclusion in Feminist Thought* (Boston: Beacon Press, 1988) and Angela Harris, "Race and Essentialism in Legal Theory," *Stanford Law Review* 42:3 (1990): 581–616; for the Afrocentric standpoint, see Patricia Hill Collins, *Black Feminist Thought* (London: Allen and Unwin, 1990).

19. Christine Boyle, "Home Rule for Women: Power Sharing Between Men and Women," *Dalhousie Law Journal* 7:3 (1983): 797. See also "Mme B.B." in 1789: "Étant démontré avec raison qu'un noble ne peut représenter un roturier ni celui-ci un noble, de même un homme ne pourrait avec plus d'équité représenter un femme puisque les représentants doivent avoir absolument les mêmes intérêts que les représentés; less femmes ne pourraient donc être représentées que par les femmes" (quoted from Maïté Albisure and Daniel Armogathe, *Histoire du féminisme francaise du moyen âge à nos jours* (Paris: Des femmes, 1977), 232, in Françoise Gaspard, Claude Servan-Schreiber, and Anne Le Gall, *Au pouvoir citoyennes! Liberté, Egalité, Parité* (Paris: Le Seuil, 1992), 125 and Françoise Gaspard, "De la parité: genèse d'un concept, naissance d'un mouvement," *Nouvelle Questions Feministes* 15:4 (1994): 42. Phillips, *Politics of Presence,* 52, also quotes a group of Frenchwomen in the same year ("a man, no matter how honest he may be, cannot represent a woman") and Williams, *Voice, Trust, and Memory,* 133, quotes the Reverend Antoinette L. Brown in 1852 ("Man cannot represent woman"). In the eighteenth century the concept that A. H. Birch, *The Concepts and Theories of Modern Democracy* (London: Routledge), 72 calls "microcosmic" representation (legislatures being ideally "an exact transcript" of the society) was still current and invoked even by some of the framers of the U.S. constitution (Pitkin, *Concept of Representation,* 60ff; Bernard Manin, *The Principles of Representative Government* (Cambridge: Cambridge University Press, [1995] 1997), 109–14). The quotations from 1789 are best understood through this historical lens.

20. The state of Illinois practiced cumulative voting until the process was eliminated in 1982 in a cost-cutting effort that reduced the size of the assembly. The system produced greater proportional representation in the state legislature but reduced voter choice, because for strategic reasons the two major parties often ran altogether only three candidates for the three seats available in each district (Jack Sawyer and Duncan MacRae, "Game Theory and Cumulative Voting in Illinois: 1902–1954," *American Political Science Review* 56 (1962): 936–46; Greg Adams, "Legislative Effects of Single-Member vs. Multi-Member Districts," *American Journal of Political Science* 40:1 (1996): 129–144).

21. See Joseph Zimmerman, "Fair Representation for Women and Minorities," *United States Electoral Systems: Their Impact on Women and Minorities,* eds. Wilma Rule and Joseph F. Zimmerman (Westport, CT: Greenwood Press, 1992) and Joseph Zimmerman, "Alternative Voting Systems for

Representative Democracy," *P.S.: Political Science and Politics* 27:4 (1994): 674–77 for the positive and negative features of cumulative voting and different forms of proportional representation.
22. See Phillips, *Politics of Presence,* 57 for enabling devices; Kymlicka, *Multicultural Citizenship,* 62 for the Canadian Royal Commission.
23. Robert Darcy, Susan Welch, and Janet Clark, *Women, Elections and Representation* (Lincoln: University of Nebraska Press, l994), 104ff, direct attention to the eligible pool. They indicate, for example, that the percentage of women in U.S. state legislatures rose from l970 to l984 in tandem with the percentage of women in the law (Figure 5.1).
24. " . . . la démocratie constitue une aspiration universelle, l'universalité englobe les femmes et les hommes, il n'y a donc pas de démocratie représentative si la représentation n'est par paritaire" (Gaspard et al., *Au pouvoir citoyennes!,* 130).
25. "La parité, encore une fois, se distingue du quota par sa philosophie même. Celui-ci, en politique, repose sur l'idée pernicieuse qui consiste à mettre les femmes sur le même plan qu'une classe, qu'une catégorie sociale, qu'une communauté ethnique ou confessionnelle. Or les femmes ne sont pas une minorité. Elles sont partout. On les retrouve dans toutes les classes, dans toutes les catégories sociales. Elles son catholiques, protestantes, juives, musulmanes, agnostiques. . . . Et on ne sourait les comparer à aucun group de pression dont less commanditaires—petits commerçants, adventistes, sourd-muets ou autres handicapés—demanderaient à être mieux représentés qu'ils ne le sont" (Gaspard et al., *Au pouvoir citoyennes!,* 165–66). The text continues, making the relationship with universality even clearer, "Il n'est pas dans la fonction des assemblées representatives de faire une place *ad hoc* à telle ou telle catégorie particulière, fût-elle d'un groupe sociale constitué. Ce serait dériver vers un 'corporatisme social qui briserait l'unité du suffrage universel'" [Ibid., quoting George Vendel]. "Les femmes ne sont ni une corporation ni un lobby. Elles consititue la moitié du peuple soverain, la moitié du genre humain. La moitié et pas davantage, même lorsqu'elles sont, en raison de la démographie, de ses accidents ou de ses particularités, plus nombreuses que les hommes" (Ibid., 166).
26. Ibid. In 1994, Gaspard repeated the argument that because women claim parity on the basis of being "half of humankind," they claim only 50 percent of the seats and not the 53 percent that would be their due on the basis of proportional group representation. Here she explicitly included "le choix d'une vie de couple échappant à la norme (gays et lesbiennes)" among the groups to which the relations between men and women are not comparable ("De la parité," 41).
27. See Joan W. Scott, "'La Querelle des Femmes' in the Late Twentieth Century," *New Left Review* 226 (1997) 3–19 for the anti-American tenor of French arguments against group representation.
28. In spite of the desire of many members of the parity movement to avoid essentialism (Gaspard, "De la parité," 41–42 and *passim*), one of the two

original parity associations was identified with "*l'essentialisme radical*" (Ibid., 34), and some of the central documents of the parity movement have a slight essentialist flavor. For example, "Le Manifeste des dix pour la parité" (signed by Michèle Barzach, Frédérique Bredin, Edith Cresson, Hélène Gisserot, Catherine Lalumière, Veronique Neiertz, Monique Pelletier, Yvette Roudy, Catherine Tasca, and Simone Veil, *L'Express* June 6–12 (1996): 32–33), attacks republican Jacobinism as having been above all "une affaire des hommes." "Centralizateur et hiérarchique, donneur de leçons et arrogant autant qu'éducateur, rhétorique et rationalist jusqu'à l'abstraction chimérique, le jacobinisme est en quelque sorte un concentré de qualités viriles," in contrast to "la sensibilité, le concret, le souci du quotidien." The qualities here associated with men and women undoubtedly describe slight average tendencies of at least upper-class men and women in France, quite possibly derived from social learning. Citing them in this short two-page manifesto, however, might lend itself to an essentialist interpretation.

29. Adelaide Haas, "Male and female spoken language differences: Stereotypes and Evidence," *Psychological Bulletin* 86 (1979): 616–626, citing Otto Jesperson, *Language* (New York: Henry Holt, 1922), catalogues proverbs from many countries criticizing women's talk (e.g., the French *Ou femme il y a, silence il n'y a* ["Where there's a woman, there's no silence"]).

Chapter Three

The Politics of Parity: Can Legal Intervention Neutralize the Gender Divide?

Claus Offe

The problem I want to discuss in the following essay can be stated in three steps.[1] First, in modern liberal democratic societies institutional spheres and fields of activity have been, and largely remain, gendered, in spite of the vigorous efforts of social movements and moral mobilizations aimed at neutralizing the gender divide. To be sure, increasing rates of mobility do occur between these gendered domains of social activities, although they differ widely across countries and social classes. By "gendered" domain divisions I mean that many fields of activity (such as primary school teaching, managerial activities, military professions, the exercise of official political power) are assigned to either men or women. This gendered division of labor and access to status is not only empirically the case; it is also widely believed to be a desirable, normal, unavoidable, or unalterable fact of social life. Such beliefs are even widely shared by men *and* women. Gendering of domains occurs far beyond any natural determination by which functions are assigned to either of the two sexes in human reproduction, although much of the pattern of division of labor prevailing between the sexes can still be read to be derived from and as an extension of the distinction between the "female" activities that take place in the "home" and those "male" activities that have to do with controlling the world outside of the home—a seemingly archaic pattern of "gathering" versus "hunting." At any rate, the activities of caring, household, and family work are still largely ascribed to the female gender, while the spheres of occupational careers, the acquisition of market income, much of the cognitive and aesthetic culture, and political power are considered to be male domains.

Between these two domains, not only a division, but also an asymmetry obtains. While many women are at least nominally entitled to and actually desire access to the domain coded as "male," most males do not exhibit the reciprocal desire to access the "female" coded domain of activities. But it is also obvious that unless the latter crossing of the boundaries separating the spheres occurs to a substantial extent, the former crossing cannot occur to the extent desired by many women aiming at the neutralization of the gender code for domains of activity. Unless males desire or accept a role in the "female" coded sphere of activities that we associate with household and caring, females are "caught" in precisely this sphere. More women want to enter into the domains coded as male than men want to move in the opposite direction. Many women experience this asymmetry of desired access as a serious problem of social injustice and illegitimate male power.

Second, the normative intuitions associated with the principle of liberal democracy imply that problems of illegitimate power and social injustice must be addressed through the institutional means of politics, state power, and legislation, as well as the administration of justice. Except for the most minimalist conceptions of democracy that limit the understanding of equality to the notion of equal participation at the *input* point of the political process (for instance, voting rights), any more demanding conception of liberal democracy would also imply some notion of equality enhancing the *output* of legislation. Concerning inequalities governing gender relations, as well as inequalities governing relations of wealth, income, access to education and the labor market, or ethnic and religious minority status, constitutions as well as many pieces of statutory law (beginning, for instance, with mandatory elementary schooling) are intended to favor outcomes that have the potential of neutralizing inequalities by providing resources to those who are illegitimately deprived of them or denied access to them. It cannot be left to civil society's free actors, or their interests, tastes, and prejudices, to treat, exploit, or discriminate against others at will or to exercise the freedom of action and contract that they enjoy relative to most women.

Third, as politics in general and the making and administration of the law more specifically are largely male-dominated fields of activity, a familiar bootstrapping problem of institutional design and innovation emerges. A new regime must be established by the means and within the constraints of the old. Thus, problem-solving through legislation and institutional innovation becomes possible only after a major part of the problem has been already solved. That is, institutional alterations within the male dominated sphere of politics and legislation are contingent upon the presence of moral and political forces that can make men cede some of their de facto gender privileges and prerogatives. The degendering of politics, as it were, must be performed by the means available within the institutions and routines of gendered politics.

It can hardly be denied that progress has actually been made concerning the political inclusion of women into a polity, both de facto and de jure. This applies to all three of the categories of rights and liberties that citizens enjoy. It first applies to the civil liberties of women (their participation in the professions, higher education, and economic life, as well as the definition and protection of women's rights within the family); it also applies to political participation and representation; and finally it applies to social rights, ranging from survivors' pensions to local social services. But even if it is agreed that much of the road has been traveled, it is uncertain how much still lies ahead. Moreover, it is not clear whether the momentum built up so far in the process of civic, political, and social inclusion of women will actually facilitate the abolition of the remaining gender barriers or whether, in a less optimistic perspective that is familiar to mountain climbers, the last stretch of the road will pose the most difficult impasses.

Apart from the thorny problem of power and implementation, the question guiding the search for innovation is plainly this: how can the female preference for reciprocal permeability of the boundary dividing the two domains be represented in and promoted through politics and legislation? Are new mechanisms and procedures of female interest representation called for? How would they work and what effects are they likely to generate? And how can they be justified from within the constitutional premises and normative principles of the liberal democratic regime? The better the answers posed to these questions, the more easily the bootstrapping act of implementation will actually be accomplished.[2]

Three Families of Rights

To start with the latter question, let me briefly recall some normative principles of political liberalism. Liberalism is a doctrine that emphasizes equal individual rights framed by citizenship (or the "right to have rights"). Liberalism is critical of group privileges. Liberal rights based on citizenship come in three families.

1. Civil liberties: rights to be unconstrained by state interference in the enjoyment of life, liberty, and property, as well as, more controversially,

to be unconstrained in the use of these rights by third-party interference. At any rate, only marginal and impoverished versions of the liberal doctrine of liberty would claim that it is only state violation of liberties, not also third-party violation, that must be prohibited through effective state action.
2. Political rights: the rights to assembly, association, participation, communication, petition, and voting, all aiming at some measure of accountability of the holders of political power.
3. Positive or "social" rights: rights designed to provide security and freedom from the kinds of fear and anxiety that come with insecurity, vulnerability, and dependence. Social rights imply rights to services, provisions, and transfers that are deemed essential preconditions for equal opportunities and the autonomous exercise of the rights contained in families (1) and (2).

Given the proclamation of these rights within the liberal polity, the standard problem consists in determining, in a fair, objective, and hence unobjectionable way, the extent to which this demanding notion of equal liberty pertaining to all citizens is or is not actually implemented regarding the social implications of gender difference and gendered domain divisions. What is the proper test by which a valid answer to this question can be found?

An answer to this second-order problem of testing the actual validity, or chance of implementation, of rights is harder to come by if we move sequentially from family (1) to family (2) and family (3). Concerning family (1), we would probably agree to check whether actually all citizens, irrespective of gender and other dimensions of difference and inequality, can make effective use of their liberties, whether the state actually refrains from infringing upon them, and whether complaints concerning such infringements, should they be attempted, can be actually and effectively brought to properly established, sufficiently independent, and professionally staffed courts that follow rule of law principles and thus are capable of taking remedial action in cases of gender discrimination.

Greater difficulties occur in testing the actual validity of family (2) rights, or political rights. Whether or not the rights to vote, to associate, to assemble, to compete for elected office, to be represented, and to receive as well as to initiate public communication are equally and fairly enjoyed by all citizens within an equitably designed and gender-blind public sphere is a question that typically involves ambiguities and judgments of an essentially contested nature. These judgments tend to be themselves influenced and arguably biased by the entrenched interests of institutional actors, such as the media, associations, and political parties, so that any assessment advanced can be suspected to be not an argument *for* a point of view, but an argument *from* a point of view that is essentially informed by gendered perspectives. For example, a controversy will typically question the extent to which statistical gender differences (in party membership, representation in legislative bodies, or the holding of political office) can be causally attributed to male power and social discrimination, or whether, alternatively, such differences follow from autonomous choices that members of gender categories make in using the equal rights available to them. For equal rights of men and women do not have to lead to gender-neutral behavioral outcomes concerning the kind and extent of the actual use of these rights, as the perfectly "voluntary" nonutilization of some rights (due, for instance, to gender differentiated conceptions of preferred kinds of activities and life plans) cannot be analytically excluded as a possibility.

Even greater, by yet another order of magnitude, are the difficulties encountered when trying to assess whether social rights are adequately granted and effectively implemented. Are female gender-specific dependencies, vulnerabilities, and disadvantages, most prominently those having to do with childbearing, sufficiently taken into account in order to allow for the chances of social participation—occupational, political, and otherwise—to be gender-balanced? How much and what kind of compensation (in terms of family law, family allowances, service facilities, programs promoting labor market participation of women, etc.), as mandated by the principle of equal citizenship rights, is adequate and sufficient? These questions, as any analogous questions concerned with providing social rights, are almost essentially contested and extremely difficult to answer in an unequivocally fair and neutral way. Any judgment on these matters is contingent not upon a fair and disinterested applications of agreed-upon standards, but upon political power, and hence ultimately upon the rules and social mechanisms that regulate the access to power positions and a mandate to make collectively binding decisions.

Methods of Resolving Political Conflict

Within any constituted political community, there is a limited repertoire of methods of political conflict resolution. These methods are designed to institutionalize power conflicts and to generate outcomes that are compatible with the continuity of the political community (or, in the extreme case, the foundation of a new one). None of the elements of this established institutional repertoire is self-evidently suitable for the resolution of macrolevel gender conflict. These elements are negotiated compromise, separation, majority rule, adjudication, deliberation, and the elimination of issues from the agenda through the use of "gag rules." Let us consider them one by one.

1. Compromise: This method is applicable only after a second order consensus is established concerning (a) the legitimate representatives of the conflicting groups in question and (b) the issue or set of issues that the conflict is "about." Gender conflict is unsuitable for this method of conflict resolution because gender categories (unlike workers or employers) do not have an associational presence or the capability of being processes through collective action. No woman in a leadership position of some women's association can conceivably claim a mandate to speak and decide for "all women," in the way that an industrial dispute can be processed through the bargaining between representatives of workers and management. For that, the social category of women is too encompassing and multidimensional, and representational claims will typically end up in sectarian political pathologies. Also, the issues at stake cannot typically be represented in quantitative terms, so that the two parties involved could arrive at a mutually agreed-upon solution "halfway" between the original positions adopted when bargaining starts.

2. Separation: Deep conflict and persistent incompatibilities can be resolved—for instance, in the case of ethnic and religious cleavages—through secession and separation. Milder forms of conflict, as in the case of linguistic cleavages, can be dealt with through territorial division of a federal sort. To be sure, separation is a valuable method of resolving otherwise irresolvable microlevel conflict between two persons, as in the case of divorce. Also, gender specific domains (rooms, clubs, educational facilities, associations, commercial organizations, etc.) have been set up in various cultural contexts by feminist associations and movements. But concerning macrolevel social organization and conflict resolution on an encompassing political level, the method of separation fails and the notion of installing separate "gender republics" turns out to be at best a literary utopia.

3. Majority rule: This method is plainly inapplicable to macrolevel gender conflict. If we were to use it at the constituency level, we would be caught in a deadlock of (near-) structural parity. Conversely, applying it at the level of representative bodies and legislatures, the objection would be compelling that majorities are gender-biased through unequal chances of males and females to find access to these bodies.

4. Adjudication through third parties: Courts and trials are means of conflict resolution that are based upon the presumption of neutral-

ity and noninvolvement. As in all bipolar conflicts, there is no conceivable equidistant third party that could credibly lay claim to neutrality and fairness (by virtue, as it were, of being neither male nor female).

5. Debate and deliberation: This method is good for the resolution of conflicts of ideas, norms and principles, with the presumed inherent and symmetrical potential that the better reasons given persuade and help ultimately to win over the other side, the assumption being that all sides involved partake in the human capacity of reason and hence the ability to tell a better argument or proposal from a less reasonable or less consistent one. As gender conflicts are typically framed as "identity" conflicts, with the reasons given by either side being coded by the other side, at least under postmodern epistemological premises, as inherently gender specific and gender biased, little can be accomplished by the methods of political discourse and public deliberation.

6. Privatization and gag rules: These methods have been valuable means to resolve conflicts over religious beliefs. They presuppose a consensus that the substance of conflict is either not capable of being resolved through political means or not sufficiently relevant to be made the object of collectively binding decisions, or that attempted political conflict resolution will by some necessity intensify rather than settle the conflict. After these premises have been challenged by feminist movements, and as numerous accepted matters of public policy do without doubt affect citizens of different sexes differently and specifically, such second order consensus concerning matters that do not properly belong on the political agenda and are thus to be banned from it is unlikely to be restored. The option to relegate gender conflict to either the microlevel of individual coping or the mesolevel of associative arrangements or pre-political movement politics within civil society seem largely foreclosed.

So far, I have established two points. One, the question of whether rights (as they pertain to gender specific life chances and the fair access to domains and life chances) are adequate or not is not to be determined by legal reasoning, but by political power that can always be effectively suspected to inform such legal reasoning. The status quo of normal politics, the institutional routines of policymaking, and the orderly administration of justice fails as gender issues are involved, as, given the empirical prevalence of males, male interests, and allegedly male modes of discourse, one party involved in the issue dominates the terms of any conceivable resolution. But second, the procedures by which political power is generated and employed within the framework of a liberal democracy do not yield mechanisms by which gender-specific rights can be promoted and the conflict over such rights resolved. Hence we might conclude that in order to change substantive rights, we need to change procedures and mechanisms of conflict resolution in a way that improves the prospects for such rights being legislated. Only if the rights of women are strengthened at the procedural level will legal arrangements at the substantive level be moved forward. Thus, as the setup of normal politics favors men and the established procedures of conflict resolution are unpromising for any effective and unbiased processing of women's interests, the only answer seems to be special representation rights for women in the political process and the adoption of hitherto unknown methods of conflict resolution. In order to improve outcomes, both agents and rules must be altered.

Special political representation rights can come in a variety of forms. First, they may be adopted by either political parties or constitutional organs such as the legislative assembly, the executive branch of government, or the electorate itself. Second, they can be limited in time or declared permanent. Third, they can aim at 50 percent gender parity or prescribe less demanding measures of representation (but why not, as a radical remedial measure, even more than 50 percent for specified periods of time or subject matters?). A wide variety of proposals and demands have emerged, as well as been partly adopted, since the late 1970s.

Rather than describing and reviewing the features of these alternative and/or cumulative arrangements, my present intention is just to assess the justifications available for special political representation rights.[3] A full assessments of the virtues and potential drawbacks of such rights would have to come up with answers to the following questions:

> Is the adoption of such rights permitted or even mandated by the constitutional order?
> If so, is the adoption of these rights actually desired by those whom they are meant to benefit, namely women?
> If so, can it be demonstrated that the policy outcomes that are brought about under the procedural auspices of these rights are actually different from those generated in the absence of these rights?
> If so, do the observable direct and indirect, intended as well as unintended results of female special representation rights justify the adoption of these rights from a consequentialist point of view?

Group rights are designed to strengthen groups and protect them from group discrimination. But distinction must be made between statistical discrimination and social discrimination. The possibility, to say the least, cannot be excluded that some (statistical) discrimination is not causally attributable to the interests of one category of people (males) who take an active (if sometimes "unconscious") interest in keeping other people (females) out. In other words, some of the choices people make and by which they end up in different places in the social structure may well be genuinely their "own" choices—which they are perfectly entitled to make according to the principles of a liberal social order and liberal justice. It may well be the case that women sometimes find it contrary to a life form considered by themselves as corresponding to their female gender identity—a form of life, that is, that has not been imposed upon them but that they have chosen voluntarily, to prefer informal over formal sorts of collective action. It is hard to define how we recognize and validate such voluntary self-exclusion, motivated perhaps by the perception, shared by some feminists, that female participation in typically "male" positions and activities will not liberate women but rather assimilate them to styles of conduct and thought that they consider essentially alien to their conception of their preferred form of life. It is also hard to categorically deny that such reasoned and authentic self-discrimination might in fact occur. But then again, the very term "autonomy"—with the implication of "voluntarily made" choice—is notoriously vulnerable to sociological deconstruction. Whenever we find that people follow preferences that we, the observers, disapprove of, the temptation is to deny the autonomous character of the formation of such preferences and invoke categories such as "manipulation" or "adaptive preferences" of the "sour grapes" type.[4]

A mirror image of this fallacy of representing perfectly authentic choices as the outcome of male discrimination and men's interest in the preservation of privilege is the equally present possibility that rights are being demanded not for the sake of enhancing justice by invalidating an unfair gender divide, but for the less lofty concern with creating shortcuts for the promotion of status interests behind a smokescreen of inauthentically invoked universalist principles. A case of "interests hidden behind the invocation of principle" would also be at hand if granting special representation rights is conceded by male elites not as a matter of principle, but as a matter of electoral tactics and as an intended appeal to the female electorate, or, for that matter, as a politically rather inexpensive move of male elites to exonerate themselves from the accusation of male chauvinism. This consideration would also explain why it is precisely in politics that women seem to have made the greatest progress in terms of entering allegedly "male" domains, whereas institutional sectors in which popular votes are insignificant in determining career success (such as management or academia) are less hospitable to such progress.

Women may sincerely want to stay out of the "male" domain of activities, and some women may challenge the gender divide for the sake of their personal interest (or political elites for the sake of electoral success) rather than justice-related motivations. In the first case, the status quo is (mis)represented as being the outcome of males' interested discrimination; in the second, a demand for a radical departure from the status quo is (mis)represented as the proponents' desire for social justice. In either of these cases, it is not easy to disentangle autonomous choices and commitments from interest-driven considerations. While I do not have the slightest intention of claiming that either of these two reciprocal suspicions can be widely validated, the question that I am concerned with here is, given the hardly deniable possibility of either of these two suspicions of inautheticity being warranted, how can they conclusively be invalidated so that the moral respectability of the demand for special representation rights can be defended against such kind of suspicions?

What I am thus going to do for the rest of these notes is propose a testing procedure the results of which are intended to throw some light on the two issues of status or other strategic interest versus autonomous commitment that I have just introduced. The demand for female special representation rights (quota or gender parity in parties, legislative bodies, or executive branches of government) would appear the more justified the more consistently the answer to the following set of questions is yes.

The first question is whether there is, on the level of observable political opinions, preferences, and behavioral patterns a distinctively "female" pattern that would be introduced into the political process through special representation rights and that would be denied its proper weight of if such rights continue to be denied. Do women exhibit a distinctive political profile, or is the range of female preferences as diverse as it is among male-dominated elites? The problem can further be subdivided into political preferences at the mass and at the elite levels: to what extent do women voters differ from male voters, and how does this preference translate into preferences of male and female elite members? Furthermore, do gender differences apply to the style and routines in which politics is conducted or/and does it also apply to the preferred outcome of the political process? As I said, I try to design a test rather than provide an answer to the questions raised. But if I were to risk a speculation about the answers the test would yield, my hunch is the following: that gender differences of political preference profiles are not very marked, except for strongly gender-related issues, such as legislation on divorce and abortion. These differences are not robust, but fluctuate in time and across countries. It is hard to pin down any "common cause" of women that would come anywhere near to uniting one gender category against the other gender category. Philosophical "female morality" theories have been tried and have largely failed. Differences at the elite level are even less significant compared to those at the mass level, which would suggest socialization, assimilation, and selection effects operating on those women who do succeed in winning access to elite positions. Supposing that all of this were true (which, again, I do not claim to be able to demonstrate), much of the moral and political appeal of the idea of gender parity and gender-based group rights would fade away. Politics and political outcomes would simply not differ very much with or without a regime of parity and quota rules.

This is so because there is little identity of interests that would unite all women and only women. Arguments claiming such unity of interest are typically framed retrospectively, namely in terms of complaints and grievances about what must be considered, from today's moral point of view, grave injustices that have been inflicted upon women by previous generations. But contrary to the appeals sometimes voiced by self-serving vanguard speakers and movement entrepreneurs, there is no intergenerational identity of "womanhood," no suprapersonal and intertemporal entity such as some "Women Inc." At least from the point of view of the principles of moral presentism and moral individualism, no legitimate compensation claims, in terms of compensatory legal entitlements, can be established for past injustices if those affected by these injustices are no longer alive. At any rate, the burden of proof that (future) political outcomes will differ once statutory quota or parity rules are introduced rests with the proponents of the regime change. If they fail to demonstrate such difference, the suspicion would gain support that other concerns than those of promoting justice motivate their advocacy of regime change.

The second component of my test concerns a measure of the authentic commitment to universalist principles. The intuition underlying the respective question is this: if it is for the sake of overcoming representational injustices that consist in the selective and discriminatory outcome of the individualist "one person, one vote" game of liberal representative democracy, then gender is clearly not the only divide that generates distorted elite composition. True, women are missing "at the top" if their share in the constituent population is taken as a yardstick. But people are defined not only by gender, but by age, ethnicity, social class, health status, region, educational status, etc. All of the underrepresented social categories defined by these dimensions (except for young people below statutory voting age) enjoy full active citizen rights, but do not find representation within the ranks of political elites nearly in proportion to their numerical strength. If representational justice is invoked by and for women in the name of universalist principles, do proponents of these demands also consider and advocate the need for improving representational justice on behalf of these other social categories? If so, a complex system of multiple quota and parity arrangements would have to be proposed. If not, an argument would have to be provided that demonstrates the greater injustice implied by the gender divide compared to, say, the ethnicity or sexual orientation divide. Unless such an argument cannot be provided and advocacy for gender parity is still not complemented by advocacy for the representation rights of these other social categories, an inconsistency arises. This inconsistency suggests an explanation either in terms of the status interests of women aspiring to political elite positions or/and in terms of male dominated electoral tactics aiming at the female vote.

The third question is this. Does a majority of women actually support the demand for quota or parity? Again, I have no data to offer concerning the empirical distribution of opinions among women on this question. To be sure, should the answer be no, some proponents of the intended reform of representation rules will remain unimpressed and perhaps even denounce those women who do not support this demand as opportunists or unenlightened victims of male brainwashing. The claim is that female voters are blinded (by traditions, culture, irrational preferences) to their "true" interests; hence, they must be encouraged and educated to come to a better understanding of their interests, and giving them a representational "head start" is a way to do so. For whatever it is worth, this is a paternalist or preceptorial argument that does not sit well with the mainstream of the liberal tradition that assumes that every person (under the condition of the three families of rights being guaranteed and enforced) must be assumed to know best what is good for him or herself.

This easy way out can perhaps be foreclosed if we look for reasoned and deliberative arguments that are advanced by women against parity or quota proposals. In fact, it is not difficult to find such arguments, as proposed by women, in the light of which the quota proposal appears an ill-considered and potentially backfiring institutional arrangement. For one thing, the claim can be substantiated that while a quota or parity seemingly constitutes a victory over male domination, the victim remains strong enough to engage in what can be termed second-order discrimination. That is to say, the (putative) beneficiaries of special representation rights can always be discredited as not having "earned" their career and status through talent, skill, and effort, as is supposedly the case with men, but as having been illegitimately endowed with it through privileged access. A milder form of such retaliatory move consists in relegating those women who have "made it"—with or without procedural advantages granted to them—to substantive domains that are somehow related to what is still considered an essentially "female" sphere of concerns. To wit, and as unsystematic evidence seems to demonstrate, there are many more women at the cabinet level endowed with the less visible, less prestigious, and perhaps also less secure ministerial portfolios for family affairs, youth, health, culture, and perhaps the environment or development aid than there are female ministers of defense, finance, foreign affairs, or the interior. Should this turn out to lead to a robust generalization, the conclusion would be supported that gains of women in terms of access are paid for in terms of second-order discrimination at the status level achieved. In view of these effects, women aspiring for political leadership position may well choose to try to "make it on their own"—perhaps following the role model of Margaret Thatcher?—rather than risking vulnerability to retaliatory forms of discrimination.

The other argument that can raise doubt concerning the wisdom of quota or parity provisions is known from affirmative action and "reverse discrimination" debates. It applies to women as it does to race and ethnic minorities. The argument is that quota provisions are a cheap and deceptive way to cover up the unresolved problem that those women who are at the same time mothers and wives face considerably greater difficulties in rising to positions of political decision making compared to men of equal talent and ambition. Rather than addressing this problem through "causal" therapies that would facilitate female careers, quota provisions constitute a "symptomatic" care that leaves opportunity structures unchanged but cosmetically alters the appearance of outcomes.

Finally, the market-liberal argument cannot be dismissed that if the majority of women were actually to prefer representational parity, it would not be necessary to introduce the respective rules governing the composition of legislatures or cabinets. For political parties, assuming they are rational vote maximizers, would adopt parity rules as a matter of strategic prudence so as to attract a larger portion of the female vote. The evidence shows that this strategic imperative has in fact been heeded, though to a widely varying extent across parties. In Germany, it is only the Green Party with its affinity to feminist causes that has adopted, on the level of party statutes, strict gender parity in the nomination of candidates for general elections. The impact of this practice upon electoral success is hard to determine and certainly not spectacular and, at any rate, insufficient to induce liberal and conservative parties to follow the example of their left-libertarian competitor, while the Social Democrats have adopted a milder version of quota rules.

In sum, we can conclude from these considerations that there are reasons for women, the alleged beneficiaries of representational parity statutes, to consider this innovation and its presumable effects a mixed blessing. The failure of the electoral marketplace to induce all political parties to adopt statutes and rules suitable to equalize the gender composition of representative bodies can hardly be explained by male intransigence alone. It must also be explained in terms of female doubts concerning both the moral plausibility and the instrumental desirability of the proposed innovation of representation rules.

Returning for a moment to normative questions, as opposed to the empirical one just discussed, the parity mandate is dubious both in the light of arguments from duty and arguments from desirable consequences. To start with the former, let us imagine, not unrealistically, a situation in which a political party has 20 percent female members and 80 percent male members—say a total of 100. As it comes to nominating candidates for the next election, it turns out that half of the female members (10) and three quarters of the male members (60) declare their willingness to be nominated. Let the total number of candidates to be nominated be 4, which under the parity mandate—self-imposed by the party, let us assume—means 2 women, 2 men. As a consequence, every woman willing to run has a 0.4 chance of being nominated, while the chance of each man is more than 12 times less likely, namely 0.03. The moral plausibility of this distribution of opportunities is less than compelling, or so the males may feel. To be sure, this gross inequality may be gradually neutralized in the course of time, as more women enter the party and qualify for nomination, while men eager to start a political career may leave. This is where consequentialist considerations come in. Suppose the appeal to female voters of the party having adopted this regime of candidate selection and faithfully implementing it is so great that the party actually gains in electoral support. Incidentally, this differential gain is a "positional" good that would wither away as parity rules are not adopted at the level of party statutes, but through laws applying to all parties. Conversely, it could also be the case that among the 60 men willing to be nominated are—according to a generally shared view—3 charismatic figures who are sure vote-winners, while there is no person of similar electoral prospects among the 10 women. Should this case obtain, the party would be forced to let parity considerations prevail over its prime organizational objective—namely winning votes. This is a clear case of a conflict between rules and the attainment of organizational goals, with a built-in incentive of revoking the (self-) imposed rules in order to make room for purposive rationality. In anticipation of this type of antinomy, legislative assemblies, whether male-dominated or not, will hesitate to mandate parity or quota mandates in the first place because they realize that the application of such rules to the sectoral and limited rationalities of political parties—or for that matter, of university departments or business enterprises—is besides the point, or *unsachlich,* as Max Weber would have said. It is an interference with the goals and objectives that the respective organizations are expected and committed to serve.

Should the empirical answers to the three sets of questions I have raised turn out to be nearly as ambiguous as my own half-informed guess would predict them to be, the case for quota and other special representation rights appears weak indeed. That conclusion would raise the subsequent question of whether there is anything that can be done about the persistent gender divide in political representation. Alternatively, the possibility suggests itself that the institutionalization of (female) group rights is simply an unpromising strategy, while approaches other than those prescribing legal mandates are more likely to succeed in neutralizing the gender divide.

The debate on the gendered division of labor, or so it appears to me, is overly obsessed with legal intervention as a means to social change. There are great differences across nations concerning the level of female labor market participation, participation in tertiary education, female shares in professorial positions, and female shares in political elites. I believe that only a marginal part of this range of variation can be accounted for in terms of laws that were adopted for the purpose of either keeping women out or integrating them into the labor market or other domains. Determinants other than the law condition the rigidity and the durability of the gender divide in social life. Examples are the religious structure of a country, with Protestant countries being much more open to gender equalization than Roman Catholic ones; the price level of the real estate market and the extent of residential and schooling segregation (United States); whether a country has been involved in the World War I, which has triggered a large scale inflow of women into the labor market substituting for military personnel (the Netherlands is a negative example); whether abundant and cheap domestic labor is available that can be bought by the middle class to free women for nondomestic activities and lifelong careers (Brazil); whether there is an extensive as well as service-intensive welfare state employing mainly female labor (Sweden); or whether cultural patterns prescribe that the hot meal of the day is eaten at home rather than at school and at midday rather than in the evening (Germany). Correlatively, the extent to which the law can influence and change the level of social participation of women, be it in the labor market, academia, management, or politics, also appears to be limited. As a rule of thumb (or null-hypothesis), I suggest that one cannot legislate parity, or the greater permeability of the gender divide, into being parity in the "male" coded world of power, income, and careers, nor a fortiori parity in the "female" coded world of caring, household, and family. To wit, the income incentives for fathers to take up parental leave do not seem to have been successful anywhere.

Instead, what helps to overcome gender discrimination and injustices are microlevel discourses, the cultivation of sensibilities through social movements, role models, mass media, and educational practices. They contribute to the sharpening of awareness, to the unfolding of largely sublegal civilizing processes, the promotion and gradual spread of standards of decency and civility. Such intangible forces of cultural change strengthen capacities for self-policing within civil society, as a consequence of which certain discriminatory modes of speaking and acting in intergender relations come to be recognized as inappropriate. The same happens with patterns of recruitment and promotion. Such pattern of reflective awareness, though unevenly distributed and often defective, contributes more to the gradual overcoming of gender injustices than do the bureaucratic activities of "equalization officers" (*Gleichstellungsbeauftragte*) mandated by German law for universities and other public sector employers. The problem here, as in many other policy areas, is that legal standards cannot effectively be enforced by state agencies, at least not without the risk of counterintentional second-order effects, such as retaliatory actions directed at those who are the intended beneficiaries of legal intervention. Instead of parity statutes, we need to rely on the forces of civil society to overcome patterns and practices of discrimination, in politics as elsewhere.

Notes

1. This is the revised and expanded version of the paper I presented at the opening panel of the conference that is documented in the present volume. Because I was assigned the task by the organizers to ask questions rather than to present findings, this paper comes without references. Very helpful comments and suggestions were received from the participants of the conference, especially from Jytte Klausen and Jane Mansbridge. The author also wishes to acknowledge the careful and critical reading of the manuscript by Susanne Fuchs.
2. Such bootstrapping acts have actually been performed in the past. An example is the transition from a male-only system of voting to the granting of female voting rights. These rights have obviously been granted by male-dominated legislatures and constitutional assemblies. Moreover, they have been advocated and eventually implemented by leftist and liberal political parties who could be almost certain that, given typical party preferences exhibited by women at the time, they themselves would not stand to benefit from the institutional innovation of the extension of the right to vote to women.
3. I write "political" as opposed to special representation rights in the job market, in the leadership of organizations, or in higher education.
4. Jon Elster, *Sour Grapes: Studies in the Subversion of Rationality* (New York: Cambridge University Press, 1983).

Chapter Four

The French Parity Movement

Françoise Gaspard

At the beginning of the 1990s the French feminist movement seemed particularly weak, almost invisible, as if it had gone out of fashion. There no longer seemed to be any obvious objectives capable of mobilizing and unifying activists to fight for the equality of women and men. The dominant republican ideology required that intellectuals, like responsible French politicians, remain especially reluctant to take any positive action that might contradict the universalist ideal. And in contrast to the increased attention in other countries to the underrepresentation of women in institutions over the previous decade, the movement in favor of parity in France was particularly inactive. Hence, it is quite astonishing to see now the success that the demands for parity have had in France—that is to say, for the equal representation of women and men in decision-making positions, in particular, in elected assemblies. In fact, in less than a decade, what was regarded as a marginal demand and a break with national tradition spawned a militant mobilization that achieved inscription of the demand for parity in the Constitution and in the law. How may we explain this quite sudden and astonishing success? How was this idea imposed on the political agenda in spite of vigorous resistance? What were the consequences of the revision of the Constitution voted in the spring of 1999 and of the laws flowing from it?

The disparity between the general position of women in French society at the end of the 1980s and their persistent marginalization in the political decision-making process is one of the major reasons for the support for parity in public opinion. At the time, the French lived under the fiction of equality between women and men. Formal equality had been established (or almost); what more could women ask for? Certainly, inequalities persisted in real life, but they were progressively receding, said the optimists. French women became citizens only after the Second World War, and they waited until the 1970s before civil law recognized them as equal to men in the family. In this case women just had to be patient, as they often have had to be; they would soon catch up. But this perspective did not take into account the profound transformations women had undergone over the previous 30 years in their lives, their perception of themselves and society, and consequently their relations to men. The "catch-up" view did not appreciate women's growing intolerance of their own marginalization in the political, administrative, or economic world.

Every year since 1971 more young women than young men have entered into the university system and continued their studies. While the latter remain the majority in the so-called hard sciences (mathematics, physics, technology), the former predominate in literature, the human sciences, law, business and medicine.[1] The education of young women has further increased women's participation in the labor market, which has always been quite high in France. Over the course of these last three decades, in spite of the economic crisis, women's labor market participation has taken on a permanent character. In the past, motherhood had interrupted women's salaried work. Women would stop working to raise their children and then return to employment when the children reached adolescence. Now, 80 percent of French women between 25 and 49 years of age are gainfully employed. Many no longer consider the occupation of a salaried position as a moment in their lives, but they value it as a career that they can (and want) to pursue, despite the difficulties of balancing paid work and motherhood.[2]

Along with advances in education and employment, a 1967 law allowing French women to use contraceptives significantly contributed to the social transformations of the last decades. Initially, women of the middle classes, better informed than those of the lower classes, were the first to benefit from this law. But the use of contraception has now become universal, largely due to the actions of family planning centers, the availability of information in the schools, and the low cost of the birth-control pill. In 1974 a law legalizing abortion was passed, as a result of feminists' strong mobilization efforts. In reality, this legislation simply expanded access to abortion and enabled women to avoid unwanted pregnancies.

Educated in the same schools with boys,[3] engaged in active professional lives, able to decide to have children or not, and if so, then to determine the moment when they will have them, French women acquired a quite unanticipated autonomy. Most women have ceased to be financially dependent on their spouses. A recent study by the National Institute of Demographic Studies indicates the point at which this autonomy has become a reality: the number of marriages in France is rapidly declining to the benefit of "free unions." Fifty-two percent of women bringing their first child into the world are not married, and births outside of marriage have increased from 6 percent in 1967 to 40 percent in 1997. This revolution seems to be for the most part linked to the fact that women no longer feel the need to be protected by a legal connection; they no longer depend on a spouse in order to live and raise their children. The decline in the number of marriages corresponds, in fact, to the decline in the number of women who stay at home. This latter group has fallen from 3 million in 1990 to 2.4 million in 1999.

French women have achieved not only near legal equality but also rights that allow them to demonstrate their independence. Nevertheless, their wages remain 20 to 30 percent lower than those for men doing equivalent work, and if men hold equal or superior credentials, they are still preferred to women in the labor market. Moreover, women occupy the majority of temporary and part-time positions, most often not by choice. In spite of their academic success and their growing presence in professional life, women rarely advance into positions of authority. Not one woman heads a top 200 French company, and women make up only 7 percent of all managing executives in the country's top 5,000 firms. In the highest levels of public administration, even though equality has been a principle of administration since 1945, women are the exception (among ambassadors 4 percent are women, among the heads of central administration management fewer than 10 percent are women). Only a short while ago it seemed "natural" not to question these disparities. And when questioned, they were explained away as being progressively overcome, or as resulting from women's refusal to accept such responsibilities.

At that time no one questioned the sex of those in authority in the public sphere. Even French feminists, whose job was to think about social change, were not at all (or very little) interested in this question. Societal change was nevertheless of a sufficient scale to justify an analysis of the causes of men's persistent dominance in positions of power, and to test the heuristic value of the concept of gender—indeed, to enrich it. The concept of gender allows us to escape from a structuralist interpretation of women and men and their relations, to say and to see that the attributed personas of woman and man are neither fixed nor subject to linear evolution. We can see that over the course of one or two generations, gender relations in French society have changed because women have changed, and more than men. The contraceptive revolution, in particular, introduced a considerable rupture that proved difficult to mend. The national strike of November 25, 1995, protesting against the government's proposed restrictions on access to contraception and abortion, gave evidence to that effect. The Right was returned to power in 1993 and Jacques Chirac was elected president in 1995. On the initiative of women's movements, more than 100,000 people descended on the streets of Paris and in numerous other French cities. One had not seen so many French women mobilized since the strike of October 6, 1974, when women had demanded the right to abortion and to expanded access to abortion services.

The events of 1995 revealed that young women in particular regarded the equality with which they had grown up as nonnegotiable. They unexpectedly discovered that a return to the past was possible at a time when feminism seemed to them, only a short while ago, to belong to the past. They suddenly felt the necessity to reflect collectively on their situation. In universities, women students on their own initiative created small groups, the goal of which was not only to preserve the rights acquired by preceding generations but also to denounce misogyny, often with humor. At the same time, in contrast to similar groups in the 1970s, these women students wanted their groups to be mixed. They could not conceive of the possibility that a struggle for a more egalitarian society could be waged without the participation of men, without men's cooperation, and without changing them first of all. These young women assumed that their issues mattered. Because they saw themselves as future leaders and made their professional careers a high priority, they were intrigued by the idea of parity—even if the means to get there provoked many furious debates amongst them. Through their own experiences, supported by statistics, they discovered that there were still as few women in important decision-making positions as in their mothers' time.

At the start of the 1990s women's groups and organizations began to use the word *parity,* and under the pressure of a series of national and international political events, the parity movement was born. The year 1995 may be considered the movement's point of departure, at least in France. But equal representation of women and men in elected assemblies was not then a completely new idea; it had first emerged in supranational organizations. In 1989, inspired by the broad reflections on the nature of democracy initiated by the collapse of the communist regimes, the Council of Europe held a seminar in Strasbourg to discuss important questions. Do the old democracies make good role models for countries in transition? Is it not necessary at a time when these new countries aspire to rejoin Western Europe to carry out a self-critique? Free universal suffrage is one criterion of democracy, but in the West electoral participation is declining, betraying many citizens' doubts about their own system of government. The rise of populist parties was disquieting. And corrupt "affairs" undermined the ideal of the people's representative, necessarily honest and devoted to the public interest. Finally, the question arose: can a democracy in which women are absent (or almost absent) from the deliberation on questions concerning the community's future really be considered democratic?

Since 1995 the European Commission also has put this question on its agenda, within the framework of the Third Program, to find a path to equality of opportunity for women and men. The question of sexual equality was not originally within the community's domain, according to the Treaty of Rome (which is still the Charter of Europe extended from 6 to 12 states), except in the matter of salaries. In order to avoid unfair competition between countries in which women's labor is abundant and underpaid and countries in which it is neither, it was decided that one of the objectives of the Common Market would be equal pay for equal work. Despite these regulations, over the course of more than a quarter of a century the differences between men's and women's salaries have not been substantially reduced. In order to understand the causes of this continuing disparity, was it not necessary to look at who makes the laws and negotiates the salary agreements in each country? The commission then launched a program to study the place of women in positions of political, economic, and social decision-making power. Over the next five years the program was to determine the gender composition of power in the European Union member countries.

With the exception of the new "alternative" political movements, ecologists in particular, the question of the near-complete absence of women from the political world was at the same time a taboo subject. The activists in the French political parties who dared to touch on it were dismissed as feminists from another age; the parties had other concerns. Because feminist movements had declined, political organizations did not have to consider the question of sexual equality. The issue even disappeared from electoral platforms. Once the Left won the French presidential and legislative elections in 1981, receiving considerable support from women voters, it forgot its promises; without a sound many feminists themselves withdrew from the parties in power.[4] One hardly dared suggest the introduction of a quota system for parties or on the electoral lists, let alone oversee its implementation. North European social democratic parties had, in fact, pushed earlier for quotas, a claim at the heart of the parties of the Left in the 1970s. Since 1974 the Socialist party has had a quota rule in its statutes. At first the quota required that women occupy a modest ten percent of managing positions and party electoral lists for proportional polls, but this has been progressively raised to 30 percent.[5] At the beginning of the last decade, one could nevertheless conclude that quotas were not generally respected, at least for the lists of candidates in elections. Other than a small minority among female party members, activist feminists had never unanimously supported quotas. They argued that the 10, 20, or even 30 percent mandate functioned as a ceiling—once attained it would never be surpassed, serving as a fixed apportionment of women. Moreover, many women found it humiliating. Some argued that such quotas were ridiculous because statistically women made up about half of the population; others stressed that quotas threatened to discredit those women who managed to get elected on their own merits. Women who were recruited in order to achieve the 10, 20, or 30 percent quotas were in the end generally chosen by men working in a system that isolated women, especially those who might pose a threat to those men's power.

The word *parity* met with rapid success because it allowed us to escape the logic of quotas, which were always fixed at a level that kept women in the minority. The word *parity* is itself a synonym of equality—of "perfect" equality, according to the Larousse dictionary. In reality, we were very far from the parity ideal. In November 1992, the European Commission held a conference in Athens on the theme "Women in Power," which triggered a social movement and a movement of opinion throughout Europe, and in France in particular. For the first time, the press and various non-governmental organizations (NGOs) were given a statistical table showing the numbers of women in the political decision-making bodies in Europe and an early analysis of the reasons behind the disparities. Having always considering itself the country of the Rights of Man, France now found itself at the bottom of the list, along with Greece, with respect to the participation of women in national legislatures.

In the face of such surprisingly brutal numbers, it became difficult to blame women, or their political "backwardness," for a situation that defied political scientists' traditional explanations. Neither the number of years of universal suffrage, nor the country's dominant religion, nor the participation of women in the labor force, nor even the country's mode of election served to explain the disparities between European countries in terms of the place of women in each country's national parliament.[6] Sociologists and political scientists were forced to study and investigate more closely the reasons for the persistent masculinity of power. Many colloquia and seminars were convened to address this question. It appeared that the principal cause of the rarity of elected women was to be found in the functioning of the political parties, in particular in the candidate selection process. This was especially true in the case of France, where the parties are not mass organizations; parties function as clubs in which the elected (hence mainly men) dominate numerically and are in a position of power. The party is an instrument to assure their reelection and, if possible, to win more elected offices. Consequently, it is difficult for activists to break into party electoral lists. Incumbents possess numerous advantages.[7] They wield the social capital of fame and can claim responsibility for all accomplished work. They also benefit from a political system that allows them to accumulate multiple elected positions. Activists are forced to succumb to this principle of reality: they prefer that their party win the election than that more women are elected. The 1993 parliamentary elections furnished proof that this system allowed the political elite to reproduce itself, or almost; election after election, the percentage of female elected deputies remained almost the same, rising from 5.6 percent in the National Assembly after the 1988 elections to 5.9 percent in the new assembly. This percentage was even more scandalous because nearly the same number of women had been elected deputies to the first National Assembly following the introduction of universal suffrage in 1945. Those activists concerned about parity were forced to call for a law requiring parties to nominate and have elected as many women as men. The first national public strike for the demand was spectacular. On November 10, 1993, the newspaper *Le Monde* published a page-long manifesto symbolically signed by 577 people (288 women and 287 men)—the number of deputies sitting in the National Assembly. The proclamation asserted that without imposing a constraint on the parties' candidate selection process, it would be difficult to imagine a change in the assembly's sexual composition.

The popularity of the demand—the media provided much coverage of this manifesto—required the politically accountable to give some signs of effort. Thus, during the European elections of 1994, several party lists, including that of the Socialist Party, maintained gender parity. During the presidential campaign of 1995, the principal candidates were forced to use the word *parity,* which had until then been applied only to the formation of social parity (negotiations between employers and labor unions were often referred to as "parity negotiations") or relations between national currencies. Several candidates, including Jacques Chirac and Lionel Jospin, even worked to augment the participation of women at all levels of public and political decision-making. A new stage seemed to be reached when the first government designated by the new president of the Republic, Jacques Chirac, included a larger proportion of women (36 percent), a record in the history of the Republic. Nevertheless, a few months later, on the occasion of a cabinet reshuffle designed to "tighten" the government in order to improve its effectiveness, the women were sacrificed, their percentage dropping to 12 percent. This affair provoked considerable reaction and the drafting of a common text by women of the Right and Left who had held ministerial positions, published by an important weekly paper, calling for parity.

The Socialist Party (PS), severely beaten in the 1993 legislative elections, was looking for new ideas. Its leader, Lionel Jospin, was convinced of the necessity to rediscover the support of the feminine electorate and equally of the necessity to feminize the management and representation of his party. He had planned to force the party to ensure that women would represent at least 30 percent of his party's candidates to be presented at the legislative elections scheduled for 1998.[8] Such quotas had, of course, been much decried. But Jospin presented this one as an important first step toward parity. In order to achieve this objective, the PS adopted a method comparable to one that the British Labor Party was introducing at about the same time: on the basis of a national accord with the PS departmental leaders, only women candidates could participate in the internal primaries in one electoral district out of three.[9] The proposal was contested on the grounds that it discriminated against men. Some men also complained that it was absurd because the party would never find enough women. Nevertheless, the PS adopted the principle, and one observed that not only was there no lack of women candidates but that in many "women only" electoral districts, there was a plurality of female candidates. Nearly half the women candidates declared that they would not have stood for election had the electoral district not been reserved, because they believed that a man would have been in a better position to win or that they had not thought to run before. The women candidates won in larger numbers than was foreseen.[10] Nevertheless, even though the Left won these elections, the number of women elected was modest: in 1993, 35 women, or 6 percent of the National Assembly, were elected. Following the 1997 legislative elections, there were 62 women elected, or barely 11 percent.

The Left returned to power. In his inaugural address before Parliament in June 1997, the new prime minister, Lionel Jospin, announced that his government would propose a revision of the Constitution to allow for laws designed to prescribe parity in elected assemblies. The government's demand for parity awakened the old conflict between "egalitarian" and "difference" feminists. The partisans of parity were accused by the egalitarian current of defending a naturalist concept of human gender, of "biologizing" society and the citizenry. In fact, one found among the "paritistes" women who defended parity in the name of "differences between the sexes," for example, Sylviane Agazinski.[11] Others, however, supported the egalitarian current, for example, Éliane Viennot.[12] The tension between equality and difference is an old story when it is a question of equality between women and men.

Joan Scott has judiciously chosen for a title of a recent work a phrase from Olympe de Gouges, who on the eve of the French Revolution already summed up women's dilemma: "only paradoxes to offer."[13] Women have in fact only paradoxes to offer. How is it actually possible to ask for equality *for women* without asking *as women,* since it is as women that equality is refused them? The philosopher Françoise Collin was one of the first to criticize parity.[14] She argued that "this strategy targets not a biological category but an identifiable social group." She does not imply that this group be endowed with a definable and immutable identity, but observes only that it exists in fact and is reparable as such. The constitution of this social group is not an invention of feminism, or of "paritistes," but first of all a product of the social mechanisms and secular politics of our society, and of all the previous history that has made women into a marginalized group.[15]

Jospin's June 1997 announcement of the revision of the Constitution re-ignited the debate, quickly mobilizing the adversaries of parity. Thirty-four philosophers, jurists, sociologists (among them 23 women) put together a resolution denouncing the government's project with great virulence.[16] Interestingly, most of these authors were situated on the left of the political chessboard. In their view, legislation designed to guarantee equal access of women and men to mandates and appointments would put the Republic in danger and betray the universalist ideal. The political scientist, Évelyne Pisier, writes "that difference blossoms in actions, but does not cede one inch on the principle of equality before the law." On the other hand, the philosopher Élisabeth Badinter labeled the proposed measure a "regression," agreeing with Alain-Gérard Slama, a political scientist and editorial contributor to *Le Figaro,* that such legislation recalls nothing less than the Vichy regime and fascism. A deputy of the Right took up the same argument, equating the government's proposed revision with the Nuremberg Laws. Clearly strong passions infused the debate.

Surprisingly, the intellectuals arguing against the parity amendment ignored the fact that the word *woman* was long ago imbedded in French law. The French Constitution's preamble includes the statement that "the law guarantees to the woman, in all domains, rights equal to those of the man."[17] Sex is also already present in the law, even omnipresent. It is one of the fundamental categories of civil law and lies at the foundation of our daily lives and social existence. Without her or his consent, each individual is attributed a sex (boy or girl) at birth. This sex, declared to the civil state, accompanies each person throughout her or his life and determines much of her or his social development. Another controversy that has agitated the intellectual milieus—same-sex marriages—has also shown the centrality of sex in the law. Curiously, it has also revealed that those denouncing parity as the "biologization" of society are opposed, with the same vigor, to the legal recognition of lesbian and gay couples. They argue that this would imperil the difference between the sexes, which must have its place, according to sociologist Nathalie Heinich, in her essay on the "context of the laws of the family."[18] She suggests that we should ignore sex in public matters but preserve its normative role in civil law.

Other parity opponents argue that parity legislation would open the door to all "communitarians." Parity, it is argued, would justify claims of Muslims and Jews, young and old, to obtain representation corresponding to their numeric presence in society. This is strange reasoning, because women do not constitute a "community" but are a part of all communities. Women are, as I have argued elsewhere, a "category" in law, and they cannot escape this juridical identity by religious conversion, intermarriage, or changing their social status. French law avoids any reference to a citizen's origins, social status, skin color, or religion. France considers all persons to be equal in their rights and duties. But because of their sex, women have been sent back to nature, excluded for a century and a half from the citizenry, dominated, domesticated, and treated as "minors" once they were married. Unlike men, women acquired legal equality only recently, gradually, and not through a single decision that would have made of them the equals of men.

Society does not evolve "naturally." One of the founders of the Third Republic, Léon Gambetta, loved to say, "that which constitutes true democracy is not to acknowledge all are equal but to make them." Progress requires a program of political action. In a democracy the law's function is to shape the rules necessary to reduce inequality. The Left has long believed in using legislative power to promote equality, which in most cases implies introducing constraints on citizens' behavior. For example, the French republicans of the 1870s believed that providing all children with access to free education was a means to create equality. This led to a "scholarly obligation." Requiring parents to send their children to school provoked a debate: was it not a limit on the liberty of families, and more exactly on paternal authority? We know that even today not all children would be educated if school were not obligatory. It is not then for reasons of "nature" that positive action to provide women access to decision-making positions should be taken, but in order to correct the effects of history that have excluded or marginalized them.

The revision of the Constitution in June 1999 makes it possible to create laws obliging political parties and groups to present as many women as men during elections, at least for certain elections. The plan is, in fact, technically complex. It is possible to make simple rules for elections held on the basis of proportional principles with party lists but it is difficult in the case of plurality elections. Now, the two types of election are in use in France. The adopted law requires party organizations in communes with more than 3,500 inhabitants to present parity lists. The same applies to regional elections and a number of Senate seats elected by party list, as well as for European parliamentary elections. The part of the law requiring parity not only of candidacy but also of result does not apply to national parliamentary elections. Deputies are in fact elected in single-member districts. Instead, the government proposed a financial sanction (parties in France are in part publicly financed): parties that do not present 50 percent women will have their public funding reduced.

Both female and male politicians, who supported parity before the Parliament as a principle, have criticized the enacted parity legislation. Without a doubt it would have been preferable that the laws proposed to Parliament were conceived as a strategy and not as a dogma justified by the biological difference between the sexes. Thus, I did not think, as did also many legal scholars, that the time had come to pass a constitutional amendment, because it was not necessary.[19] The government could have simply asserted, by virtue of the Preamble of the Constitution, that it is the role of the law to guarantee sexual equality. It could have also stressed that the jurisprudence of the 1982 Constitutional Council had been displaced, when in 1983 France ratified the 1979 International Convention on the Elimination of Discrimination Against Women, without opposition from the Constitutional Council. The states that introduced this convention into their law empowered themselves to take measures of positive action to create equality, notably in representation. At a given historical moment, parity can be a means to experiment with equality between the two socially and juridically constructed genders as they are inscribed today in the law, which can and must evolve. Such a law, conceived as temporary, would have stated that it did not institute the "difference between the sexes" as an intangible norm but aimed at correcting the consequences of a juridicosocial construction by experimenting with numerical equality in representation.

One thing is certain: the parity movement has in Europe in any case, and in France in particular shown that the absence or the scarcity of women in the elected assemblies is the product of exclusion and a mark of an archaic political culture. Parity in decision-making positions at the local, national, and international level will mean neither the end of male domination in all its manifestations nor the end of the story. It will not put an end to all injustices, inequalities, and violence. But it may be a means to deepen democracy.

Notes

1. Christian Baudelot and Roger Establet, *Allez les filles!* (Paris: Le Seuil, 1992).
2. Margaret Maruani, ed., *Les nouvelles frontières de l'inégalité, hommes et femmes sur le marché du travail* (Paris: La Découverte, 1998).

3. The French government resolved to mix genders in schools in 1959, but this was not implemented across the entire educational system until the 1970s.
4. Jane Jenson and Mariette Sineau, *Mitterrand et les Françaises: un rendez-vous manqué* (Paris: Presses des sciences politiques, 1995).
5. On this point see "Actualité de la parité," *Projet féministe* 4–5 (1996).
6. Proportional representation is reputed to be more favorable to the representation of women. In 1986 France experimented with this type of polling in the elections to the National Assembly, but the number of women elected did not increase.
7. In 1999 men constituted 92 percent of mayors and 94 percent of county counselors, two strategic elected mandates that help lay the foundations for one's candidacy to become a deputy or senator.
8. The President of the Republic, Jacques Chirac, decided in April 1997 to dissolve the National Assembly and to precede to the anticipated elections, which took place in May and June 1997.
9. The department is a French administrative unit that goes back to the Revolution of 1789. The departments are divided into electoral districts for elections to the National Assembly.
10. See Françoise Gaspard and Philippe Bataille, *Comment les femmes changent la politique et pourquoi les hommes résistent* (Paris: Editions de la Découverte, 1999).
11. Sylviane Agacinski, *Politique des sexes* (Paris: Seuil, 1998).
12. See in particular Elianne Viennot, *La démocratie "à la française" ou les femmes indésirables* (Paris: Publications de l'Université de Paris 7-Denis-Diderot, 1995).
13. Joan W. Scott, *Only Paradoxes to Offer: French Feminists and the Rights of Man* (Cambridge, MA: Harvard University Press, 1996).
14. Françoise Collin, "La parité, une autre démocratie en France," *Les Cahiers du GRIF* 47 (June 1993): 137–141.
15. Françoise Collin, *Le différend des sexes* (Paris: Editions Pleins Feux, 1999), 72.
16. Micheline Amar, ed., *Le piège de la parité, Arguments pour un débat* (Paris: Hachette-Littératures, 1999).
17. This article appears in the preamble of the Constitution of 1946, which is part of the French "constitutional bloc."
18. Nathalie Heinich, "Les fins, les moyens, les principes, trois lignes de clivage," in *Le piège de la parité,* 145–150.
19. Françoise Gaspard, "La parité, principe ou stratégie?" *Le Monde Diplomatique* (November 1998).

Part II

Parity as an Electoral Issue

This page intentionally left blank

Chapter Five

Constitutionalizing Equal Access:
High Hopes, Dashed Hopes?

Isabelle Giraud and Jane Jenson

In November and December 1999 the *Délégation aux droits des femmes et à l'égalité des chances entre les hommes et les femmes* of France's National Assembly held hearings on two pieces of draft legislation. These bills were the result of a decade-long effort by activists within the parity movement to promote gender equality in all elected bodies. One step in that direction seemed to come on July 8, 1999, when the Constitution was reformed; Section 3 of the French Constitution now provides a general guarantee that "the law will further equal access of women and men to elected office and functions." The report of the *Délégation,* published in January 2000, documents a long and detailed debate over the issues involved in activating that constitutional amendment.[1] It reveals the gaps between the original goal of creating parity—that is "50 percent women and 50 percent men"—and the legislation currently under discussion, which would increase the presence of women in electoral politics but not necessarily result in parity.[2]

In their testimony before the parliamentary body, expert witnesses criticized the draft bill for insufficiently promoting full gender equality. For example, in her testimony the well-known feminist researcher and political scientist, Mariette Sineau, criticized the draft bill for two reasons. First, it reserved its strictest requirements for elections using lists, and therefore excluded important non-proportional representation (PR) elections, especially those to the National Assembly, whose overwhelmingly masculine composition had provoked the parity movement in the first place.[3] Her second major critique was that the bill focused on nominations, ignoring the issue of whether elections would produce more elected women.

The *Délégation* agreed with her; its first recommendation was that "parity" be understood as equality of results.[4] The National Assembly also moved in that direction by voting to amend the government's legislation.[5] On January 25, 2000, it voted on first reading to require that Euro-parliamentary elections and Senate elections (for senators elected by PR) have "tic-tac" lists (that is, alternation by sex), while lists for municipal and regional elections must have as many women as men, in every group of six candidates. As for the all-important National Assembly, however, the amended draft bill would require the parties to nominate only as many women as men, within a 2 percent range, or risk a fine. Moreover, because the fine is not very onerous, results such as a 60–40 split would result in only a 10 percent reduction in public finding. Such measures can do little to guarantee parity in results; the emphasis remains on equality in nominations, not outcomes. Therefore the law, even as amended, falls short of the original goal of instituting gender parity.

In her testimony to the *Délégation,* Geneviève Fraisse (*Déléguée interministérielle aux droits des femmes* from November 1997 until November 1998, and currently a deputy in the European Parliament) asked the deputies to recall that parity in electoral politics was but a means to a larger end. She spoke of the need to promote gender equality everywhere—in social, work, and associational life. However, the draft bill could only address electoral politics, given the preexisting limits set by the constitutional amendment. Therefore, her testimony could do little more than remind the deputies why some activists, especially those making claims for parity in other European countries, had mobilized in the first place. Their goal was to create gender equality in all spaces in which power is exercised, and not only in electoral politics.

This chapter does not analyze the ins and outs of the ongoing debate, which is by no means settled yet. Rather, it asks two questions. First, why are so many of the people who mobilized throughout the 1990s to promote equal rights for women now disappointed or critical of the direction the reform has taken? For example, in 1998 Françoise Gaspard, an early and prominent activist for parity, spoke out against the strategy of pursuing a constitutional amendment. Instead, she favored investing scarce political resources in pressure for immediate legislation (which would be necessary in any case), rather than taking so much time to hold out for constitutional recognition.[6] A second but closely related question asks: why have the very hopes for parity in France been focused on the limited goal of electoral politics?

Since 1997 the European Union has embraced, via the Treaty of Amsterdam, a constitutional commitment to broad-based equality rights, building on earlier actions of the courts and other institutions, including the

Equal Opportunities Unit of the European Commission. Since 1994 the German Basic Law recognizes the legitimacy of affirmative action to overcome "existing disadvantages," whereever they may exist. Since 1982 the Canadian Constitution guarantees women (as well as a range of other groups) protection from discrimination and enshrines affirmative action as a constitutional right.

In contrast, because of its location in Section 3 of the French Constitution, the only equality that French women are specifically guaranteed by this reform is access to elected office. None of the other domains in which social and economic inequalities exist, nor even the nonelected functions of politics, are subject to this commitment to equal access. This reform, as Geneviève Fraisse reminded French parliamentarians, falls short of the pledge to promote "equality in decision-making" in all sectors (business as well as politics, for example), made by the European Network of Women in Decision-Making. Since its Third Action Plan in 1990, Europe's Equal Opportunities Unit continually has identified the absence of women in decision-making positions as a major blockage to the achievement of the equal opportunities guaranteed by Article 119 of the 1957 Treaty of Rome. Both the Declaration of Athens (1992) and the Charter of Rome (1996) had called for parity in decision-making and not only in politics.

The French reform is more modest than the constitutional and extra-constitutional guarantees that have been introduced in other liberal democracies, such as Canada. The Canadian Charter of Rights and Freedoms (1982) and Quebec's *Charte des droits et des libertés* (1975) provide a general protection against discrimination. Of course, this is not the case in the United States, where the Equal Rights Amendment (ERA) failed and where the percentage of women in elected office is closer to that of France than to most European countries and Canadian jurisdictions.

Thus, in comparative terms, the limited ambition of the French reform merits attention. In consequence, this chapter considers both why the parity movement's ambitions were restricted to electoral politics and why, even within that understanding of parity, the result has been less than many activists hoped.

Gender Parity in a Neoliberal Citizenship Regime

The answers to these two queries will be found in the ways in which the run-up to the reform guaranteeing equal access to elected office fit within the restructuring processes of the French citizenship regime over the last decade and a half.[7] The equality promoted by actors within this regime was increasingly limited to the institutions of liberal democracy, while any attention to social justice concentrated more on promoting the "inclusion" of the marginalized than on fostering socioeconomic equality. If in the past liberalism may have failed women, the recent reform of the French Constitution and the subsequent proposals for changing the electoral law complement and support the vision of citizenship promoted by neoliberalism.

The postwar divisions and discourses of class-based politics attenuated over the 1980s and 1990s, as the French Left and Right competed at the political center. In part, the institutions of the Fifth Republic account for this convergence, including the compromises necessitated by cohabitation, but they go far beyond that. New ideological templates hold sway.[8] For example, the Socialist Party in the 1990s, and particularly with Lionel Jospin as first secretary, has committed itself to promoting democratization with the fervor previously reserved for achieving social and economic equality. The distinction between left-wing and right-wing politics, which had shaped French political life for most of the postwar years and was deeply inscribed in partisan politics with the consolidation and rise of the Union of the Left in the 1970s, no longer holds. The Left of the Left gave way with the collapse of the Communist Party, while the Right struggled with its demons on the Far Right. Policy differences between the two political families blurred during the presidencies of François Mitterrand, as governments submitted to the discipline of European integration, while seeking a replacement for the failed Keynesianism of the union of the Left.[9]

The parity movement, as we will demonstrate below, was both a symbol of and support for this new politics. Its claims made sense in the new political landscape. The movement was cross-partisan, supported by women coming from parties of the Right as well as the Left, and indeed bridging the deep divide that had characterized the second wave of French feminism from the mid-1960s until the early 1990s.[10]

Moreover, the parity movement was a full partner in the European adventure; some of its financial support and much of its visibility came originally from being the French partner in a broad European initiative to promote gender equality in decision-making. And finally, as we will demonstrate in detail below, the concept of parity was sufficiently flexible that it could be reworked in debates about liberal democracy so as to shore up the institutions threatened by a crisis of representation. In this sense it provided a defense against the ambient criticism of liberal democratic institutions and promised reforms that would reinforce rather than menace them.

During the transition from the postwar citizenship regime to a neoliberal one, issues of representation and the legitimacy of representative institutions have held center stage. The problems identified in this crisis went far beyond the absence of women in elected office, however. They included accusations and findings of corruption, as well as complaints about a widening gap between the voters and elected officials. In other words, French liberal democracy, as that of many other countries, suffered from a crisis of confidence. This was the scene into which the parity movement entered. Its proposals for feminizing the institutions of liberal democracy, replacing the old gang with visibly different elected officials, and dramatically changing the way political parties behaved was a positive and appealing vision in those troubled times. Embracing the demand for parity, as we will see below, allowed the still-male-dominated political forces to be seen to be addressing a fundamental problem of widespread concern to the population.

We use the rest of this chapter to demonstrate that the door by which the demand for parity entered debates about the "modernization of politics" (*modernisation de la vie politique*) and the place it came to occupy in that discussion help account for the final result, which is a narrow focal point on electoral democracy and legislation which focuses more on access than on results. Indeed, at each stage of the decade-long mobilization, the larger politics of representation worked to narrow the meaning of equality to the political and to silence claims seeking redress of other types of discrimination and other forms of inequality, whether social or economic.

A First Step: Reclaiming the Revolutionary Tradition, Debating Republicanism

All social movements have their organic intellectuals, those who participate in its construction of claims to legitimacy and arguments in support of change. For the parity movement, feminist philosophers and historians have played a central role, although it has often been other social scientists who popularized their ideas.

The arguments for gender parity have been constructed out of a vision of French "exceptionalism." Despite the precocious movement to universal male suffrage at the heart of republicanism, France is described as the shameful "red lantern of Europe," bringing up the rear in terms of the number of women holding elective office.[11] Such characterizations of the problem owe a good deal to the intellectual space for mobilization that was opened by the celebrations—and controversies—surrounding the bicentenary of the French Revolution in 1989.

That year brought the publication of one of the classic works of the parity initiative, *Muse de la Raison. La démocratie exclusive et la différence des sexes,* written by political theorist Geneviève Fraisse. She identified the absence of elected women and their more general exclusion from sites of power as a direct legacy of the French Revolution and its core vision of universality. Because this was a French problem (rather than a general one of liberal democracy), it would also require a French solution—that is, a frontal assault on the assumptions of universality, so central to the country's republican tradition.

The next year two important multivolume historical collections appeared. Each was immense (five volumes in one case, three in the other), and both brought together in one place all the material necessary to begin reclaiming and rewriting the history of French women.[12] The Revolution was once again a key moment, as historians retrieved and popularized Olympe de Gouges's *Déclaration universelle des droits de la femme,* recounting her death by guillotine during the Terror and analyzing the sexist treatment of French queens in revolutionary discourse.[13] De Gouges would be constantly cited throughout the subsequent struggles. For example, Elisabeth Guigou, the minister of justice, opened the parliamentary debate on the constitutional amendment on December 15, 1998 with the classic De-Gougien quote, "If a woman has the right to climb the scaffold, she should equally have the right to take the rostrum."[14]

In subsequent analyses, the history of French feminisms in the nineteenth and first half of the twentieth century was rehabilitated. Women's struggles for suffrage and political rights were celebrated at the same time that the long history of the country's exceptionalism was described. Indeed, certain historians constructed an explicit parallel between interwar suffrage claims, which foundered in the political crises of the 1930s, as well as explaining certain black moments of French history (such as February 6, 1934) as the result of a masculine monopoly of political power.[15]

Others went back to the nineteenth century in search of ancestors. The claims for political equality of Jeanne Deroin (1830s) and Julie Daubié (1870s), for example, were rediscovered.[16] Three figures in particular became important to the iconography of the parity movement: Maria Deraisme, Hubertine Auclert, and Marguerite Durand. All three had promoted a rights-based vision of feminism and had considered political rights an important tool for women's emancipation. Indeed, Auclert is frequently cited as a direct ancestor of the parity movement. In the 1880s she called for equality of representation in addition to female suffrage.[17]

Why did this rewriting of women's history and the reexamination of France's republican history matter? A first reason is because it allowed the movement to begin to construct a broad cross-class base of support as well as to bridge the cleavages that had previously made French feminism one of the most ideologically divided of the second-wave movements.[18] In the

1960s and 1970s the central wing of the women's movement—which itself scorned even voting in elections until 1981—had tended to dismiss these female ancestors as examples of "bourgeois feminism," if they were allowed to be named feminist at all.[19] Their discovery and embrace signaled a major change.

This work of rehabilitation continued through the 1990s. For example, in an important collection edited by Éliane Viennot in 1996, Christine Bard provided a sympathetic reading of the suffrage movement of the interwar years. In the past this movement had been dismissed as maternalist, as well as dominated by Catholic or other right-wing organizations. Bard's work showed how, in the sexist circumstances of the time, the suffrage movement had proceeded more from strategy than a commitment to traditionalism or maternalism. In addition, she recovered the history of interwar feminists, such as Monette Thomas, who had called for "proportional representation" of women in Parliament.[20]

Reclaiming and accepting this part of French women's history's meant that several doors swung open. One message was that a variety of routes had been followed in making claims for political representation, and that such variety was legitimate. Sectarianism was giving way to ecumenism as well as to non-partisanism. Women coming from the Left claimed republican feminists as their model, thereby aligning themselves with center-right women in history and opening the way to a similar cross-party alliance in the present. Second, none of these female ancestors had had a broad-based movement behind them. Taking them as a model thereby legitimated an elite-led movement with only a tiny popular base. Third, the new interpretation of what had been a maternalist movement, strategic or not, meant that a hand was tendered to contemporary women who sought a role in politics in order to realize a family-centered or even essentialist agenda. For example, at a UNESCO meeting on parity in June 1993, Simone Veil said, "I believe that men and women are rich in their differences and that they are complementary. It is, moreover, in the name of these differences and of all that women can offer that it is necessary to demand equality in politics." As the journalist Christiane Chombeau remarked, "a few years ago, Madame Veil's views would have provoked protests in a meeting of women. Instead, thunderous applause greeted this claim to a right to equality in difference."[21]

The results of this smoothing over of old divisions, both within feminism and across the political divide, were frequently evidenced.[22] In November 1992 the first European Summit of Women and Decision-Making was held in Athens. A number of French women, from both the Right and Left, were actively involved. Simone Veil (member of a center-right party and former president of the European Parliament) and Édith Cresson (former Socialist prime minister) were the official French representatives. In 1993 a Manifesto of 577 (289 women and 288 men) was published in *Le Monde* in support of parity-based democracy, demanding "as many women as men" in all elected bodies. Signatures came from all political horizons.[23] In June 1996 ten female ex-ministers from governments of the Right as well as the Left published a Manifesto for Parity in *L'Express.*

A second reason that this rewriting of history and philosophy matters is because it anchored the claim for parity within the republicanism of the neoliberal citizenship regime. As a political principle, republicanism is shared by both the left and center of the political spectrum. Therefore, by tagging republicanism as exclusionary, the parity movement could directly appeal to that tradition on its own terms. Despite being cast by some as an enemy of republicanism, the parity movement is hardly that.[24] From the beginning it has located its claims within the revolutionary tradition, domesticating it so that it resembles a well-known social situation that is already associated with the two sexes, the family. The first text published in *Le Monde* revealed this amalgam of revolutionary, republican, and homey discourse. "A true democracy is built on the real, not a false, political equality of all its children. This is the way to translate a revised and corrected republican motto: Liberty, Equality and Parity."[25]

The discourse of parity is individualist, as many good republican discourses are. If parity were instituted, each individual would still be responsible for her success. New rules would simply guarantee access for both sexes to a level playing field. Where the parity movement differs from classical republicanism, however, is in its insistence that rather than the "abstract" and de-sexed individual so often imagined by male-stream texts, any individual is always either male or female. Therefore, equality demands that no one suffer from this inevitable difference.[26]

In addition, with its anticategorical stance, the movement bars the door to any notion that the universality of republicanism should attempt to accommodate to the myriad of differences which many ethnic and other groups in France seek to have recognized—or the "politics of diversity" that North Americans treat as normal. The movement itself abhors "slippery slope" arguments that might to claims for better representation for other groups.[27] It does so by insisting that sex is a case apart. It is never comparable to ethnicity, race, class, or language.

Both the individualism and the clear distinction between sex and other "differences" means that the movement for parity began to find a welcoming political opportunity structure. This solid anchor within the republican discourse meant that the parity movement could begin to develop allies within the political elite.

Finding Allies:
The Crisis of Representation

One of the political spaces in which such alliances across the elite were forged was the public debate over the "crisis of representation." It provoked a good deal of discussion in the winter of 1992–1993 and eventually led a number of male politicians to adopt new practices with respect to the institutions of democracy. Some of the prescriptions for the malaise included a dose of "parity." However, by the mid-1990s the term *parity* had come to mean many things, some of which had little to do with the equal presence of women and men in elected bodies.

By December 1992, notions were gaining ground that the political world was closed, that the elite had lost touch with ordinary citizens and politicians were making decisions that did not reflect constituents' views, that many elected officials were corrupt, and that they clung to outmoded distinctions, such as left and right. The time had come, according to those intervening in this debate, to move away from old practices. In this controversy, the Greens, whose positions blurred the usual left-right distinctions, were frequently cited as examples of all that might be good in the transformation of political parties.[28]

The consensus that ultimately emerged from the debate was that it was necessary to replace the old and tired party hacks with a new generation and that the political institutions should be reformed to make them more open and less likely to be taken over by a small and isolated elite. For example, the *cumul des mandats,* which permitted a single person to hold several elected positions simultaneously (for instance, that of mayor, deputy, regional councilor, Euro-parliamentarian all at the same time) came in for criticism as concentrating power too much. Feminists had long been critical of the same institution, describing it as a blockage to access.[29] The two arguments could merge into a call for institutional redesign.

The groups and associations promoting parity that were created in 1992 and 1993 picked up and elaborated such themes precisely. The point of departure for their claims was the crisis of representation. As *Au pouvoir citoyenennes!* put it: "This book deliberately engages with the thinking about the content of the democratic system, about its improvement and its functioning."[30] Instituting parity would automatically bring a significant renewal of political personnel; the National Assembly in 1993 still was 94 percent male. The old and tired could be replaced, and the new politics could begin.

This debate about the crisis of representation was followed by the establishment of several associations that explicitly positioned themselves as able to correct the weaknesses of the institutions. In 1993, 14 existing women's associations, representing elected women, Catholic women, and the center-right (among others), formed *Elles-aussi*. Described as dedicated to achieving parity, it would conduct a national campaign to mobilize, support and prepare women to become candidates in upcoming elections.[31] Simultaneously, Yvette Roudy created the *Assemblée des femmes* as a group within the Socialist Party. Despite being an internal body, the group was open from the beginning to interested women who were not party members. Academics were included in this category. Madame Roudy justified founding the *Assemblée des femmes* by the fact that political parties' misogyny—reflected in their failure to nominate women—cut them off from their political base.

Simultaneously, there was a debate about the institutions of representation going on within the Socialist Party, and this soon had important consequences. Defeated in the 1993 legislative elections, the party organized a vast process of internal reflection, with assizes held at all levels from the local to the national throughout the spring of 1993. In July in Lyon, the leadership of the party faced a disgruntled, even angry base that accused it of being too distant, unconcerned, and unresponsive. Propositions circulated widely calling for better control of the leaders by the base and in general for internal democracy. Into this unstable situation erupted about a dozen Socialist *paritaristes* who demanded implementation of the quota of 30 percent women candidates. Rather than being rejected, their proposal was readily accepted by the leadership, for whom it was a way to signal a commitment to better representation. Thus, the first secretary, Michel Rocard, incorporated the 30 percent quota into his proposals presented at the end of the congress.

Change began to come fast and furious. Michel Rocard announced that his 1994 Euro-parliamentary list would alternate the sexes.[32] The list was almost half female and half male.[33] Indeed, fully six lists looked quite *paritaire*.

Then, during the 1995 presidential elections, candidates were compelled to reveal their positions on how to improve the political representation of women.[34] Several activists of the parity movement organized an event for March 8, during which they interrogated all the candidates. The Communist called for a referendum, the Green for a constitutional reform, Lionel Jospin (PS) proposed an *estates-general* of women to discuss the matter, while Jacques Chirac called on the parties to encourage female candidates. Édouard Balladur, who had forgotten to put the matter on his electoral platform, announced that day that he supported minimalist quotas for municipal and regional elections.

Following the election of Jacques Chirac in May, Prime Minister Alain Juppé appointed the most feminized cabinet in French history; 29 percent of its members were women. By November of the same year, he had dismissed 8 of the 13, provoking an outcry throughout the ranks of women politicians and among parity activists.

Such unanimity in outrage arose directly from the stance of the movement at the time. While there might be differences in the philosophical grounding of various tendencies, as described above, there was very little talk of the policy content that might follow from electing more women. Moreover, because of the non-partisanship that was at the center of the movement, women from the Left as well as the Right found it logical to defend the *Juppettes,* as the women fired from the cabinet were sometimes termed.

Consideration of policy content could not be completely avoided, however. The parity activists and the movement itself stumbled for a moment in fall 1995. In response to a call from the CADAC (*Coordination pour le Droit à l'avortement et à la contraception*), 40,000 women and men, many in family groupings, joined the demonstration in Paris on November 25 in defense of the right to abortion and contraception. While access to abortion had been deteriorating over the years, due in part to the violent actions of the pro-life forces, the precipitating factor creating this large turnout and drawing the support of unions, parties, and women's groups was the draft legislation put forward by an RPR (*Rassemblement pour la République*) deputy, Christine Boutin.[35] It was hard, in this case, to defend the principle that policy content was not the issue when discussing representation. Many had to acknowledge that an elected woman might adopt positions worse than those of many men.

The problem intensified as the National Front took to nominating women. Nonetheless, parity activists continued to refuse to enter what they saw a trap. For example, they used the following argument to explain their principles to those scandalized by the National Front's substitution of Catherine Mégret, self-acknowledged as having no qualifications for the position, as mayor when her husband was relieved of his duties by the courts:

> But in mixing together everything, and using the argument that a "good" [male] candidate is preferable to a "bad" [female] candidate, one is quite simply undermining the basic idea of parity. The claim of parity, we should remember, is based on the self-evident assumption that there must be as many women as men in public life, from all the political parties that participate in elections.[36]

By the late 1990s, then, as it took off and gained popularity, there were two dimensions of the parity movement that helped confine the definition of equality to electoral equality alone. The first was its non-partisanship and cross-ideological composition. Some women were *paritaristes* because they believed in women's differences; Simone Veil was not alone in making an argument for women's "different viewpoint" and the need to represent it.[37] Others, however, were in the movement because they believed profoundly that true equality required recognition of gender difference and measures to overcome discrimination. Into this fragile coalition, constructed around a non-partisan grouping of elite women, discussion of social issues or of policy matters would only bring disruption and therefore weakness. Therefore, success depended on keeping all eyes focused on the one position everyone accepted—that French politics would be better if more women held elected office.

The second dimension of the movement that generated this limited focus was the articulation of the movement's claim with the analysis of the crisis of representation. This opening in the political opportunity structure allowed claims for better representation of women to be heard by mainstream and male politicians facing their own crisis of confidence. If they could modernize politics by feminizing it, everyone would benefit. However, this discourse also imposed limits. The crisis of representation was itself confined to electoral politics and its institutions, such as political parties; it was not taken as a sign of the need for broader social change or for equalizing other sites of power. Therefore, having hitched its wagon to the "crisis of representation" horse, the parity movement was on a ride through the institutions of liberal democracy. It lost any capacity it might have had, or some activists might have wished for, to speak convincingly of promoting other forms of equality and countering other forms of discrimination.

These are the reasons that the definition of parity used in the French debates was often substantially narrower than that used in European discourse, in which parity implied access to various sites of power. Nevertheless, some activists did promote this broader understanding of parity, calling for a feminization of and greater gender equality in all sites of power. For example, Monique Dental, *chargée de mission à la recherche et statistiques* for the *Service des droits des femmes* and president of *Réseau pour la parité "ruptures,"* wrote in 1997:

> We think of parity as the basic principle of an approach to citizenship education.... Parity must be extended to the following domains:
>
> establishment of education for parity . . .
> measures to allow economic and social parity . . .
> measures to introduce parity in the household . . .

measures for cultural parity . . .
parity in politics.³⁸

A similar position was promoted by Geneviève Fraisse when she was an interministerial delegate (*déléguée interministerielle*).³⁹ Françoise Gaspard used a stretch version of the concept when she wrote in 1997, "Parity in representation, in consultative bodies and the administration is obviously not an end in itself. It is, however, beyond an indicator of equality, one means among others to reinforce democracy and to advance women's situation which continues to be marked by inequality, domination, and subordination."⁴⁰ Moreover, and perhaps somewhat ironically, one of the major institutional innovations of these years, the *Observatoire de la parité,* created in October 1995, continues to promote a broader vision of equality-seeking. This new institution is charged with making propositions to the government on a wide variety of dimensions of parity, including at work and in international affairs.⁴¹

However, these were not the conceptions of gender equality that the major institutions of French politics worked with as they took control of the "parity agenda" after 1998.

"Modernization of Politics" within the Old Institutions of French Democracy

A new competition regarding how to modernize French politics broke out in 1997 and 1998, after the surprise victory of the Jospin-led Socialists in the legislative elections unexpectedly called by Jacques Chirac in spring 1997. Prime Minister Jospin and President Chirac each tried to position himself as best able to bring true "modernity" to French political life. While this debate had its roots in the earlier fears of a crisis of representation, it took on some new twists after 1995. In all of this we can discern the solidification of the citizenship regime focused more on political forms and less on social issues and broad definitions of equality. This is the citizenship regime within which the practices of "parity politics" are currently taking form.

As part of his efforts to renovate and rebuild the post-Mitterrand Socialist Party, in October 1995 First Secretary Lionel Jospin defined "renewed democracy" as his priority.⁴² This time the "crisis of democracy" was analyzed in relation to social exclusion and social rights, as well as to the weaknesses of local democracy and absence of voting rights for noncitizens in local elections. The modernization project, for its part, put the principle of gender parity (*parité homme-femme*) on a short list of institutional reforms, which also included incorporating a "dose of proportional representation" into elections to the National Assembly.

The first secretary had made a formal commitment to parity in 1995. Nevertheless, he was not able to impose this commitment on the party as it prepared for the next legislative elections. Instead, in 1996, taking his inspiration from the British Labour Party, Jospin pressed the PS to implement the quota notion that had surfaced in 1993.[43] In preparing for the elections (then expected for 1998), the party agreed to reserve 30 percent of seats for female candidates.[44] In part, such a change was possible because there were a large number of ridings "available"; the party's sitting Socialists had been defeated in 1993.

Despite being less than a *paritaire* position, the initiative did provoke change. The Communists and the Greens also took care to nominate women to 40 percent of their constituencies, and the result was that for the first time ever, the National Assembly opened its doors to more than 10 percent elected women.

When he became prime minister, Jospin continued to use the *paritairiste* discourse. In the first elaborated statement of his program as prime minister, on June 17, 1997, he promised a constitutional amendment to institute "parity." On March 8, 1998, he reaffirmed his "determination" to inscribe "the goal of parity" in the French Constitution, because "women represent a crucial element in the renovation of political life."[45] However, as the prime minister indicated at the time and would note several times in subsequent months, he faced certain challenges in reaching this goal. Among these were the opposition of the president, Jacques Chirac.

The latter had spent the months after the 1997 elections trying to recoup some political capital. He found himself in the familiar difficulties of cohabitation, that peculiar institution that results from the character of French presidential regime, in which the president and the prime minister share executive power. When they are from different parties, and certainly when they are from different political "families" as Chirac and Jospin are, policy coordination is never simple.

Chirac had never been a real supporter of the notion of parity. As indicated above, he had done the minimum in 1995, promising a subvention to those parties that placed women on party lists. For his part, however, Jospin continued to use all opportunities to promise a constitutional reform.

As the pressure mounted, within the government and outside, Jospin again took a strong position, which forced the president to respond. On April 1, 1998, the prime minister announced he wished to propose a constitutional amendment that would include a commitment to furthering access by women and men to positions of "political, employment, and social responsibility."[46] This was a commitment to a general democratization of power, and it also included the notion that some men might need support in taking up positions of responsibility. In light of the far reach of the reform, the prime minister suggested the proper place for this gesture was in Section 1 of the Constitution, in which France is described as adhering to the basic principles of a single, democratic, and social Republic that guarantees equality before the law.

The president demurred. For several months he had been running on a platform of reforming democracy so as to "revitalize political life." As he fought off the rising popularity of the prime minister, his focus turned to local governments and reinforcing morality in politics. To do so, he recommended opening political life to women and young people, among others. As a journalist remarked, he was forced to take action by the cohabitation; he could not afford to allow Jospin to bank all the advantages of the draft law on parity.[47]

However, he would not accept the notion of "parity," nor did he agree with the notion of reforming Section 1. He preferred Section 34, which simply lists the domains in which the legislature may make law, including elections. Therefore, in spring 1998 he announced he was ready to support a law guaranteeing "equal access" of women and men to positions of "political, employment and social responsibility."[48]

Neither proposal went very far, however. The *Conseil d'État* in its opinion concluded that employment and social equality were already included in the Preamble of the Constitution and therefore no further change was necessary. Thus, with the stroke of its pen, the Conseil d'État brought an end to any further discussion within the government of broadening the definition of equality to include other dimensions of possible discrimination.[49] Other institutions continued to narrow the application of the law.

The president made two other important adjustments to the draft bill presented by the prime minister. Apparently, Chirac's soundings had led him to conclude that the Right remained profoundly hostile to the idea of parity, which it saw as nothing more than a 50 percent quota, and it had always opposed quotas. Therefore, the wording "equal access" came from Chirac, as did the verb of the constitutional reform. If the original wording had included the notion that the law would "guarantee" access, the compromise bill introduced the current wording, that the law would "further" (*favoriser*) it.

The final step to producing a circumscribed law, applying parity in nominations to some elections but not those of the National Assembly, involved a promise by Lionel Jospin. Before the Right and many deputies of his own party would accept the constitutional amendment and the draft legislation implementing it, he had to promise to back away from his longstanding commitment to reform the electoral law. If in 1995 the Socialist program included a commitment to a "dose of PR," throughout the fall of 1998, the Socialist prime minister confirmed over and over that the constitutional amendment would not bring a subsequent reform of electoral law. The National Assembly was reminded of this solemn promise again on January 25, 2000.[50]

Here we see the institutional limit of making change by reforming electoral law. Those who are most at risk in any changes are those who must vote the law. Thus, while the deputies of the National Assembly did vote to impose parity in a range of other elections, in ways that might produce equality of results, when it came to the National Assembly, they voted only to require better results for nominations. The deputies voted to impose a fine on parties that did not fall within the range of equality in nominations. In other words, nothing in the law voted on first reading would prevent parties from placing their female candidates in the least desirable ridings or simply paying the fine. The obligation inscribed in the law is much weaker in the case of legislative elections than for the others.

This is a disappointing outcome for some parity activists. After all, it was the dismal showing in the French National Assembly that had been cited for decades as making France the "red lantern" at the end of the European train. The other elections had already begun to be feminized, even if equality had not been achieved.

In conclusion, we find that as the parity movement lost control of the agenda to its allies and supporters within the government and Parliament, the claim was transformed from one of "as many women as men" to one of improving the chances of women and men getting elected to the National Assembly, with the first step as improving their chance of being nominated. The second part of our argument is that the French debates have been confined to considerations of political equality and have left aside economic and political equality for institutional reasons, as well. Most dramatically, it was the Conseil d'État that determined those dimensions of equality were already sufficiently protected by the general guarantee of equality. However, the absence of significant opposition to this declaration among *paritaristes* is also explained by the ways in which the movement and its allies have linked their actions to the more limited understandings of equality that were simultaneously fashioning France's neoliberal citizenship regime. As the arguments for parity were incorporated into the ongoing debates about the "crisis of representation," they were detached from their origins in a feminist project for social transformation and became an instrument for rescuing the liberal democratic institutions of France.

Notes

1. *Rapport d'information fait au nom de la Délégation aux droits des femmes et à l'égalité des chances entre les hommes et les femmes,* Document # 2074 of the *Assemblée nationale,* January 18, 2000. One draft bill considered mechanisms

that would "further equal access of women and men to elected office and functions" (*projet de loi* #2012—December 9, 1999) and the other did the same for New Caledonia, French Polynesia, and the islands of Wallis and Futuna (*projet de loi organique* #2013).

2. This definition of parity as absolute symmetry (as many women as men—d'autant de femmes que d'hommes) is often lost in the debates, as will become clear below. Therefore, it is worth recalling that in the past the standard definition of parity was "la présence dans toutes les assemblées élues, de 50% d'hommes et 50% de femmes." Janine Mossuz-Lavau, *Femmes/Hommes pour la parité* (Paris: Presses de Sciences Po, 1998), 10. In effect, the legislation is a sort of quota system to increase the representation of women rather than to establish either true parity or a recognition that the "individual" always has a sex. Such a demand for recognition motivated some parity activists, although by no means all. For this important distinction between "quotas" and "parity," see Bérengère Marques-Pereira, "Quotas ou parité. Enjeux et argumentation," *Recherches féministes* 12:1 (1999): 103–22.

3. For those elections not using proportional representation, the idea was to sanction parties that did not behave in egalitarian fashion by reducing their public funds from the electoral finance regime. This is a much blunter instrument than requiring parties to alternate candidates by sex on the list.

4. *Rapport d'information,* 31.

5. See Clarisse Fabre, "Les députés ont adopté le projet de loi instituant la parité," *Le Monde, édition électronique,* January 26, 2000.

6. Françoise Gaspard, "La parité, principe ou stratégie?" *Le Monde Diplomatique* (November 1998): 26–27.

7. The concept of citizenship regime is developed in Jane Jenson and Susan D. Phillips, "Regime Shift: New Citizenship Practices in Canada," *International Journal of Canadian Studies* 14 (Fall 1996).

8. Bruno Théret, "La Régulation politique. Le point de vue d'un économiste" and Bruno Jobert, "La régulation politique. Le point de vue d'un politiste," *Droit et Société* 24 (1998).

9. George Ross and Jane Jenson, "France: Triumph and Tragedy," in Perry Anderson and Patrick Camiller, eds., *Mapping the West European Left* (London: Verso, 1994).

10. See, for example, the rapprochement that occurred in 1995, as part of the preparations of France's participation in the UN's Beijing conference, especially the conclusion to the proceedings, reported in *La place des femmes. Les enjeux de l'identité au regard des sciences sociales* (Paris: La Découverte, 1995).

11. From the beginning of the parity movement the 95 percent male National Assembly and Senate were described as shameful French exceptionalism. Comparisons with other countries (sometimes somewhat dismissive of them) were common. For example, in her overview of the 1993 elections, journalist Christine Leclerc wrote, "Although a macho country and an

emerging democracy, Spain has three times more elected women" (*Le Monde*, February 19, 1993).

12. These were the five-volume collection edited by Georges Duby and Michelle Perrot, *L'Histoire des femmes en Occident* and the three volumes edited by Marie-France Brive, *Les femmes et la Révolution française, Actes du colloque international* (Toulouse: Presses universitaires du Mirail, 1990). The latter resulted from an international colloquium held in April 1989.

13. See, for example, Danielle Haase-Dubosc and Élaine Viennot, *Femmes et pouvoirs sous l'Ancien Régime* (Paris: Rivages, 1991).

14. "La femme a le droit de monter à l'échafaud, elle doit avoir également celui de monter à la tribune;" quoted in *Le Monde*, December 26, 1998.

15. See, for example, Christine Bard, "L'étrange défaite des suffragistes (1919–1939)," in Éliane Viennot, ed., *La démocratie à la française ou les femmes indésirables* (Paris: Cahier du CEDREF, 1996), 234–37.

16. Michelle Riot-Sarcey, "Femmes, pouvoirs," in Michelle Riot-Sarcey, ed., *Femmes pouvoirs*, Actes du colloque d'Albi des 19 et 20 mars 1992.

17. See, for example, Gaspard, "La parité. Principe ou stratégie?" 26, and Mossuz-Lavau, *Femmes/Hommes pour la parité*, 34.

18. Françoise Picq, *Libération des femmes: Les années-mouvement* (Paris: Seuil, 1993).

19. Claire Duchen, *Feminism in France: From May '68 to Mitterrand* (Boston: Routledge, 1986).

20. For an example of the ways C. Bard's work was used, see Mossuz-Lavau, *Femmes/Hommes pour la parité*, 34.

21. *Le Monde*, June 6–7, 1993.

22. For a useful overview of the steps in the movement's history, see Janine Mossuz-Lavau, *Femmes/Hommes pour la parité*, chapter 2, and Jocelyne Praud, "Women and political citizenship in France: the fight for gender parity in public life in historical perspective," paper presented at the annual Meetings of the Canadian Political Science Association, Québec, July 30, 2000.

23. *Le Monde,* November 10, 1993.

24. Joan W. Scott rightly points out that the movement is universalist. "'La querelle des femmes' à la fin du vingtième siècle," *Parité Infos* 19 (1997): 5. See the original formulation in Naomi Schor, "French Feminism is a Universalism," *Différences* 7 (1995): 15–47.

25. "Une démocratie véritable se fonde sur l'égalité politique effective et non fictive de tous ses enfants. Voilà ce que traduirait une devise républicaine revue et corrigée: liberté, égalité, parité," Françoise Gaspard and Claude Servan-Schreiber, "De la fraternité á la parité," *Le Monde*, February 19, 1993. The same combination of reworked republican imagery is also evident in the first book-length argument for parity: Françoise Gaspard, Claude Servan-Schreiber, and Anne Le Gall, *Au pouvoir citoyennes!: Liberté, Egalité, Parité* (Paris: Seuil, 1992).

26. See Éliane Vogel-Polsky, "La parité ne se limite pas à un problème de représentation des femmes dans les sphéres de pouvoir. Elle répond à une

question préalable fondamentale: qui est la personne humaine de la Déclaration universelle de 1948," in *Sextant* 7, 17–39.
27. See Marques-Pereira, "Quotas ou parité," for a comparison of the English-language and French treatment of difference around matters of quotas.
28. This description is derived from an analysis of the texts published in *Le Monde* in December 1992 and January 1993.
29. Mossuz-Lavau, *Femmes/Hommes pour la parité*, 24. This was also a major point in the Manifesto published by 10 female ex-ministers in 1996. See ibid., 41–42.
30. Gaspard, et al., *Au pouvoir citoyennes!*, 14.
31. *Le Monde*, January 16, 1993.
32. There is some dispute over who influenced this decision. Françoise Gaspard states that Rocard himself decided (see "La parité. Genèse d'un concept, naissance d'un mouvement," *Nouvelles Questions Féministes* 15:4 (1994): 39); Yvette Roudy claims that Rocard followed her advice; see *Mais de quoi ont-ils peur?* (Paris: Albin Michel, 1995), 15–18. According to Antoinette Fouque, she was the one who made the difference. In March 1993 she met Rocard and demanded a parity list; see her "Demain la parité," in M. de Manassien, ed., *De l'égalité des sexes* (Paris: Centre nationale de documentation pédagogique, 1995), 89–103.
33. There was a notorious break of the order exactly at the point at which the cut-off was expected to be, thereby favoring male candidates.
34. An all-candidate meeting was organized by the *Conseil national des femmes françaises* on April 7, 1995.
35. See, for example, Maya Surdut, "Allocution ouverture," *En avant toutes! Les assises nationales pour les Droits des femmes* (Paris: Le temps des cerises, 1998), 18.
36. Claude Servan-Schreiber, "La fausse-vraie maire de Vitrolles: une insulte pour toutes les femmes," *Parité-Infos* 17 (1997): 5.
37. See also Régine Saint-Criq and Natalie Prévost, *Vol au-dessus d'un nid de machos* (Paris: Albin Michel, 1993), 141, 149.
38. "Nous concevons la parité comme principe fondateur d'une démarche d'éducation à la citoyenneté [. . .] Elle doit donc être déclinée dans les domaines suivants:—l'instauration d'une éducation à la parité [. . .]—des mesures permettant la parité économique et sociale [. . .]—des mesures pour introduire la parité domestique [. . .]—des mesures pour la parité culturelle [. . .]—la parité politique [. . .]. En avant toutes!" (1998, 198).
39. Geneviève Fraisse, "La double évidence du féminisme," *Le Monde*, January 20, 1998, 15.
40. "La parité dans la représentation, dans les organes consultatifs et dans l'administration n'est évidemment pas une fin en soi. Elle est cependant, outre une mesure d'inégalité, un moyen parmi d'autres de conforter la démocratie et de faire avancer la condition des femmes qui demeure marquée par l'inégalité, la domination, la subordination." Françoise Gaspard, "Les Françaises en politique au lendemain des élections législatives de 1997," *French Politics and Society* 15:4 (1997): 11.

41. It is worth noting that the *Observatoire* also is inscribed with the non-partisan representation of parity. It has two *rapportrices* on gender parity: one from the Left (Gisèle Halimi) and one from the Right (Roselyne Bachelot).
42. He was also forced to make a few feeble concessions to his party's left wing. The major "concession" was a commitment to require that all layoffs fall under the jurisdiction of the labor inspectors. Michel Noblecourt, "Les propositions du Parti socialiste pour rénover la démocratie," *Le Monde,* April 7, 1997.
43. Gaspard, "Les Françaises en politique au lendemain des élections," 3.
44. Philippe Bataille and Françoise Gaspard, *Comment les femmes changent la politique et pourquoi les hommes résistent* (Paris: La Découverte, 1999), 15–16.
45. Michèle Aulagnon, "Lionel Jospin réaffirme sa 'détermination' à inscrire la parité dans la Constitution," *Le Monde,* March 10, 1998.
46. In addressing the National Assembly, he said that "la loi ou la organique peut fixer des règles favorisant l'accès des femmes et des hommes aux responsabilités politiques, professionnelles et sociales," quoted in Clarisse Fabre, "Lionel Jospin: inscrire dans la Constitution l'égalité des sexes," *Le Monde,* April 3, 1998.
47. Pascale Robert-Diard, "Jacques Chirac se pose en modernisateur de la démocratie," *Le Monde,* December 5, 1998.
48. Raphaëlle Bacqué, "Le principe de l'"égal accès" des deux sexes aux fonctions électives pourrait s'inscrire dans la Constitution," *Le Monde,* December 19, 1999.
49. It is not at all clear that even Jospin was committed to a call for parity in all spheres. In an interview on the issue of parity and France's "backwardness," he framed the problem solely in political terms. See Bataille and Gaspard, *Comment les femmes,* 158–59. A more likely hypothesis about the appearance of the "in all domains" definition of parity in March-April 1997 is that the prime minister's office was in dialogue with the *Déléguée interministérielle,* Geneviève Fraisse, whose position was close to this one.
50. Raphaëlle Bacqué, "Le mode de scrutin législatif ne sera pas modifié au nom de la parité. Le premier ministre a écarté cette éventualité," *Le Monde,* December 11, 1998.

Chapter Six

Breaking the Barriers:
Positive Discrimination Policies for Women

Pippa Norris

Women's social and economic position has gradually improved in many societies due to long-term secular trends, such as developments in female enrolment in higher education and adult literacy, labor force participation, and real GDP per capita.[1] Nevertheless progress in female empowerment in elected office has lagged behind in many established democracies such as Japan, France, Greece, and Israel, as well as in many transitional and consolidating democratic states (see Figure 6.1). At the start of the twenty-first century the glass ceiling for women's political empowerment in elected office remains almost uncracked: nine out of seven members of national parliaments worldwide are male, and women make up more than one third of the legislature in only a few nations.[2] Yet against this backdrop, in recent decades countries as diverse as South Africa, India, Norway, Britain, New Zealand, and Argentina have experienced a decisive political breakthrough for women parliamentarians due to positive discrimination strategies implemented via party regulations or electoral laws. In a model of punctuated equilibrium, changing the rules for political recruitment has often—although not always— opened the door for women to enter elected office.

Given this context, this chapter examines three central questions: what are the major policy options available to increase women's representation— in particular, how have positive discrimination strategies been used worldwide? Second, given that we would expect resistance by incumbents, why are such strategies adopted and implemented? This chapter presents a case study of one such breakthrough—the British Labour party's adoption of all

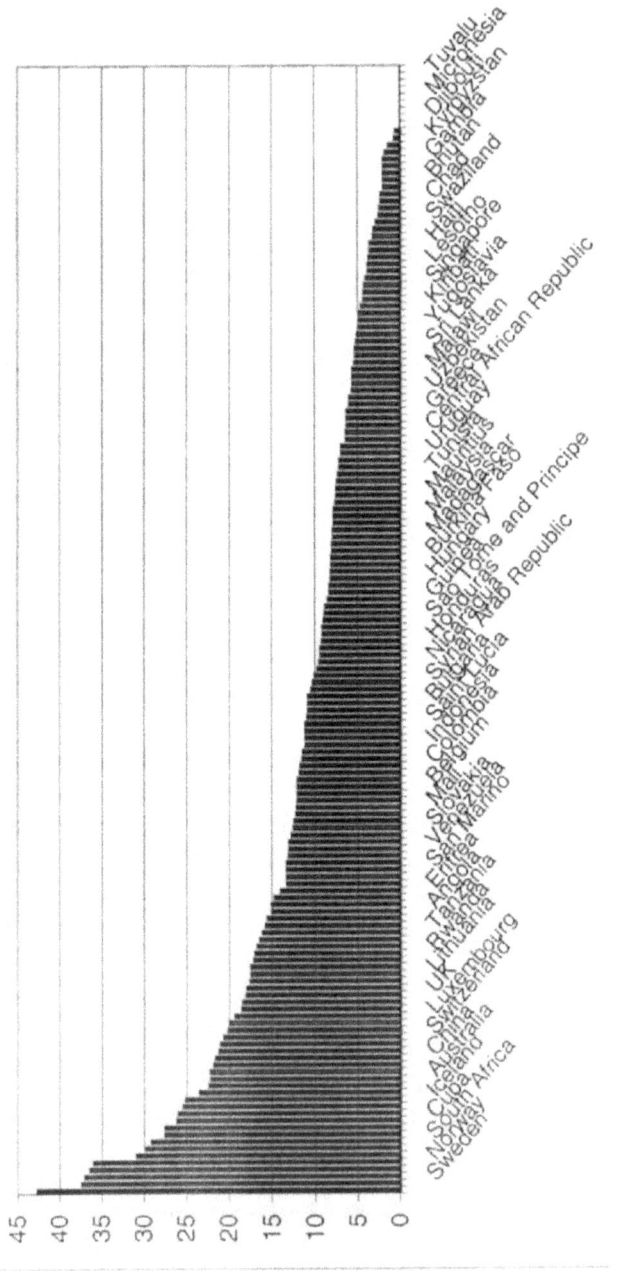

Figure 6.1 Percentage of Women in Parliaments Worldwide, 1999.

women shortlists in the selection process for parliamentary candidates in the run up to the 1997 British general election. As a result, after decades of modest progress, at best, the proportion of women at Westminster doubled overnight, to 18.2 percent. Lastly, under what conditions do these strategies prove most effective and, in particular, can their use in Britain provide lessons for "best practice" that are applicable elsewhere? The chapter concludes that positive discrimination strategies can produce a sharp increase in women's representation under certain conditions, namely where parties combine a political culture sympathetic to these policies with a bureaucratic organizational structure which implements formal party rules. In this context, changing the rules can transform the structure of opportunities for women, particularly in elections which experience a substantial landslide throwing out incumbent politicians. Under other conditions, these strategies may merely prove symbolic, altering the rhetoric more than practice.

Policy Options for Gender Equality

Worldwide, three different types of recruitment policies are available to increase women's representation, reflecting different cultural values and beliefs (see Figure 6.2). Rhetorical strategies, articulated in leadership speeches, party guidelines, or official party platforms, aim to change the party ethos by affirming the need for social balance in the slate of candidates. Parties may wish to widen their electoral appeal through altering their public profile in Parliament, for example by attracting more women, ethnic minorities, or other types of candidates. Rhetorical statements may prove only a symbolic fig leaf of political correctness, or they may represent the first steps toward more effective reforms if they influence the selectors who choose parliamentary candidates, and if they encourage more women applicants to come forward.

Affirmative action programs aim to encourage applicants by providing training sessions, advisory group targets, financial assistance, as well as a systematic monitoring of the outcome. These meritocratic policies aim to achieve "fairness" in the recruitment process, removing practical barriers that may disadvantage women or other groups. The policies can be gender-neutral, such as providing training in public speaking and media presentation equally to all candidates, or they can be specifically designed to correct certain imbalances in women's representation, for example targeting funding for women aspirants. Affirmative action programs can also be applied to the party selectors—for example, training them to be aware of the need for equal opportunities or providing standardized checklists of the qualities used for evaluating applicants. Gender quotas fall into this category if they are advisory rather than binding.

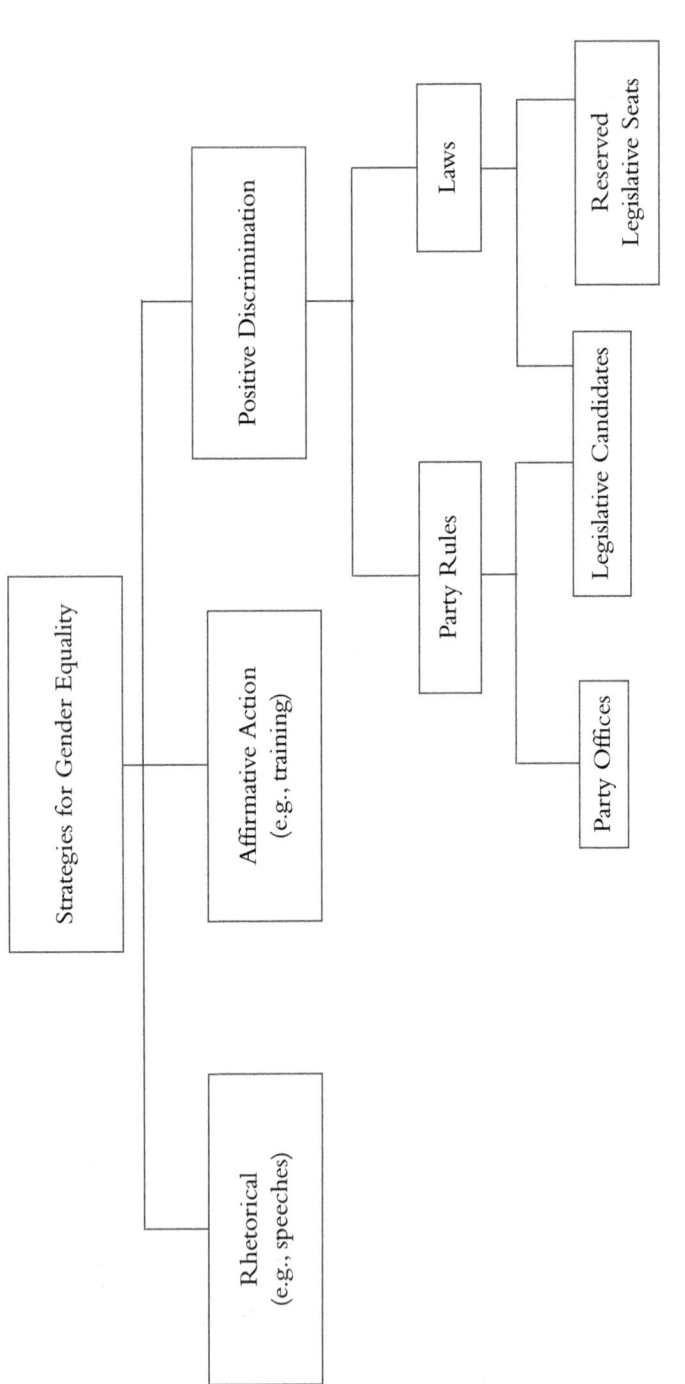

Figure 6.2 Policy Options to Increase Women's Representation

Positive discrimination strategies, in contrast, set mandatory group quotas for the selection of candidates from certain social or political groups. Although the term *quotas* is often used loosely, these strategies vary in three important ways. First, quotas can be set at different levels, such as 20, 30, 40, or 50 percent. Second, these quotas can be applied to different stages of the selection process, including to internal party offices, shortlists of parliamentary applicants, electoral lists of parliamentary candidates, or reserved parliamentary seats. Lastly, binding quotas can be implemented either by law or by internal party rules. In general, *ceteris paribus,* the higher the level of the specified quota, the closer the quota is applied to the final stages of election, and more binding the formal regulation, the more effective its impact. Thus the strongest version would be legal measures specifying in the constitution that a high proportion of all parliamentary seats should be reserved for women, while the weakest would be party regulations specifying that women should be at least 10 to 15 percent of local party chairs, secretaries, or convention delegates.

Positive discrimination aims to achieve equality of outcome or results. This has made left-wing parties, with a more egalitarian ideology, more comfortable with this strategy. Most advocates admit that these strategies are not procedurally "fair" for individual applicants. Some groups are thereby ruled into the recruitment process, while others are automatically ruled out, by virtue of certain ascriptive characteristics such as gender, race, ethnonationalism, region, language, or religion. The process discriminates positively in favor of certain individuals on the basis of characteristics seen as common to their group.[3] Nevertheless, proponents argue that underrepresented political minorities need positive discrimination, at least as a temporary stopgap measure to overcome the historical disadvantages they face in winning elected office.

A worldwide comparison indicates considerable variance in the type of positive discrimination measures implemented via laws or internal party rules. Broadly categorized, they are:

A. Reserved Seats

The strongest measures specify certain reserved seats in parliaments for women. In India, for example, the seventy-fourth amendment to the Constitution adopted in 1993 requires that one third of the seats in local municipal bodies (village councils) are reserved for women.[4] Other countries with legal requirements of reserved seats for women in national parliaments include Bangladesh (set at 9 percent of all seats), Eritrea (9.5 percent), Tanzania (6 percent), Taiwan, and Uganda.[5] Reserved seats are also used to ensure the representation of specific ethnic, religious, or linguistic minority groups in parliament, such as scheduled tribes and castes in India, the aboriginal community in Taiwan, Hungarians and Italians in Slovenia, and the Maori population in New Zealand. The main advantage of these measures is that if effectively implemented, this guarantees the inclusion of women or other groups in office. Possible disadvantages are that legal regulations may be difficult to pass politically, given the power of incumbents, it can be argued that the use of reserved seats limits the electorate's choice of candidates, the system may be seen as less fair than other ways to promote minority representation, and the level of the quota may reinforce the status quo, acting as a ceiling rather than a floor for any minority group.

B. Legal Gender Quotas in Party Lists

Alternatively electoral laws may specify that party lists of parliamentary candidates should contain a certain proportion of women or minority groups. In multimember districts, in which election is determined by rank order on the ballot paper, laws may also sometimes regulate the position of female candidates throughout the party list, for example that women should be every other name on the ballot paper (a technique otherwise known as "zippering"). In the past, Communist parties in Central and Eastern Europe often used gender quotas, for example for representatives of official women's organizations. These were subsequently dropped in the post-Communist parliaments, producing an immediate fall in women's representation just at the time when these bodies gained in legitimacy and authority. More recently, ten Latin American states passed electoral laws in the 1990s in stipulated that all party lists had to contain a certain proportion of women candidates, although parties could determine their rank order. Due to problems in implementation, only the Argentinean law has fully achieved its objectives, but in other states in the region during the last decade these reforms have boosted women's presence in Congress by about 5 percent on average.[6]

C. Party Rules

More often, rather than state regulation, quotas are implemented by internal party rules and procedures. This is the most common mechanism and it has been used with different degrees of success all over the world including by the ANC in South Africa, CONDEPA in Brazil, the PRD in Mexico, the Social Democrats in Germany, and Labour parties in Australia and Norway.[7] A worldwide review conducted in the early 1990s, by the *Inter-Parliamentary Union,* found that 22 parties employed gender quotas when selecting candidates for legislative elections, while 51 parties used them for elections to internal party posts. These measures were commonly introduced in Western Europe during the 1980s by parties of the left (see Table 6.1). The impact of these strategies has often increased women's representation significantly, as shown by case studies of Norway and Germany.[8] A recent study, comparing women's representation in a dozen advanced industrialized societies in the late 1980s, found that women composed 28 percent of MPs in parties with gender quotas, compared with only 22 percent of MPs in parties lacking such rules.[9]

Why Are Positive Discrimination Policies Adopted?

So why are positive discrimination policies adopted, given that we would expect resistance from incumbent office-holders, and how do they work? Here we can turn to a case study of Westminster. During the 1980s and early 1990s Britain continued to lag behind most European Union countries in the representation of women, and the general pace of progress remained glacial. If secular trends from 1945 to 1992 had continued on a linear basis, women would not have achieved parity with men at Westminster until the middle of the twenty-first century. One key barrier to change has been the structure of opportunities in British political life. About 140 new MPs usually enter the House every general election; opportunities are restricted by predominance of the two major parties, the rate of retirements from the Commons, and the limited number of marginals won or lost in general elections. If women fail to become adopted as Labour or Conservative parliamentary candidates for winnable seats, they have almost no hope of electoral success at Westminster.

In an attempt to speed change the fall 1993 Labour conference approved a policy of positive discrimination for women. When selecting candidates for the 1997 general election, Labour agreed to introduce all-women shortlists in half their "inheritor" seats (vacancies created when a Labour MP retires), and half their "strong challenger" seats (defined in the conference motion as Labour's "most winnable" seats). The policy of "all-women shortlists" meant that local party members could still decide which parliamentary candidate would be adopted in their seat, for example whether on the left or center of the party, whether a local or carpet-bagger, and whether a social worker, trade union official, or lawyer, but the shortlist in these constituencies would be restricted only to women applicants. Labour's policy of all-women shortlists was officially dropped in January 1996, after legal challenge but not before the party had selected many women candidates for target seats. The landslide Labour victory on May 1, 1997, sweeping out the Conservative government, produced record numbers of Labour women MPs (101). As a result, the proportion of women MPs at Westminster doubled overnight, from 9.2 to 18.2 percent. To encapsulate the radical nature of this change, half of all the women who have ever been elected to the House of Commons are currently in parliament. Women are also one third of the Blair cabinet, including five Cabinet ministers. Nor have positive discrimination strategies been confined to Westminster. For selection to the new Scottish Parliament, the Welsh Assembly, and the Greater London Assembly, Labour used a policy of "twinned constituencies," selecting one man and one woman in each pair of seats. The result was in the first elections to these new bodies, women represent 37 percent of the Scottish Parliament and 40 percent of the Welsh Assembly, and will probably be well placed in the May 2000 London elections.

Party Culture

The move toward positive discrimination was consistent with the dominant culture within the British Labour party, reflecting the values shared with other parties of the center-left. Just as social democratic parties believe in interventionist policies to reduce social and economic inequalities, through the welfare state, so they are more likely to feel that interventionist strategies are appropriate to achieve gender equality. Some suggest that the adoption of all-women shortlists was due to a small, well-motivated radical faction within the Labour Party, which managed to achieve its goals at the expense of the more moderate majority, and opinion within the party was certainly divided, but it is more accurate to understand quotas as broadly in line with grassroots attitudes.

In personal interviews, a minority of Labour politicians expressed private reservations about how gender quotas work in practice.[10] Some feared that women might desert the party in response to the new pressures on them created by quotas. One MP said,

> This is why I worry about the quota system because putting pressure on some of our women will drive them out, it'll drive them out of the party. If you sit in a big ward, and there's sixty men and two women, and you've got to have half your officials women, half of them going to constituency as delegate, you'll have to go, and the women don't want to go. They want to be part of the movement but they don't want the spotlight on them, they don't want to be forced into positions like that.

One woman MP thought that quotas were unfair to men who had spent years in party service. Asked about the all-woman shortlists, she said,

> I think it's balmy and so do women in my party. They don't believe in this nonsense. It's crazy why should we have an all-women shortlist. It's the same as an all-male shortlist. One woman on the shortlist, yes. All women on the shortlist, definitely not. I'm against quotas too. I think the idea the party has that party officers of the party should be women is crackers. Why should men who've been doing the job for years stand down so that they can have half the women as officers, when you can't find a woman who wants to do it. It's crazy. Give women the chance by all means. Encourage them. But not at the expense of men.

Another MP thought it would benefit only the professional lawyers and teachers, who would probably make it anyway, at the expense of working-class candidates.

> I'm all for positive discrimination but I think what you've got to be careful of is you don't just make fast tracks for certain, well-heeled, middle-class people inside our party, whether they're black, women, or whatever. And that's the danger. I've got West Indians and Asians within my constituency. Some of my best friends. They don't want black sections.

Others anticipated conflict within the grassroots. They approved in principle, but expressed more ambiguous feelings about how quotas would be implemented in practice. As one ex-MP remarked:

> The danger is, bluntly, that not very good women will be selected, and that won't help the position of women in parliament. The plus side is you've got to do something like that, otherwise you are just not going to get women there. But the problem is, it has not been thought out properly . . . the mechanics have not been thought through, and the mechanics are going to be the downfall of the system if we're not careful.

Yet despite these voices, the majority expressed more positive views, seeing the principle of quotas as a necessary, albeit temporary, move in the right direction. Many dismissed the argument that there were not enough good women to become party delegates or candidates:

> A lot of socialist parties have direct discrimination and certainly I do think increasingly you ought to have quotas in some form. I mean, people always resent it, because they say you've got a stupid woman doing that instead of an intelligent man. But, frankly, we have so many stupid men at all levels, that I don't see why we shouldn't have a few stupid women. You've got to have a bigger representation of women, and therefore to start off with [positive] discrimination is the best way to do it. . . . But it won't last forever.

Some women felt that it might not be necessary to have special measures in districts where women were already doing relatively well, such as in London, but quotas would help give women opportunities for safe seats in the Labour heartland.

Systematic survey evidence suggests that, despite some reservations, the principle of gender quotas fits the mainstream culture among Labour activists. This was shown in the 1992 British Candidate Survey, when Labour party members and politicians (applicants, candidates, MPs) were asked, "Do you approve or disapprove of the following proposals for increasing the number of women in Parliament? . . . Positive quotas/affirmative action for women." Tables 6.1 and 6.2 show that the principle of positive quotas/affirmative action was widely supported by most groups within the party; two-thirds of all members approved, as did three-quarters of all politicians. Support was strongest, as might be expected, among women, the middle class, the better educated, and younger groups within the party, but on balance no group proved overwhelmingly negative.

The 1997 British Representation Survey found that Labour attitudes toward this strategy were fairly stable. According to this evidence, the policy passed by conference is in accordance with the Labour Party culture. In interviews, people expressed some reservations about how all-women shortlists worked in practice, but the principle was widely supported. In contrast, Liberal Democrat, Nationalist (Scottish National and Plaid Cymru), and Green politicians were evenly divided between those who approved and disapproved of this proposal, while there was almost no support (6 percent) for this measure among Conservatives, who favored more meritocratic policies (see Table 6.3).

Party Organizations

Attitudes toward quotas are strongly influenced by party cultures. Whether quotas are implemented depends upon the type of party organization. The Labour Party has a formal bureaucratic organization that places considerable emphasis on formal constitutions, structural solutions, and the power of the rulebook. Changing party rules often can and does change the internal power structure. Positive discrimination operates most effectively in organizations in which the selection process is rule-bound and decentralized. In the Labour Party, decisions about candidates are taken primarily at constituency level, under binding, standardized procedures established by national bodies.[11] Gender quotas implemented by party rules have also proved effective in other formal-localized parties, such as the Social Democrats in Germany, Norway, and Sweden. In contrast, in loosely organized parties, like the French UDF, the Japanese LDP, or the old Italian

Table 6.1 **Support for Gender Quotas among Labour Party Members, 1992**

	Strongly Approve	Approve	Strongly Disapprove	Disapprove	No
All	33	33	26	9	419
Men	26	36	21	11	255
Women	42	27	24	6	164
Middle Class	33	31	28	8	344
Working Class	25	39	21	14	56
Graduate	36	29	28	7	196
Non-Graduate	27	36	26	11	186
Union Member	33	32	27	9	314
Non-member	30	35	25	11	84
Older	20	39	30	12	122
Middle-aged	37	30	26	7	195
Younger	35	27	25	13	79

Note: "Do you approve or disapprove of the following proposals for increasing the number of women in Parliament? Positive quotas/affirmative action for women?"
Source: The 1992 British Candidate Study.

Table 6.2 **Support for Gender Quotas among Labour Party Politicians, 1992**

	Strongly Approve	Approve	Strongly Disapprove	Disapprove	No
All	44	31	18	7	534
Men	35	35	21	9	395
Women	69	20	9	3	137
Middle Class	45	30	17	7	479
Working Class	24	36	31	10	42
Graduate	46	32	16	6	368
Non-Graduate	96	28	23	10	163
Union Sponsored	38	32	23	7	136
Non-Sponsored	46	31	16	8	397
Older	34	33	25	8	110
Middle-aged	44	33	16	7	225
Younger	50	27	16	7	199
MPs	31	31	32	5	

Note: "Do you approve or disapprove of the following proposals for increasing the number of women in Parliament? ... Positive quotas/affirmative action for women."
Source: The 1992 British Candidate Study.

Table 6.3 Support for Policy Options, 1997

	Conservative	Labour	Liberal Democrat	Nationalist	Green	All
Party training programs for women	69	98	98	92	95	89
Better childcare facilities in Parliament	66	98	98	98	100	89
Changing hours of parliamentary sittings	57	91	97	97	100	83
Positive quotas/affirmative action	2	74	47	48	59	43
Financial support for women candidates	3	56	90	19	46	32
All-women shortlists	0	53	4	8	38	21
Reserved seats for women	0	22	3	6	24	10

Note: "Do you approve or disapprove of the following proposals for increasing the number of women in Parliament?" The proportion of MPs and parliamentary candidates within each party who "agreed" or "strongly agreed" with the proposals.

Source: British Representation Study, 1997 (N.999).

Christian Democrats, which are largely coalitions around factions or particular leaders, changing the formal party rules has little effect because they are unlikely to be implemented. In decentralized and weak party organizations, like the U.S. Democrats and Republicans, it makes little sense to consider positive discrimination strategies for legislative elections, since parties no longer control the recruitment process.

The short-term context leading to reform in fall 1993 was the gradual mobilization of women activists around this policy during the 1980s and 1990s and the structure of opportunities provided by internal party reform. Labour women were able to take advantage of the process of party modernization, initiated by the leadership in the mid-1980s, to advance their concerns onto the mainstream agenda. One of their most persuasive arguments, after successive Labour Party defeats in the polls, was the electoral reward of reform. In the conventional wisdom, Labour needed to break out from its declining working-class and inner-city base, expanding voting support among women voters. The way to achieve this aim, research for the Shadow Communication agency suggested, was for Labour to develop a less male-dominated image.[12] This argument influenced the leadership, particularly since other pressures were opening the door to reform of the selection process.

Introducing quotas at all levels of the party has been a gradual process of incremental change.[13] Traditionally, Labour has always been more sympathetic than the Conservatives toward positive discrimination. In 1918 four places were reserved for women in Labour's National Executive Council (increased to five in 1937), in early recognition that special arrangements were needed to facilitate female participation. But it was not until the 1980s that the patterns of race and gender politics led to demands for positive discrimination at all levels of the party. It was easier to establish gender quotas for internal party offices than for Parliament, since members of constituency executive and general committees wanted to safeguard the principle of local autonomy in selecting "their" prospective Parliamentary candidate. Since the mid-1980s, Labour women have used the process of party reorganization to advance proposals for increasing women's representation.

In April 1983 the National Executive Committee (NEC) published its *Charter to Establish Equality for Women within the Party,* stating the objective of increasing women's involvement at all levels of the party. This was the first significant step toward recognizing the issue's validity, although the proposals were essentially voluntary. Subsequent attention passed to the policy of developing a ministry for women, and further internal reforms lay in abeyance for a few years. Then in 1987 the Labour conference passed new rules for the compulsory shortlisting of women, implemented two years later. The rule specified that where a woman was nominated in a constituency, at least one woman must be on the final shortlist for interview. If no woman had been shortlisted by the regular procedure followed by the Executive Committee, the final name on the shortlist was dropped and a ballot was held to determine which of the nominated women should be included.

In 1989 the conference overwhelmingly carried Composite 54, which accepted in principle that quotas were the way forward, and called on the NEC to present proposals on how quotas could be implemented at every level: for all party committees and local delegations, for the NEC, and for Shadow Cabinet. The Labour rulebook lays down that women should be at least half the statutory branch officers and branch delegates to the constituency party. Constituency parties have to select a woman conference delegate at least every other year. Affiliated trade unions are required to include women as conference delegates in proportion to their membership in the union. There are a series of quotas to ensure that women are elected to Labour's National Executive Committee.[14]

By 1990, after a process of consultation, the party endorsed the aim of women forming 40 percent of Labour MPs by the year 2000. To achieve this ambitious goal, the fall 1993 conference took this process a step further, with the critical decision to implement all-women shortlists in half of Labour inheritor and strong challenger seats. Once quotas had been accepted at all other levels of the party organization, it seemed difficult to resist the logic of using them for parliamentary office. In addition, the earlier move to increase the number of women as conference delegates from constituency parties, as well as their increased membership among trade union affiliates, caused a significant shift in the social composition of the party conference. Many women recognized this sea change, opening speeches with "I'm a quota" as their first statement. The composite motion for all-women shortlists passed in 1993 after relatively little debate by a solid majority of votes (54 to 35 percent). The conference was distracted at the time by a heated controversy over the appropriate influence of affiliated trade unions in the selection process, although once passed the motion quickly produced some bitter counterattacks.[15]

To implement the policy, from 1994 to 1996 Labour held regional "consensus" meetings to determine which seats in each region should have all women shortlists and its National Executive Committee (NEC) intervened where regional targets were not achieved. The NEC had the power to impose all women shortlists where a constituency proved recalcitrant. This decision came as part of a range of measures designed to improve women's representation in the party. New rules about the representation of women in internal party positions were important in the implementation of the candidate quotas. Under the regulations at least three of the seven constituency party officers had to be women. All seven officers were invited to consensus meetings so it became a simple matter to check that the composition of officers met the requirements. In addition, new women constituency officers were often (but not inevitably) sympathetic to the idea of promoting women candidates. Efforts to improve women's prospects had the full support of the party leader, John Smith, the Labour Coordinating Committee, various trade unions responding to claims by women members, and a number of internal feminist women's advocacy groups including Labour Women's Network, EMILY, and Labour Women's Action Group.

Early in 1996, with 34 women selected on all-women shortlists, two disgruntled male aspirants won their case against the policy at an Industrial Tribunal held in Leeds on January 8, 1996 (*Jepson and Dyas-Elliott vs. The Labour Party and Others*). The Industrial Tribunal accepted the argument that the selection procedure by a political party facilitates access to employment and was therefore subject to the UK Sex Discrimination Act, which prevents (positive or negative) discrimination on the grounds of sex.

Anxious to complete its selections in good time for the general election, and concerned not to jeopardize the positions of women already selected under the policy, the NEC decided not to appeal the decision. Instead they established a working party to identify effective and legal ways to maximize the number of women candidates nominated and selected in the remaining vacant Labour seats. This decision disappointed feminist advocates in the party who believed that the party leadership was lukewarm toward issues of women's representation and too unwilling to take controversial decisions to improve it. After the tribunal decision, few women were selected for target or inheritor seats as the tendency was for selections to go to the candidate who fought the seat in 1992. After the legal challenge, Labour politicians were still evenly divided about use of all-women shortlists (see Table 6.3 above), although women candidates were most likely to favor this policy.

Although the policy had to be abandoned in 1996, the all-women shortlists were successful in achieving their objectives. All the women candidates chosen by this process were elected. The timing of the quotas was especially important. If the 1997 general election had been missed, later opportunities might not be as effective.

The Consequences of Gender Quotas

What were the consequences of the use of gender quotas? The defeat for the Conservative government, and the Labour landslide under Tony Blair, in the May 1, 1997, British general election, broke numerous historic

Table 6.4 Number of Women Parliamentary Candidates and MPs, Britain, 1987–1997

	Conservative		Labour		Liberal Democrat		Nationalist	
	Candidates	MPs	Candidates	MPs	Candidates	MPs	Candidates	MPs
1987	46	17	92	21	105	2	15	1
1992	63	20	138	37	143	2	22	1
1997	67	13	159	102	122	3	23	2
1997 (%)	(10.3)	(7.9)	(24.8)	(24.2)	(19.0)	(7.2)	(21.2)	(33.3)

Note: "Nationalist" includes Scottish National Party and Plaid Cymru.
Source: House of Commons Research Papers. 1999. *Women in the House of Commons.* London: House of Commons Information Office.

precedents.[16] In total 259 new members entered Parliament, the highest number since the war, due to the combination of record retirements and defeats.

Most strikingly, there was only a modest increase in the total number of women standing; British parties nominated 371 female parliamentary candidates, compared with 366 in 1992. But nevertheless because of the key position of Labour women in target seats, women made substantial gains; 120 women MPs swept into the House of Commons, representing 18.2 percent of members. Female representation doubled, bringing Britain into line with other EU member states, although remaining below Scandinavian levels. The success rates for women differed dramatically by party (see Table 6.4). For Labour, the election produced a record-breaking 102 women MPs, or one quarter of the parliamentary party. The change was not just in the House of Commons: five Labour women were appointed as secretaries of state, four became ministers of state, and another nine became parliamentary under-secretaries. Moreover women were not just appointed to "women's ministries": Mo Mowlam was made secretary of state for Northern Ireland (then subsequently the Cabinet Office), Margaret Beckett became president of the board of trade, Dawn Primarolo entered the Treasury, Ann Taylor became Leader of the House. In total, women made up more than a fifth of the Blair government.

As in the past, what was important was where the Labour candidates were standing, as British political parties have tended to place their women candidates in unfavorable seats. In 1997 many of Labour's 159 women candidates were well situated to win since they fought fourteen seats where Labour MPs were retiring, and half of Labour's 86 target marginals. What mattered was less the number of Labour women candidates per se than the type of seats they fought. The shift in votes for women and men standing in each party was identical: women candidates neither gained nor lost more support than average.

In contrast, neither the Conservatives nor the Liberal Democrats altered their candidate selection procedures to increase the nomination of women. Following their devastating defeat, in total only 13 women Conservative MPs were returned, representing 8 percent of the parliamentary party. The party had made limited efforts to promote women candidates although they made periodic exhortations that more women should come forward, and training for women candidates was offered by the party women's section, often with disapproval from other leading officials. Officially the Conservatives were opposed to positive action and they were critical of Labour's policy.

The Liberal Democrat fielded 122 women candidates but almost all fought hopeless seats. No women were selected to replace the 6 MPs who stood down, although 2 were well placed in classic Liberal Democrat marginals. Liberal Democrats opposed positive discrimination measures such as compulsory quotas but they do insist that women be placed on shortlists should these contain at least two aspirant candidates. A significant number of their shortlists, however, contain only one name, and there are no special rules to help to place women in winnable seats. Only three Liberal Democrat women candidates were returned (representing in total 7 percent of their party's MPs). The SNP returned their two sitting women MPs, while Plaid Cymru's women candidates fought seats that would have required a swing of more than 25 percent to win, and none were returned.

Conclusions and Discussion

The process of adopting all-women shortlists in the Labour Party has had a major influence on Westminster backbenches and government office. A combination of factors, notably the predominant culture of the Labour Party and the process of organizational reform, produced a structure of opportunities that allowed women within the party to mobilize within a broad alliance to achieve a policy of positive discrimination in the selection process. The strategy of all-women shortlists, although subsequently abandoned, have had long-term consequences for women's representation in at least three ways.

First, the surge in women Labour MPs has increased the pressures on the Conservative Party to respond to the obvious gender disparities in parliament. Although the process currently remains under review, and few visible gains for Conservative women candidates are evident at the time of writing, the party is reconsidering its selection process.[17] The culture of the Conservative parliamentary party remains supportive of strategies like candidate training programs designed to achieve equality of opportunity, but is clearly opposed to positive discrimination strategies. Other parties also remain divided in their support for further reforms designed to achieve gender parity, with far greater approval across all groups for strategies, like improving parliamentary childcare facilities, rather than for more radical proposals, like reserved seats for women.

Secondly, the parliamentary Labour Party has been altered by this breakthrough, although it remains to be seen whether the momentum for increased female representation will be maintained. The issue of reforming the parliamentary selection process remains under internal review, but in the midterm period there seems to be little political impetus toward the reintroduction of all-women shortlists for Westminster, and a number of the Labour women MPs who first entered in 1997 have already announced plans to stand down in the next general election.[18] On the other hand, Labour's use of "twinned" constituencies for the new elected bodies in Scotland, Wales, and London has produced substantial numbers of women representatives. The issue has also increased pressure on the new Ministry of Women to improve the policy performance of the Blair administration on gender-related issues, with some notable achievements such as the legislation on minimum pay, which has had a significant impact on women's pay.[19]

Lastly, Parliament itself has been transformed. At the turn of the century, the House of Commons looks more like society, and there has also been some substantive changes to the predominant parliamentary culture. Analysis of the attitudes of the 1997 parliament shows that although politicians continue to differ more by party than gender, nevertheless there are certain policy issues—especially attitudes toward women's rights—in which there is a consistent gender gap within each of the major parties, and in which the claim that women speak in "a different voice" seems most plausible.[20] As such, the adoption of positive discrimination strategies to get more women into office—in Britain and elsewhere—has the potential to alter, however gradually, legislative priorities and political debates on some issues most relevant to women's lives.

What are the lessons of this case study for elsewhere? Previous comparative studies have demonstrated that neat but oversimple monocausal explanations of the proportion of women in elected office are inadequate, since many factors have contributed toward this phenomenon, notably the type of majoritarian or PR electoral system, the structure of the economy, such as the share of women in professional and managerial occupations, and cultural attitudes toward the role of women in politics.[21] In many previous global studies, however, the role of positive discrimination strategies designed to promote the recruitment of women has tended to be underemphasized, in part because of the difficulties of comparing how these policies operate within the "black box" of candidate recruitment processes in different parties in many countries.

If, as we have demonstrated, positive discrimination strategies succeeded in producing an immediate boost to women's representation at Westminster, doubling the proportion of female MPs in the 1997 election, could they have the same effect if adopted elsewhere? The answer depends upon the conditions that allowed all-women shortlists to be implemented within the Labour party. If other parties have a political culture that shares the commitment to greater gender equality in political representation, and a bureaucratic mass-branch organization in which party rules matter, then it does seem likely that changing the rules can have an immediate impact upon the recruitment process. This suggests that many social democratic parties in Europe, particularly those in opposition seeking to maximize their electoral support, will be most sympathetic to such strategies. But there is no single policy option that works in every situation for every party in every country. In other circumstances, reformers should look to alternative mechanisms, like equal opportunity training programs for candidates, or to reforms to the electoral law to achieve their objectives.

Notes

1. United Nations, *Human Development Report 1999* (New York: United Nations, 1999).
2. In 1999 worldwide women represented 13.9 percent of the members of lower houses of Parliament and 13.6 percent of upper houses. Inter-Parliamentary Union, *Women in National Parliaments* (Situation as of April 15, 2000), http://www.ipu.org/wmn-e/world.htm. For discussions of the full range of political, social and cultural reasons for this phenomenon see Joni Lovenduski and Pippa Norris, *Gender and Party Politics* (London: Sage, 1993); Azza Karam, ed., *Women in Politics: Beyond Numbers* (Stockholm: IDEA, 1998): http://www.int-idea.se/women/; Andrew Reynolds, "Women in the Legislatures and Executives of the World: Knocking at the Highest Glass Ceiling," *World Politics* 51(4), (1999): 547–572; Lane Kenworthy and Melissa Malami, "Gender Inequality in Political Representation: A Worldwide Comparative Analysis," *Social Forces* 78(1) (1999): 235–269.
3. For a discussion, see Judith Squires, "Quotas for Women: Fair Representation?" in *Women in Politics,* Joni Lovenduski and Pippa Norris, eds. (Oxford: Oxford University Press, 1996) and Drude Dahlerup, "Using Quotas to Increase Women's Political Representation," in *Women in Politics: Beyond Numbers,* Azza Karam, ed. (IDEA: Stockholm, http://www.int-idea.se/women/).
4. Shirin Rai, "Cass, Caste and Gender—Women in Parliament in India," in *Women in Parliament: Beyond Numbers* (IDEA: Stockholm, 1998).
5. Dahlerup, "Using Quotas to Increase Women's Political Representation"; Andrew Reynolds and Ben Reilly, *The International Idea Handbook of Electoral System Design* (IDEA: Stockholm, 1997; http://www.idea.int), 97–100.
6. Mark Jones, "Assessing the Effectiveness of Gender Quotas in Open-List Proportional Representation Electoral Systems," *Social Science Quarterly* 80 (1999): 341–355; M. Jones, "Gender Quotas, Electoral Laws, and the Election of Women—Lessons from the Argentine Provinces," *Comparative Political Studies* 31(1998): 3–21; M. Jones, "Increasing Women's Representation Via Gender Quotas: The Argentine Ley de Cupos," *Women & Politics* 16 (1996): 75–98; Mala N. Htun and Mark P. Jones, "Engendering the Right to Participate in Decision-Making: Electoral Quotas and Women's Leadership in Latin America," paper presented at the 95th Annual Meeting of the American Political Science Association (1999).

7. Reynolds and Reilly, *International Idea Handbook*.
8. Richard E. Matland, "Institutional Variables Affecting Female Representation in National Legislatures: The Case of Norway," *Journal of Politics* 55(3) (1993): 737–55; Eva Kolinsky, ed., *Women in West Germany: Life, Work, and Politics* (Oxford: Oxford University Press, 1989).
9. Miki Caul, "Women's Representation in Parliament," *Party Politics* 5(1) (1999): 79–98.
10. Data and interviews for this research are derived from two main sources. The 1992 *British Candidate Study*, funded by the ESRC, was co-directed by Pippa Norris and Joni Lovenduski. The *1997 British Representation Study* was conducted under the direction of Pippa Norris (Harvard University) in collaboration with Joni Lovenduski (Southampton University), Anthony Heath (Nuffield College/CREST), Roger Jowell (Social and Community Planning Research/CREST), and John Curtice (Strathclyde University/CREST). The research was distributed and administered from the School of Economic and Social Studies at the University of East Anglia and funded by the Nuffield Foundation. The 1997 BRS survey used a mail survey sent to all candidates selected by the main British parties (Conservative, Labour, Liberal Democrat, SNP, Plaid Cymru, and Green) by June 1, 1996. Fieldwork was from June 18 to July 3, 1996. In total 1,628 questionnaires were distributed, producing 999 replies, representing a response rate of 61.4 percent. The survey includes 179 MPs elected in 1992 and 277 MPs elected in 1997. The response rate produced a fairly even balance between parties although the rate of return was higher among candidates than incumbent MPs. Full details can be found at www.pippanorris.com.
11. Pippa Norris and Joni Lovenduski, *Political Recruitment: Gender, Race and Class in the British Parliament* (Cambridge: Cambridge University Press, 1995).
12. Lisanne Radice, *Winning Women's Votes* (London: Fabian Society, 1985); Rachel Brooks, Angela Eagle and Clare Short, *Quotas Now: Women in the Labour Party*, Fabian Tract 541, (London: Fabian Society, 1990); Patricia Hewitt and Deborah Mattinson, *Women's Votes: The Key to Winning* (London: Fabian Society, 1989).
13. For discussions, see Simon Henig, "The Labour Party and Women's Quotas," paper presented at the EPOP Conference (1999); Clare Short, "Women and the Labour Party," in Lovenduski and Norris, *Women in Politics;* Maria Eagle and Joni Lovenduski, "High Time or High Tide for Labour Women?" *Fabian Society Pamphlet* (London: Fabian Society, 1998).
14. Five places on the NEC are reserved for women. In addition, three Constituency Labour Party–elected members must be women, and four union-elected members must be women. For elections among the parliamentary party to the Shadow Cabinet, four votes must be cast for women.
15. Joni Lovenduski and Pippa Norris, "Labour and the Unions: After the Brighton Conference," *Government and Opposition* 29(2) (Spring 1994): 201–217.

16. Pippa Norris, "Anatomy of a Labour Landslide," in *Britain Votes, 1997,* Pippa Norris and Neil Gavin, eds., (Oxford: Oxford University Press, 1997).
17. Tessa Keswick, Rosemary Pockley, and Angela Guillame, *Conservative Women* (London: Centre for Policy Studies, 1999).
18. *The Times,* January 31, 1999.
19. For details of policy initiatives taken by the Ministry for Women, see. For details of employment and pay, see the *Equal Opportunities Commission. Facts about Women and Men in Great Britain* (EOC: Manchester, 1999;).
20. Pippa Norris, "Gender and Contemporary British Politics," in *British Politics Today,* Colin Hay, ed., (Cambridge: Polity Press, 2000).
21. Pippa Norris, "Women in European Legislative Elites," *West European Politics* 8(4), (1985): 90–101; idem, *Politics and Sexual Equality* (Boulder, CO: Rienner, 1987); idem, "Legislative Recruitment," in *Comparing Democracies,* eds. Lawrence LeDuc, Richard G. Niemi, and Pippa Norris (Newbury Park, CA: Sage, 1996); idem, *Passages to Power* (Cambridge: Cambridge University Press, 1997); Wilma Rule, "Electoral Systems, Contextual Factors and Women's Opportunities for Parliament in 23 Democracies," *Western Political Quarterly* 40 (1987): 477–98; Lovenduski and Norris, *Gender and Party Politics;* Karam, ed., *Women in Politics;* Reynolds, "Women in the Legislatures and Executives of the World"; Kenworthy and Malami, "Gender Inequality in Political Representation."

Chapter Seven

Women and the Third Way:
Collaboration and Conflict

Anna Coote

About halfway through the first New Labour government in Britain, there were signs of a renaissance in women's politics, the like of which had not been seen for 20 years. It is often said that oppressed peoples do not rise up when they are thoroughly downtrodden and hopeless, but only when their conditions show signs of improvement. New Labour's arrival in government in 1997 raised expectations among feminists, as it did in most left-leaning circles.

By 1999, a rash of debates and writings appeared as women on the Left began to respond to the emerging litany of the "Third Way"—New Labour's attempt to give its politics some intellectual coherence. The tone was of puzzlement and unease. On the one hand, women were well aware that they were better off under Tony Blair's administration than under those of John Major and Margaret Thatcher. On the other hand, there was a bitter scent of unfulfilled promise. Feminism had been beyond the pale for two decades, during which time it had exerted no influence upon the incumbent government, but had done much to make the opposition electable. Two years after Blair's landslide victory, it appeared that feminism remained in the wilderness: wanted on the voyage but not on arrival.

In this paper I want to explore the relationship between feminism and the politics of New Labour and the Third Way. What part did pro-women's politics play in the modernization of the Labour Party? What impact did it have on Parliament and government after 1997? What is it about the Third Way that makes it both a friend and a foe to feminism and why is it so confused? How has power been distributed since New

Labour's arrival in government? What are the implications for the next election and the next Parliament?

From "Modernisation" to New Labour

During the late 1980s and early 1990s, the British Labour Party under leaders Neil Kinnock and John Smith went through a profound transformation. It distanced itself thoroughly from the "old left," whose ambitions had been to vest power (variously) in the state, in workers' organizations, or in "the people." It dimmed the power of its trade union paymasters. It woke up to global capitalism and the futility of aspiring to "socialism in one country." It learned to love business, began to adapt to the postindustrial economy and accepted, *faut de mieux,* that relations between women and men in the public and private spheres had changed irrevocably.

Many feminists distrusted the modernizers and defended aspects of the "old left," especially its egalitarian tendencies. But feminism, like socialism, is a heterogeneous movement. Many other feminists played a critical role in the process of modernization. Labour's traditional heartland was the industrial working class, union-led and male-oriented—a fast-diminishing power base. The party needed to rebuild its electoral support and that meant taking on board the needs and concerns of the service sector, white-collar workers, and all human life beyond the world of paid employment. Women were of course heavily represented in each of these spheres. Feminists in or near the Labour Party took up the challenge, helping to broaden its political focus and to redefine its image and appeal.

After Labour's crushing defeat in 1987, which returned all of 21 Labour women to Parliament, two feminists close to the party leadership wrote in a pamphlet published by the Fabian Society that women would be more likely to vote Labour if there were more female candidates. Citing qualitative research into voter attitudes, they argued that a large number of women voters was more likely to trust women politicians—as were men. "A majority of men seem to share the view that, at least, women should be more equally represented, and many share the preference for women politicians. A political party which visibly has more women politicians at every level is, therefore, likely to win more support than one perceived as a more male party."[1] (More than a decade later this sounds entirely obvious, but at the time it had the force of a new idea and marked a watershed in the party's attitude to the electorate.)

Feminists called not only for special measures to get more women into Parliament and government, but also for stronger policies on issues such as childcare, education, health, and family-friendly employment. Gradually, these messages began to penetrate Labour's agenda. Men, who continued to dominate the party's decision-making machinery, responded positively for a range of reasons. The evidence about voter preferences was hard to refute. Labour was lagging behind its European counterparts, many of whom had introduced quotas or targets in the late 1980s to increase female representation. Furthermore, women's policy demands were in tune with the realities of a postindustrial economy, which Labour had to accommodate in order to survive as a political force. It may have occurred to the party's leaders that as they distanced themselves from the organized working class, they would need to consolidate support elsewhere—not least among women. And they were ultimately desperate enough for a change in their fortunes to embrace positive action. After Labour's fifth consecutive election defeat in 1992, all-women shortlists were introduced in selected constituencies to ensure that women were chosen as candidates for more "winnable" seats. This was part of a wider strategy to give the party a more feminine image. A concerted effort was made to field women in television and radio shows, in party advertising, and on political platforms.

In the1997 general election, the strategy paid off. More than one hundred women were returned to Parliament, raising the proportion of women in the house from 8 to 16 percent. As power was devolved to Scotland and Wales, women were elected in even greater numbers to the new Scottish Parliament and Welsh Assembly. This was thanks to Labour's policy of "twinning" constituencies for these elections, with each pair selecting a male and female candidate. In 1999, women accounted for 48 percent of Labour members of the Scottish Parliament and 50 percent of Labour members of the Welsh Assembly. Five women were appointed to Tony Blair's cabinet—again, an all-time high. This was not directly due to positive action, but in opposition Labour had operated a quota system, allocating at least five places for women in the shadow cabinet. Once that step had been taken, any reduction in the numbers might have proved embarrassing to the prime minister.

Positive or "affirmative" action (that is, special measures to help create a "level playing field" so that women can compete with men on genuinely equal terms) was thus part of Labour's pre-1997 modernization program. It was never an "Old Labour" strategy—indeed, it was passionately resisted by many traditionalists, whose chief concern was to defend the trade unions' powers within the party. But it was not part of the new government's agenda, either. Between the era of modernization and the emergence of New Labour under Tony Blair, a significant shift took place in the party leadership's attitude toward women. The Blair government introduced a raft of measures that were highly beneficial to women and for which feminists in the party had campaigned over many years. But even as it did so, it appeared increasingly reluctant to identify with feminism and uncomfortable about promoting a pro-woman agenda. Like raising taxes and redistributing wealth, this was something it seemed able to do by stealth or sleight of hand, but never with pride or a positive spin. Hence the unease, bordering on dismay, that feminists began to voice as the century turned. Is New Labour friend or foe to women? The answer, inevitably, is far from straightforward.

The Third Way: Friend and Foe

New Labour claims unequivocally to stand for fairness and social justice. On this basis, it is opposed to sex and race discrimination and has signed up to equal opportunity. In a Fabian pamphlet published in 1998, Tony Blair argued that the Third Way must engage fully with the implications of change.[2] These, he said, included a transformation in the role of women, questioning forms of social organization that had been in place for centuries, and offering half the population the opportunity to fulfil its potential according to its own choices. New Labour has the right language to support gender parity. But when it comes to action, the Blair government is more readily committed to *opportunity* than to *equality*.

Blair and other exponents of the Third Way have clearly signaled that fighting poverty and "social exclusion" is a top priority. The aim is to break out of entrenched patterns of deprivation, making sure that disadvantage is not handed on from one generation to the next. So the New Labour government has put policies in place to ensure that the poorest and most dependent can get help to find employment. Chief among these is the welfare-to-work program, New Labour's flagship policy for reforming the welfare state: it includes the New Deal for Lone Parents, which provides help to identify skills, training needs, childcare, and routes into paid work for single parents, the vast majority of whom are women. And because it became evident that a welfare-to-work program could not work without tackling the childcare issue, for the first time in history, Britain now has a National Childcare Strategy, designed to stimulate diverse, local childcare provision and to offset the costs for low-income families.

Part of the same package is Britain's first-ever national minimum wage, which is bound to benefit women disproportionately, as most low-paid workers are women. The minimum wage is intended to ensure that people find paid work more attractive than a life dependent on benefits. For similar reasons, New Labour has introduced a new Working Families Tax Credit to boost the income of low wage earners with dependent children, and a Childcare Tax Credit supplement, which can provide up to £105 per week toward childcare costs, depending on the numbers of children in the family. And at the same time, there have been significant increases in Child Benefit (from £11.45 in 1998–1999 to £14.40 in 1999–2000, with a further rise promised to £15.00 in 2000–2001): child benefit is usually paid to the mother and so will help raise the income levels of women with children, whether or not the women are working. All these measures, especially when taken together, are capable of making a very substantial improvement in women's lives, especially those of poor, working class, and ethnic minority women.

New Labour is comfortable with the idea of rooting out pockets of disadvantage. If women are a subcategory of a group targeted for help or improvement to attain "social inclusion," they will probably do well out of it—indeed, this is the main way in which women have benefited from the government's policies. But the prime minister has condemned what he calls "dull uniformity"[3] and shows no enthusiasm for any kind of systemic intervention to tackle entrenched patterns of advantage and disadvantage, such as those that sustain unequal power relations between women and men, and unequal pay. The specific disadvantages and imbalances of power that women suffer in relation to men are not targeted.

Absolutely central to the Third Way is the ambition to level up, not level down. New Labour wants to hold the balance between the disadvantaged and the advantaged, between the inner cities and middle England. This is the basis of its appeal to the electorate: better-off people must not lose out. However, while leveling up may work with economic inequalities (if only in times of growth), it does not work with gender inequalities, because so much depends on how time is used for paid and unpaid labor. If women are to boost their earnings, there needs to be a redistribution of time between women and men, because time is a finite commodity. So is power. Women cannot increase their political strength unless men give up some of theirs. Gender parity requires a redistributive deal between women and men. But redistribution appears to be something of an embarrassment to New Labour, an idea strongly associated with the old days of class politics and welfare socialism.

In struggling to assert a distinctive identity, New Labour must be seen to be just that—new. It therefore feels it must repudiate anything that smacks of Old Labour. This is likely to include redistribution, increased public spending, and calls for further state intervention to achieve equality. It may also include anything described by the media as "politically correct"—a slur that has haunted Labour since the days of "municipal socialism" in the 1980s, when Labour-controlled local authorities found themselves increasingly out of step with the burgeoning neoliberalism of Margaret Thatcher's Conservative government. Some of the activity that attracted the slur was dire, didactic ultraleftism that was, in its own way, oppressive. Much of it, however, was well-intentioned, egalitarian politics. Feminism and the efforts of women to use positive action to gain more representation in Parliament are associated with the pre-New Labour era and have been tarred with the "politically correct" brush. So it is one of the things from which New Labour seeks to distance itself.

While it must appear to be "new," however, New Labour cannot afford to be unequivocally modern—not, that is, if it hopes to establish a strong base in the shires of England, where notions of heritage and tradition are cherished. The Third Way must carve a path between the old and the new. Tony Blair says it is about "traditional values in a changed world."[4] What are those "traditional values"? Social justice is certainly one of them, opportunity for all, another; also included are family, community, and responsibility—with major implications for women.

New Labour has introduced measures to make working conditions more family-friendly, following its decision to sign the social chapter of the European Union's Maastricht Treaty. These will benefit women disproportionately: they include a right to up to three months' parental leave, available to fathers and mothers, limits on maximum hours, and new rights for part-timers. However, New Labour's enthusiasm for strong families and strong communities[5] may be a mixed blessing. The Blair government is heavily influenced—as no other Labour leadership in British history—by Christianity. Tony Blair (who is known to be a devout churchgoer, as are many prominent members of his government and inner circle) says that reconciling changes in the role and opportunities of women "to the strengthening of the family and local communities is among the greatest challenges of contemporary public policy."[6] The policies that potentially liberate women are thus caught in an undertow of traditional Christian values—evidenced by efforts to make divorce more difficult and strongly to endorse the family as "society's most important unit."[7] The latter is characterized as a stable marriage, in which parents supervise homework, prevent truancy, build social capital in the neighborhood, and convey appropriate values to the next generation. Family policy is treated as though it affected women and men indiscriminately. But one wonders which parent is expected to have time for all these tasks? What chance does a woman have to enjoy equal opportunities if she is encumbered by "traditional" responsibilities?

Powers and Prejudices

New Labour wants strong government. As Tony Blair puts it, "Freedom for the many requires strong government."[8] That entails concentrating power at the centre. Here New Labour is on the horns of a dilemma: it needs to devolve power to show that it is not an old-left statist government, and it needs to engage others in partnership to implement policies because it is not a top-down, tax-and-spend government committed to direct action. It wants to "steer more and row less."[9] But it cannot easily tolerate the unpredictability and messy spontaneity of local action. It cannot accommodate the consequence of empowerment, because the empowered might want to steer as well as row. There are obvious implications here for sharing power between men and women. Women are acceptable as long as they remain "on message." If they start demonstrating independent or critical thought, they will cease to be considered suitable candidates for empowerment. (The same thing goes for men, but at least men are usually judged individually. When one woman steps out of line, she is readily judged as representing women as a category.)

The Third Way, by definition, is about reconciling opposites, squaring circles, having one's cake and eating it. Arguments about whether it is or is not an ideology will doubtless rumble on. Tony Blair has indicated that he is less interested in ideology than in knowing "what works." However, the hegemonizing force of New Labour as it seeks to be neither left nor right, neither liberal nor conservative, but always a bit of both, a synthesis to embrace opposites and end arguments, is beginning to feel remarkably like an ideology. As it radiates outward from the center, there is diminishing space even for loyal dissent. Either one is in and one buys the whole package, or one is in outer darkness.

An important part of the process shaping the Third Way has been Labour's commitment to understanding the nuances of voter opinion. Learning from the U.S. Democrats, the Labour Party in opposition developed an expertise in profiling target groups in the electorate and identifying their interests and concerns. The idea that the party's electoral strength lay in consolidating and extending its traditional base, which was defined by economic interests, was no longer delivering results. Gradually, this gave way to a conviction that success lay in locating swing voters in key marginal constituencies and finding out what would make them cross the line on polling day. This has enabled New Labour to sideline old allegiances and rise above sectional interests. It can claim it is not about politics any more, but common sense, or what "ordinary folk" want.

During the 1997 election campaign, the phrase "Worcester Woman" emerged to describe the quintessentially middle-England swing voter who must switch from the Tories in order for Labour to win. Worcester Woman is in her thirties with a husband, a mortgage, a job (probably part-time), and one or two children. She is mainly concerned about the economy, schools, and health services. Gender politics do not trouble her, and she would not call herself a feminist.

A wedge can be driven between Worcester Woman and the cause of gender parity and its feminist protagonists. Feminism is and has always been ahead of popular opinion. That is one of its defining characteristics. Feminists called for the vote when most women did not know they wanted it. Now they have won it, most women would not do without it. The same could be said of equal pay and laws against sex discrimination, and possibly even the fact of having more than 100 women in Parliament. Worcester Woman would not like to lose the vote, or the right to equal pay, or anti-discrimination laws; nor, I hazard to guess, would she like to see the numbers of women in Parliament reduced. But she is unlikely to have thought much about getting more women into Parliament or on to local councils. In ditching its enthusiasm for a high-profile, pro-woman agenda, New Labour may hope to signal that it is on the side of "real women," not those politically correct feminists whose demands are at odds with "common sense."

It is hard to judge how far this has been a carefully considered political maneuver and how far it is merely an instinctive lurch by Blair's inner circle. New Labour was forged in highly charged, deeply embattled times. After its third and fourth election defeats, the Labour Party had to rid itself of associations with the past, tighten discipline, and close ranks against adversity on all sides. This has given rise to a close political culture of elite insiders. Predominantly they are young, male, white graduates who live and breathe and eat and dream in the same small biosphere.[10] They control entry and recruit those whom they trust, who speak their language, share their values, and play by their rules. The Policy Unit at 10 Downing Street has been described as a "football team"—and that is not just a metaphor. A few women are allowed in if they prove they can play the game (metaphorically if not literally), but they are not leading players. They cede rank to a generation of young males, who grew up feeling that the gender issue had already been sorted out (by their own mothers in some cases) and now think women are yesterday's problem. They enjoy power and do not want to give it up. They tend to be more comfortable with anti-racism than with anti-sexism. Anti-racism does not challenge their personal behavior because they rarely meet black people. Anti-sexism is potentially more threatening, especially to those who go home to wives or girlfriends in the evening. And women's demands usually imply a need for changes in their own behavior.

This elite enjoys a symbiotic relationship with the media, especially the political lobby, which tends to be peopled by similar sorts—men who are complacent about their masculine privileges, who disregard the women's agenda and denigrate feminism. Any woman who sticks her head above the parapet to call for a better deal for women is fair game for them. The young men at the political center can justify distancing themselves from any pro-woman cause on the grounds that this sort of thing always gets a bad press. So the two groups reinforce each others' powers and prejudices.

It is not easy for women politicians to fight for gender parity in such circumstances. If they are ambitious, they have got to try to keep in with the insiders, which means displaying the insiders' values and supporting their priorities. Its not easy to build and sustain solidarity among women in politics, especially in the House of Commons where the culture is profoundly individualist. Appointments are by favor. There are no codes of conduct, no procedures to ensure fairness in the promotions and firings that punctuate political careers. Each woman has to fight for her own place on the greasy pole.

The terms of engagement are more complex than they used to be, because many of the more obvious goals have been reached (such as establishing the principle of equal pay in law), and because, on the face of it, the government is doing a great deal for women. But the gap between women's and men's pay still yawns wide (women earn 73 percent of men's average weekly earnings), and women remain pitifully underrepresented in most places where power is held (women account for only 27 percent of local councilors and an even smaller proportion of senior civil servants).[11] The case has to be made for keeping up the momentum and finding more ways of creating conditions for genuine equality of opportunity. In the masculine undergrowth of New Labour, the tactics of passive resistance are skillfully employed. These involve agreeing with the need for equal opportunity but doing nothing about it, secure in the knowledge that nothing will change, since the men themselves hold the levers of power.

In short, there is a weak and ill-defined women's movement, fighting a close and powerful cadre of men in a hostile environment. It is slow and it is dirty. And it is not an equal contest.

Where Do We Go From Here?

The renaissance in women's politics that was evident by the turn of the century drew its force from a shared conviction, particularly among left-leaning political activists, that New Labour's appeal to women hung in the balance. Deborah Mattinson, co-author of the 1989 Fabian Pamphlet cited above,[12] wrote ten years later,

> Polling data consistently demonstrates that women remain more sceptical of Labour than men. The qualitative research evidence shows that they are anxious that the radical changes that have taken place, enabling them to vote Labour, are not lasting. A "quick fix" will be no substitute for a sustainable

new approach to politics; one that is practical, "can do" and focused on the things that matter.[13]

The message was clear: women wanted Labour to deliver for women and to be seen to do so. They scented betrayal and their votes could not be relied upon.

As women's lives continue to change, women's votes will remain volatile. Furthermore, a gendered perspective on politics points the way to addressing some of the government's most pressing social problems—which concern men and masculinity. New Labour appears to be increasingly concerned about young men not taking responsibility for their children, about boys underachieving at school, about the rising tide of young offenders, who are almost all male, about the failure of young men to get jobs, about older men disabled by work-related illnesses, and about the fact that men suffer disproportionately from heart disease, suicide, and premature death. All these factors are rooted—partly or wholly—in the ways in which time, power, and responsibility are distributed between women and men, and the subsequent impact on male identities, ways of life, and opportunities. Gendered politics and a redistributive deal between women and men are therefore necessary not only to achieve a fair deal for women, but also, ultimately, to improve the health, well-being, and life chances of men.[14]

The key to a rapprochement between feminism and New Labour lies in understanding that women's politics are integral to modern social democracy, not an add-on. They are an asset, not a threat: a key to the continuing process of political renewal, not a set of demands to be met in a one-off exercise and then forgotten. A one-dimensional politics, crafted almost exclusively by white males and reflecting their priorities, is intellectually frail and politically vulnerable.

Notes

1. Patricia Hewitt and Deborah Mattinson, *Women's Votes: The Key to Winning*, Fabian Research Series 353 (London: Fabian Society, 1989).
2. Tony Blair, *The Third Way: New Politics for the New Century*, Fabian Pamphlet 588 (London: Fabian Society, 1998), 6.
3. Ibid., 3.
4. Ibid., 1.
5. Ibid., 12.
6. Ibid., 6.
7. Ibid., 13; see also Great Britain Home Office, *Supporting Families: A survey of responses to consultation* (London: Stationery Office, 1999).
8. Blair, *The Third Way*, 4.

9. David Osborne and Ted Gaebler, *Reinventing Government: How the Entrepreneurial Spirit Is Transforming the Public Sector* (Reading, MA: Addison-Wesley, 1992), 25–49; see also Anna Coote, "The Helmsman and the Cattle Prod," in Andrew Gamble and Tony Wright, eds., *The New Social Democracy* (Oxford: Blackwell Publishers, 1999).
10. Mark Henderson and Adam Sherwin, "Revealed: the whiz-kids who really run Britain," *Sunday Times,* July 9, 1999, 14. See also Helen Wilkinson, "The day I fell out of love with Blair," *New Statesman,* August 7 (London: 1998): 9–10.
11. Office for National Statistics, Equal Opportunities Commission, *Social Focus on Women and Men* (London: HMSO, 1998), 46; Harriet Harman, *The Democratic Deficit: A Report on the Under-Representation of Women in Local Authorities in Scotland, Wales and England* (London, England, 1999, unpublished); Ross Schneider, *Succeeding in the Civil Service: A question of culture* (London, England, Cabinet Office, 1999).
12. Hewitt and Mattinson, *Women's Votes: The key to winning.*
13. Deborah Mattinson, "Worcester Woman's Unfinished Revolution," in Anna Coote and H. Wilkinson, eds., *The Bigger Picture* (London: Insititute for Public Policy Research, forthcoming).
14. See, for example, Anna Coote, ed., *Families, Children and Crime* (London: Institute for Public Policy Research, 1993); Royal College of Nursing Men's Health Forum, *Men's Health Review* (London: Royal College of Nursing, 1999).

This page intentionally left blank

Chapter Eight

Changing the Rules of the Game: The Role of Law and the Effects of Party Reforms on Gender Parity in Germany

Christiane Lemke

In recent years, the unequal distribution of power between women and men has become a key issue in European democracies resulting in new approaches to advance gender equity and to reconceptualize citizenship rights. The feminist critique of modern democracies claims that classic liberalism failed to address the gendered dimensions of political institutions and the social construction of power. Key issues raised by feminists involve the separation between the public and the private spheres, the gendered division of labor in society, and political practices resulting in an unequal distribution of power. Citizenship as an institutional practice and a set of norms is a major focus of critical reevaluation, based on the notion that the model of citizenship embraced by Western democracies lacks an understanding of the gendered construction of power. Today, a persistently low representation of women in politics, for example, is no longer accepted as a viable practice in liberal democracies, because it raises serious issues of political legitimacy.

From a comparative perspective, the Federal Republic of Germany provides an interesting case in analyzing the problem of gender equity inasmuch as the country evolved from a laggard in respect to women's rights to a vital player in Europe. For a long period of time, Germany featured predominantly strong conservative traditions with respect to women's rights. Among the indicators were a modest female employment rate, a welfare system based on a patriarchal, "male-breadwinner model," and weak anti-discrimination legislation despite the establishment of a liberal constitutional framework after World War II and the emergence of a strong civil society. Yet, when analyzing political representation and civil rights in European comparison, there are some remarkable changes in the past decade, including an increase of women in politics, stronger affirmative action policies, and a reframing of key policies regarding women's equality in the social sector. While feminists have long criticized the lack of institutional changes allowing women to achieve gender equity, more recent developments suggest a shifting of the discourse and practices. With the election of the new government in 1998, the share of women in government jumped to almost 31 percent from less than 9 percent. Likewise, women's representation in the legistlature increased significantly and now amounts to about one third. Elaborating on these shifts in Germany, this chapter is built on the argument that constitutional changes and the changing of party rules were key features in the process to advance gender equity.

Situating Germany: A European Comparison

Germany has clearly been a laggard in respect to gender equity. Historical legacies and institutional constraints hindered the reconceptualization of democratic norms and procedures along the lines of gender parity for some time. Until the beginning of the twentieth century, strong statist authoritarian and antiliberal traditions persisted in Germany. For example, women were not allowed to join political organizations, such as the emerging influential political parties and the unions in their formative years, and they were barred from attending universities until the beginning of the twentieth century. A strong women's movement emerged at the turn of the last century, but class conflict and an ideological clash between "proletarian" and "bourgeois" women's groups divided it. Political freedom enjoyed by women after the failure of the Weimar Republic and the seizure of power by the National Socialists soon overshadowed their enfranchisement in 1919. Universal citizenship was belatedly established after World War II, but strong patriarchal traditions persisted for some time, and the authoritarian legacies dominated social relations. Other factors contributed to the slow modernization of gender relations, such as the postwar economic miracle cementing traditional women's roles as homemakers, the influence of corporatist traditions in labor relations, and the ideological confrontations with state socialism in East Germany.[1]

Significant legal and policy shifts, however, contributed to the conversion of women's social and political status. According to recent statistics, Germany today ranks in the upper middle field in terms of women's representation in politics in European comparison. Women's share in national parliaments and governments has increased over the past decade throughout Europe, but in Germany the increase has been particularly swift. A recent report found parliamentary representation in 1998 to be an average of 17.5 percent (1997, 16.9 percent), with Scandinavian countries scoring much higher and Southern European countries generally lower. The increase is even more pronounced with respect to women's presence in governments; the share of female ministers was 21.9 percent as compared to 19.3 a year earlier.[2]

In Germany, the increase of women in the legislature was particularly large. After the 1983 election, only 9.8 percent of the members of the lower house (the *Bundestag*) were women. In 1987, the number increased to 15.4 percent, in 1990 to 20.5, in 1994 to 27, and in 1998 to 30.9 percent.[3] Women's representation in the German *Bundestag* is still lower than it is in the Scandinavian legislatures, but higher than in France (8.9 percent), Italy (10.8), and Britain (18.2), and above the European average. The highest rate can be found in Sweden (1991, 33.0 percent; 1994, 40.4 percent), but other countries have seen recent radical increases to, for example, Great Britain (1992, 9.2 percent; 1997, 18.2 percent) and the Netherlands (1989, 21.3 percent; 1994, 31.3 percent).[4] A high level of inclusion of women is to be expected in countries with a strong egalitarian tradition, but some of the "outlayer" cases are noteworthy because they do not conform to expectations. Britain, for example, has a low parliamentary representation despite comparatively strong egalitarian features and high female employment; Germany has an increasing representation despite strong patriarchal traditions and lower female employment rates. Germany shows some interesting similarities to the Netherlands (31.3 percent of parliamentarians are women). Despite the Netherlands' conservative tradition and strong traditional family orientation, an influential women's movement and a political system set up to arrange for compromise between different social groups allowed for gender equity and equal representation to be promoted.

As for women's inclusion in government, a high proportion of women in the legistlature usually leads to a higher female representation in government. This is particularly true in the Scandinavian countries, where women's representation in government exceeds their representation in parliament. Germany was an outlayer case until the elections in 1998, when the center-right government was replaced by the Red-Green coalition of Chancellor Gerhard Schröder (SPD). Despite the increase in parliamentary representation during the 1980s, women held only 8.8 percent of leading governmental positions under the government of Helmut Kohl (CDU) and his CDU/FDP coalition. With the Red-Green government coming to power in 1998, women's representation in national government jumped to 35 percent (see Table 8.1). It is still low compared to some Scandinavian countries—Sweden has parity in government with 50 percent women, Norway has 44 percent, and Finland 38 percent—but Germany now ranks with Denmark with 35 percent and the Netherlands with 34.6 percent.

Some of the most significant changes occurred on the state, or *Länder,* level on which women's share in parliamentary representation as well as in government positions is in several cases even higher than on the national level (see Tables 8.2 and 8.3). At the turn of the century, Germany finally takes an upper-middle position in Europe. This conversion is embedded in broader constitutional and legal changes regarding gender relations. In fact, the law has been instrumental in changing the role and status of women and advancing their position in society.

Gender Parity: The Role of Law

In Germany, the role of law has generally been supportive of efforts to change the status of women and to advance concepts of equal rights. Two institutions should particularly be mentioned here, the Federal Constitutional Court *(Bundesverfassungsgericht)* and the European Court of Justice. Whereas the first mainly supported changes in the realm of family law and the civil rights of women, the latter was instrumental in promoting changes concerning women's work and employment opportunities in Germany.[5]

A. Constitutional law

As early as 1948, Elisabeth Selbert (SPD), one of the four "mothers" of the German constitution, proposed the inclusion of an equal rights article in the constitution, or Basic Law *(Grundgesetz),* being drafted for the founda-

Table 8.1 Women in the Federal Government 2000 (Cabinet Members only)

Ministry of Justice	Herta Däubler-Gmelin (SPD)
Ministry of Family	Christine Bergmann (SPD)
Ministry of Health	Andrea Fischer (Grüne/B90)
Ministry of Education and Science	Edelgard Buhlmahn (SPD)
Ministry of Economic Cooperation	Heidemarie Wieczorek-Zeul (SPD)

Total: 14 Ministries (11 SPD, 3 Grüne/B90); Cabinet includes Chancellor Schröder (SPD), 14 ministers and the director of the chancellor's office, 3 *Staatssekretäre,* or assistant secretaries of state, in the chancellor's office.

tion of the Federal Republic of Germany in the postwar years. Supported by women's groups throughout the country, this move was successful despite fierce opposition from men and conservative representatives in the parliamentary counsel. The German constitution of 1949, said that men and women should have equal rights ("Männer und Frauen sind gleichberechtigt," Article 3). The vision of equality embedded in this constitutional provision was a big step forward, but the underlying concept understood equality primarily with reference to men's rights. Whether or not preferential treatment of women was allowed or even necessary was beyond political concepts envisioned at that time.

The granting of basic civil rights and liberties in the German constitution included protective provisions as well. In particular, the family as a social community enjoys constitutional legal protection. Because of this regulation, opponents of women's rights frequently suggested that the concept of equal rights contradicts the special role of women within the family. The notion of the "natural" differences between women and men in raising and nurturing children and taking care of the home proved to be culturally more enduring than the more modern universal caregiver model.[6] Despite the tensions inherent to these different and contrasting approaches to women's status in society, however, progress has been achieved in advancing equality over the past decades.

When affirmative action policies for women in public sector hirings and promotions were introduced in the 1980s, opposing views were held about the meaning and the mandate of the constitution in respect to equality. Legal scholars interpreted the equal rights language of the Basic Law to mean that these plans violated men's rights to be judged on merit. When other legal experts argued that the constitution not only allowed but even demanded to advance equality actively and through state programs, attention of women's rights activists shifted to amending the Basic Law to support affirmative action policies.

In 1994, in the course of constitutional changes after German unification, equal opportunity polices were finally codified as a constitutional provision. Article 3, section 2 was amended by the sentence, "The state shall promote the realization of equal rights for women and men and strive to abolish existing disadvantages" (in German, "Der Staat fördert die tatsächliche Durchsetzung der Gleichberechtigung von Frauen und Männern und wirkt auf die Beseitigung bestehender Nachteile hin"). This new phrasing was a compromise between different proposals, but it still allowed the rewriting of the equal treatment dogma and opened the space for preferential treatment for women. The shift in the conception of what is legally feasible and politically necessary to promote gender equity was supported among the broader public and generally welcomed by women's groups.

B. Family Law and Civil Rights

The traditional dependency of women on men's income has long been a major point of critique among West German feminists. Searching for alternatives, parts of the new women's movement rejected the marriage contract altogether, while other activists pushed for structural reforms. From a radical feminist approach, housework was viewed as "work" that should be paid, a view embraced in the early demand by feminists to grant a "salary" for housework ("Lohn für Hausarbeit"). Other women's rights activists pushed for incremental reforms adjusting family and labor law to a more modern conception of equality.

Compared with other European countries and the United States, Germany today has a modern family law, having abandoned its patriarchal legal traditions and respecting women's civil rights. A substantial reform of the marriage and family law in 1977 gave women more rights and improved their legal status. As a result of this reform, the model of the so-called housewife marriage was abandoned and women were to receive their own share of social security support in case of a divorce. In 1997, another significant reform removed one of the last bastions of patriarchal family

Table 8.2 Women in State Parliaments (*Länder*) in Germany, 1999

State	Members of Parliament (total)	Women (total)	Women in percent
Berlin	206	85	41.3
Schleswig-Holstein	75	30	40
Bremen	100	39	39
Brandenburg[a]	88	31	35.2
Hamburg	121	42	34.7
North-Rhine Westphalia	221	74	33.5
Mecklenburg-Vorpommern[a]	71	23	32.4
Saxony-Anhalt[a]	116	37	31.9
Hesse	110	35	31.8
Saarland	51	16	31.4
Saxony[a]	120	35	29.2
Thuringia[a]	88	25	28.4
Rhineland-Palatine	101	27	26.7
Lower Saxony	157	40	25.5
Bavaria	204	46	22.5
Baden-Wurttemberg	155	27	17.4

[a]Former East Germany

Source: Author's calculations based on Internet and survey.

rights. According to the new criminal law, marital rape has finally been declared a criminal offense, securing full civil rights for women.

However, as legal scholars point out, subtle mechanisms of discrimination continue to prevent women from enjoying equal opportunities in social and professional life. For example, the German tax system clearly favors marriage and a one-earner family. Paid employment for married women is often economically less favorable than providing the unpaid carework at home. Moreover, raising children still requires a flexible, nonemployed caretaker, since childcare facilities are underdeveloped. As a result, Germany still has a low female participation in the labor force in European comparison (44 percent), despite the high qualification achieved by women in terms of their educational degrees and professional merits.[7]

Current institutional set-ups have made role changes within the family and parity arrangements concerning child rearing rather difficult. As a result, only two percent of fathers take parental leave to take care of their children. Even among more highly educated couples the division of labor exhibits traditional patterns according to recent studies. To change men's roles is therefore viewed as a crucial and much needed concept to promote

Table 8.3 Women in State Governments (*Länder*) in Germany, 1999

State	Women	Women in percent
Hamburg	6	50
North-Rhine Westphalia	4	44
Schleswig-Holstein	4	40
Berlin	4	36
Hesse	3	33
Saxony-Anhalt	3	30
Saarland	2	29
Brandenburg	3	27
Rhineland-Palatine	2	22
Baden-Wurttemberg	2	20
Bremen	2	20
Mecklenburg-Vorpommern	2	20
Lower Saxony	2	20
Thuringia	2	20
Bavaria	2	17
Saxony	1	8

Source: Author's calculations based on *Taschenbuch des öffentlichen Lebens 1998/99* and *Kostenloser Nachtrag zur Bundestagswahl,* Bonn 1999.

gender equity, but no attempts have been made to promote these changes through specific policies.

C. Welfare, Employment and Labor Law

Comparative political science frequently refers to Germany as a model for what Esping-Andersen refers to as a "conservative welfare state."[8] Historically, the German welfare state was based on the assumption of the male-worker/income provider. In the "Golden Age" of postwar European welfare state development, the male head of the household was paid a family wage sufficient to support children and a full-time wife and mother who performed domestic labor without pay. Of course, many lives did not fit the pattern of the male-headed nuclear family—in the postwar years, particularly those of the countless war widows with children in Germany—but the normative family-wage ideal inscribed in the structure of the welfare state shaped most of the key policies up to the present time.[9] A changing labor market characterized by high unemployment, increasing job insecurity, and wages insufficient to support a family, as well as shifts in the meaning and reality of family life, produced a crisis of the welfare state that requires a rethinking of traditional conceptions of gender policies and welfare state support. When the East German states joined the Federal Republic upon unification in 1990, the concept of equality had replaced the traditional, rigid notion of different spheres of life, and women had reached some success in respect to incremental policy changes removing the discriminatory mechanisms built into the male-breadwinner-model welfare state. Today, many people no longer prefer the traditional male-breadwinner/female-homemaker model, and the sharp increase in single-parent families poses a particular challenge to traditional welfare provisions. In some regions, in particular in East Germany and in the larger cities, single parent families make up about one-third of all families, and more women expect to sustain their families single-handedly.

Despite increased job opportunities and a more widespread social acceptance of working mothers, there is still a significant gender gap in respect to poverty, however, which is even growing for some groups. Of the 2.7 million welfare recipients (Sozialhilfeempfänger) in Germany, about 22 percent are single mothers. Another 22 percent are women living alone, often widows. The German welfare state is biased toward supporting married women, but even in this group, poverty at old age is common. Eighty percent of all widows cannot live on the social security benefits provided for them on the basis of their late husbands' income.[10] A rather modest improvement was the recognition of three years spent for raising a child

(*Kindererziehungszeiten*) in the pension system since 1995, but this is certainly not enough to compensate for the lack of income. At the same time, in 1996 women's earlier retirement age (60 years) was abolished. Designed to provide support during a difficult and temporary passage in life, welfare policy reflects indeed structurally a lower status of women in society. The current feminist debate therefore focuses on non-discriminatory basic income models based on universal rights rather than on need or charity.

Opposing the ideology of difference and the claim of women's "natural" abilities for carework, the women's movement subsequently focused on improving women's access to education and the labor market. By the early 1980s, income inequality and discrimination in the workplace became a main target of policy change. Income equality was poorly developed compared to other European countries, and even today Germany shows a significant discrepancy between men's and women's income. Moreover, unemployment is higher among women than among men (10 percent as compared to 7 percent). Strategies to improve equality between women and men included the introduction of affirmation action legislation and equal opportunity offices (*Gleichstellungsstellen*) in public and state administrations. This innovation was supported by the experience in other countries, in particular the United States, and by European legislation.

The Significance of the European Court of Justice

In the field of labor law and employment it was the European Court of Justice that acted as promoter for equal rights. In response to the European Community directives of 1975 and 1976 calling for equal pay for work of equal value and equal treatment of both women and men regarding access, training, promotion, and working conditions, anti-discrimination legislation was finally passed in 1980 in the form of an EEC-Adaptation Act. The rather weak provisions set off a "ping-pong" process between the European Court of Justice (ECJ) and Germany, with the former pressing the country to adapt to European legislation and the latter reluctantly following suit. In a 1984 decision, the ECJ criticized Germany's legislation for lacking enforcement provisions, causing the German government to provide revised guidelines in 1985 for promoting women in recruitment, training, further education, and employment. The guidelines were revised again in 1990 and once more in 1994 in the second Equal Opportunity Law.

By the mid-1990s, all states, or *Länder*, had enacted equal opportunity laws (*Gleichstellungsgesetze*) for women working in public service. They provide the basis for administrative reforms, which have introduced the office of equal opportunity representatives, also known as women's representatives (*Gleichstellungs* or *Frauenbeauftragte*). An equal opportunity law for the private sector is now in preparation according to the current minister for family affairs, Christine Bergmann (SPD). This legislation is considered to be necessary, since only few women benefit from the current legislation. It should also be noted that these equal opportunity laws differ from state to state, so that there are vast differences on the *Länder*-level with respect to the provisions and the enforcement mechanisms. Overall, the effect of this legislation has been limited. According to the EU report on equality, women's income is still only 77 percent of men's (in 1987, it was 70 percent). Overall, only 4 percent of all management and leadership positions in Germany are held by women (in the United States and Canada it is about 45 percent). The efficacy of equal opportunity and anti-discrimination legislation remains therefore contested, even among women, who feel that these regulations have not sufficiently changed practices of hiring and promotion.

The European Court in its rulings has followed a non-discrimination policy forcing Germany to abandon discriminatory practices and opening up employment opportunities for women. In a most recent case, in January 2000, it even ruled that women had to be admitted to the German army, *Bundeswehr*, challenging a consensus in Germany that military careers should be reserved for men alone.[11] But the court has also opposed the more radical concept of preferential treatment for women supported by feminists in the country. In a conflict over quotas in hiring, the European Court ruled in 1995 that the equal opportunity law in the state of Bremen violated European law, because it provided for an automatic preference that discriminates against men ("Kalanke case"). The case received broad attention in Europe, since it was the first time that the court ruled over quota regulations in an EU-member country. The decision caused fierce controversy, especially among women's rights advocates in Germany, and was perceived as a setback for equal employment and affirmative action policies.

In a second, subsequent decision in 1997 involving a case in North-Rhine Westphalia, however, the court did not reject quota regulations as such ("Marschall case"). According to this ruling, preference for women is in accordance with European law as long as the decision for preferring a woman is taken on a single-case basis (*Einzelfallprüfung*) considering the merits of each individual candidate. Legislation in North-Rhine Westphalia included exactly this provision and was therefore upheld by the court. The court's decision confirmed the view that equal employment policies could be built on active preferential treatment of women, and it was therefore widely welcomed as a support for these policies.

Changing the Rules within Political Parties: From the Politics of Exclusion to the Politics of Presence

The shifts in constitutional law and legal provisions reflecting new approaches to gender equity are embedded in broader societal changes in Germany. An important feature in this development is the changing of rules within German political parties. Since the channels of access to positions of power have been pre-structured by the male-dominated political organizations, especially parties, the question for women has always been one of whether to work through these existing organizations, to form new organizations, or to eschew organization all together. Women in the postwar decades did engage in political life, both within political parties and outside of parties in numerous voluntary associations, in community work, and in charity groups. The concept of equality embraced by this first generation of women basically followed the liberal equal rights philosophy. By the end of the 1960s, a new generation of women emerged, demanding recognition of female identity and non-discriminatory policies in all spheres of life, including the collective representation of women's interests. The "autonomous" women's movement rejected political parties as part of the establishment and developed cultural—and often separatist—strategies to promote new gender relations. Due to a generational change, changes in the political outlook on parties, and the emergence of a vibrant civic culture in citizens' initiatives, political parties developed new strategies to adjust to these shifts. Pressure from outside political parties as well as from inside parties through women's caucuses caused parties to change their rulebooks. The major feature was the introduction of quotas for women's representation in the 1980s.[12]

Rule Changes

In Germany, the introduction of quota systems for party positions was part of a strategy to move from the politics of exclusion to a politics of presence in political life. Historically, women were excluded from parties, and their access to political power and public administration has henceforth been limited. Up to this day, in all political parties, membership of women is lower than that of men. The Greens have a female membership of 37 percent, the SPD 28.4 percent (1988, 25 percent), the CDU 25 percent (1988, 22.5 percent), and the PDS has a female membership of 43 percent.[13] To change the rules of representation required a concept that extended equality to matters of organizational settings moving away from an individualistic, voluntary view of political participation to a perspective of collective responsibility for guaranteeing political rights. Because of the dominant role of political parties in German parliamentary democracy, the major access to decision-making in politics is through parties.[14] Party membership is not required for many forms of political participation, such as voting, but it is essential for acquiring a position in the political decision-making process. Changing the rules of the political game was therefore viewed as a promising strategy for women to participate fully and exercise their political rights.

Parties favored different measures and policies, reflecting their ideologies and traditions. German political scientist Beate Hoecker distinguishes between strategies of mandatory positive action (Social Democrats, Greens, Party of Democratic Socialism, and Christian Democrats), supportive positive strategies (Free Democrats), and rhetorical strategies (Christian Social Union).[15] Quotas were first proposed by the women's organization within the Social Democratic party, the ASF (Working Group of Social Democratic Women). But it was the newly founded, small Green Party that first introduced party quotas in 1986. By the end of that decade, all parties had adopted quota regulations.

The Greens introduced a radical approach to the issue, proposing a 50 percent quota. According to their regulations, all odd numbers on a party list have to be filled by a woman. In the 1987 national elections the Greens were thus the only party sending more female than male representatives to the national parliament. Their bold initiative to increase the number of women in Parliament was soon followed by the other German parties. The Social Democratic Party decided in 1988 to establish an initial quota of 33 percent, followed in 1992 by a 40 percent quota for candidatures and offices, and parity by the year 2000. In 1988, the Christian Democratic Union introduced a flexible goal that women be represented in offices and mandates proportionate to their membership; only the conservative Bavarian wing (CSU) has not followed this line and simply states that "women have to be considered." The Free Democratic Party adopted a resolution under which women were to be "represented at all levels according to their membership proportion." Similar to the Greens and the Social Democrats, the post-communist PDS introduced parity quotas after the collapse of the GDR in 1990. Today, women's representation is higher in parties with strict quotas (SPD, Greens, PDS) than in those with soft goals (CDU, FDP) or rhetorical strategies (CSU).

Several reasons account for this policy to change party rules. First, party platforms and political positions are a decisive factor. As a rule, parties left of center are more inclined to include equality between women and men as well as active equality policies in their conception of democracy. Promoting gender equity implies implementing democratic values and attitudes and achieving societal justice. Gender equity is perceived as an issue of social fairness. Generally, leftist parties are also more open to feminist demands and the women's movement. With the founding of the Greens the new women's movement found it, for example, easier to channel its demands, and the Greens have included a number of feminist issues in their platform.

Secondly, the strategic positioning and the competition among parties played a major role in the introduction of quotas. In the 1980s, parties competed heavily for women voters in the electoral process. Modernization of society and generational change made votes more volatile, and the de facto exclusion of women from politics was no longer viewed as legitimate. For example, the Social Democrats realized that educated and working women represented a growing voter bloc, and modernization of society included issues of equality and fairness and, among other features, a better representation of women in politics. Moreover, the Social Democrats introduced quotas while in opposition on the national level; an influential feminist contender on the Left (the Greens) competing for votes accelerated the shift. For the center right CDU, traditional women voters were still present, but the party had lost support among the younger women. For the small parties, in particular the newly emerging Greens, attracting new younger women voters was a matter of political survival and surpassing the 5 percent hurdle to enter Parliament. Today, both small parties, the Greens and the PDS, find more support among the educated and younger women in society, whereas the SPD enjoys the support of working-class and employed women. In general, the system of proportional representation favors women, since they can choose from several parties. Once introduced, quotas serve as a catalyst for more party competition.

Representational Equity?

Ten years after the introduction of quota regulations, representation of women in the government as well as in the national parliament has increased. In all political parties, the percentage of female representatives in their respective fraction in parliament has at least tripled, with the exception of the CSU. The smaller parties PDS and Greens even send more women than men to Parliament (see Table 8.4). On the state level, the changes are even more pronounced. Empirical evidence shows that the number of women in state parliaments is higher in states in which there are left-of-center governments and stronger quota regulations (SPD; SPD/Green; SPD/PDS)—for example, in Schleswig-Holstein (40 percent), Brandenburg (35.2 percent), North-Rhine Westphalia (33.5 percent), Mecklenburg-Vorpommern (32.4 percent). Women's share in Parliament is also higher in the city states Hamburg (34.7 percent), Bremen (39 percent), and Berlin (40.3 percent), where Social Democrats and leftist parties have traditionally been strong (see also Table 8.2 above).

The politics of presence has therefore had visible success in Germany. Yet there are also serious questions to be raised. Studies show that women are often confronting individual barriers in their engagement in politics that have not been removed with the introduction of quotas.[16] Because of the traditional division of labor between women and men, women are still heavily underrepresented in the leading bodies of the political parties and are seldom included in the inner-party elites. Lacking capability or time of men to share household tasks is a barrier, and marriage and motherhood are thus the most influential factors hindering women from pursuing a career in politics even when they are interested in party politics.

Institutional barriers present another difficulty. In respect to the voting system, findings for Germany confirm that proportional representation favors women; however, in the personality vote there are very few women. Germany has a mixed system of proportional representation and majority vote for a candidate (*Direktkandidaten*), and there is a fierce struggle for a place on the party list. The power basis necessary for nomination is often weaker than that of men, due to women's absence from some of the key informal power centers, such as unions, church groups, and social clubs.[17] Up to this day, an influential paternalistic culture exists in all large mass parties making the rise of women even more difficult.[18] Once elected, women find that party quotas

Table 8.4 Men in Parliament by Political Parties

Years	*CDU/CSU* Total Percentage	*SPD* Total Percentage	*FDP* Total Percentage	*Grünen/B0* Total Percentage	*PDS* Total Percentage
1983–87	17	21	3	10	—
	6.7	10.4	8.6	35.7	—
1987–90	18	31	6	25	—
	7.7	16.1	12.5	56.8	—
1990–94	44	65	16	3	8
	13.8	27.2	20.3	37.5	47.1
1994–98	41	85	8	29	13
	13.9	33.7	17	59.2	43.3
1998–02	43	105	9	27	20
	18	35	21	57	56

Source: Beate Hoecker, ed., *Handbuch politischer Partizipation von Frauen in Europa.* Opladen 1998. The last term, author's calculations based on *Taschenbuch des öffentlichen Lebens 1998/99* and *Kostenloser Nachtrag zur Bundestagswahl*, Bonn 1999.

play even less of a role. The example of the Red/Green electoral success in 1998 shows that once women are in power, quotas are no longer considered to be binding when appointing ministers and other persons for positions of power.[19] The phrase "Frauenschicksale—Männerfreundschaften"(women's fate, male friendship) captures the problem quite well, showing that even when successful electorally, women lack the power basis within their party to move beyond representation and acquire positions of power.[20] Bonds of companionship placing men inside the circle of power were more influential than the policy laid out in guidelines and regulations.

Legally, quotas in political parties are not contested because they represent a changing of rules within an existing organization that is considered to be at the discretion of the party. However, feminists have questioned the efficacy of these strategies and pointed out their limits. For example, quotas have some unintended consequences. In times of a crisis, women are often called upon to "clean up the mess," leaving them with the most difficult and ungrateful tasks to perform. If women acquire positions of influence and power, the perverse effect is often the impression that they succeeded "just because they are women." Therefore, several women's rights activists have openly come out against quotas.[21]

Another question raised is whether women can "make a difference" and how the increased representation of women influences agenda setting in politics. Empirical proof, at least in Germany, is weak so far.[22] Yet, left-of-center governments have made a difference in the representation of women's issues on the political agenda. Historically, there is some evidence that a leftist government opens the reform space for gender equity. For example, the SPD/FDP government (1969–1982) passed liberal reforms in the areas of family law, abortion regulation, education, and women's employment and introduced concepts of equality in society. Today, there is limited reform space due to financial constraints (high budget deficit, high unemployment); but chances are that the current SPD/Green government may introduce reforms to abolish some of the indirect forms of discrimination, such as the tax law.

Conclusion:
Moving beyond a Politics of Presence

The introduction of quotas has been a jump-start for the politics of presence of women in a country with rather mixed institutional and historical legacies. Over the past two decades, legal and rules changes were instrumental in fighting discrimination and the marginalization of women. Therefore, Germany provides an interesting example of a country in which gender equity has moved forward against the odds. The big increase in the presence of women in politics is one of the important changes in the past decade. Political parties incorporated equitable representation as a policy issue in response to (a) external pressure from women's organizations and (b) electoral competition. The political decision to restructure the very institutions that are decisive for decision-making in modern democracies was an essential shift. Legal changes, including the strengthening of civil and social rights, and the introduction of affirmative action policies mark another major shift. But changing the law and party rules are not sufficient to provide for equal opportunities and to help unfold universal capacities and talents. Gender parity involves a more thorough social and cultural process-shifting from a politics of presence to a politics of redistribution to change power relations. However, without a women's movement framing political issues to advance gender equity and change roles, rather than to adjust to men's roles, the parity movement will not be successful.

Notes

1. See also Christiane Lemke, "Women and Politics: The New Federal Republic of Germany," in Barbara Nelson and Najma Chowdhury, eds., *Women and Politics World Wide* (New Haven: Yale University Press, 1994), 324–341.
2. Figures according to the EU–Commission Report on Equality, 1998.
3. Sources are until 1994, Beate Hoecker, ed., *Handbuch politischer Partizipation von Frauen in Europa* (Opladen 1998); the last two terms are my own calculations based on *Taschenbuch des öffentlichen Lebens 1998/99; Kostenloser Nachtrag zur Bundestagswahl* (Bonn, 1999).
4. Data according to Beate Hoecker, ed. *Handbuch Politischer Partizipation von Frauen in Europa (Handbook of Political Participation of Women in Europe)* (Opladen: Westdeutscher Verlag, 1998).
5. For a detailled account see Sabine Berghahn, "50 Jahre Gleichberechtigungsgebot—Erfolge und Enttäuschungen bei der Gleichstellung der Geschlechter," *WZB-Jahrbuch 1999. Demokratie in der Bewährungsprobe* (Berlin 1999).
6. "Universal caregiver model" is a term used by Nancy Fraser in her "After the Family Wage: A Postindustrial Thought Experiment," *Justice Interruptus* (New York: Routledge, 1997), 41–66.
7. The employment rate of women increased slightly to about 57 percent.
8. See Gösta Esping-Andersen, *The Three Worlds of Welfare Capitalism* (Princeton: Princeton University Press, 1990).
9. The East German path was quite different, inasmuch as the East German state promoted women's work and provided childcare facilities. Before unification, the female employment rate was 83 percent. However, wages were generally low, and there was still a segregated employment structure

as well as discrimination in the workplace, but women had their own income and could draw their (modest) welfare benefits from their work.
10. See Jutta Almendinger, Hannah Brückner, and Erika Brückner, "Ehebande und Altersrente," *Soziale Welt* No. 1 (1992), pp. 90–116.
11. In this case, a young woman was denied access to the army to pursue a career as an electronic engineer.
12. Today, 12 of the 15 EU-member countries operate some kind of quota or preference regulation for women.
13. It should be noted that only about 3 percent of Germans are members of a political party.
14. On the importance of parties and legislative recruitment, see Joni Lovenduski and Pippa Norris, eds., *Gender and Party Politics* (London: Sage, 1993); Pippa Norris, ed., *Passages to Power: Legislative Recruitment in Advanced Democracies* (Cambridge: Cambridge University Press, 1997).
15. Hoecker, ed., *Handbuch,* p. 83.
16. Hoecker, ed., *Handbuch,* 1998.
17. Drawing on Max Weber and Nicolaus Sombart, feminist political scientist Eva Kreisky, for example, describes the state as "Männerbund," a male bonding institution.
18. The current scandal within the CDU regarding illegal flows of money (undeclared donations, and corruption) sheds light on some of these structural problems facing the larger mass parties.
19. In the Green Party, the cleavage was between *Realos* and *Fundis,* within the SPD between the "new center" and the left, working-class wing.
20. Tissy Bruns, "Frauenschicksale, Männerfreundschaften," *Der Tagesspiegel* (October 9, 1998), 3. This is only one of many articles in German newspapers elaborating on the difficulties of women to acquire governmental positions after the elections of 1998. This article explicitly addresses the blockage within the parties despite party quotas.
21. A recent example is the prominent Green Party representative, Renate Künast, from Berlin.
22. A more positive example is the passing of the law banning marital rape in 1997.

This page intentionally left blank

Part III

Policy Processes

This page intentionally left blank

Chapter Nine

From Equal Pay to Parity Democracy: The Rocky Ride of Women's Policy in the European Union

Agnès Hubert

Little did those so-called Fathers of Europe know that what they considered to be a fairly minor article of the Treaty of Rome, Article 119, would later serve as a basis for changes in electoral laws and even constitutional revisions in the six original sovereign states that made up the European Economic Community. Little did they envision, when the former belligerents were negotiating the Treaty of Rome more than 40 years ago, that gender equality would develop into an important component of the European integration process.

Now, the latest treaty in the long line of constitutional documents providing a legal base to the 15-state European Union, the Treaty signed in Amsterdam in June 1997 has significantly upgraded the status of gender equality.[1] From being purely a labor-market issue (equal pay was deemed necessary for fair competition in industry), gender equality has become a general political objective of the European Union applicable to all policies and programs under the treaty.

One step forward, two steps sideways. Since 1958, the formulation of a European Union policy to advance gender equality has followed a stop-and-go trajectory. It has been irregular, has rarely come as a natural development within the process of the construction of a united Europe and as a general rule, as in most other regions and countries of the world, has reflected decision-makers' ambivalence about integrating the changing roles of women in society. Still, the commitment of member states to strong supranational institutions at the European level has served the cause of women in the member states. Questions of gender equality have never disappeared from the European Union's agenda.

Describing the main developments of this policy, I will delve into two particular occasions during which women and other gender-minded actors overcame the threat of reversal, employing the leverage capacity of the European Union's institutional framework: first, in 1961, when "technical difficulties" were invoked to justify governments' decisions to bypass their original commitment;[2] second, in the mid-nineties, when the judiciary questioned and limited the binding tools developed to implement gender equality, "positive actions."[3] On both occasions the interactions between institutions and actors were decisive in pushing policy forward.

The second argument I wish to make takes us deeper into the mid-nineties. As affirmative action, including quotas and binding commitments to counteract indirect discrimination in the labor market, were being questioned, gender equality policy was moving on to new ground: inter alia, the concept of parity democracy offered a fresh approach to gender equality policies. Since the early nineties, women's underrepresentation in decision-making positions in elected assemblies, governments, and large corporations has become a more urgent economic and political issue. The expression "breaking the glass ceiling," born in the United States, pointed to the structurally embedded obstacles facing women attempting to climb the ladder of power. In the European Union the concept of "parity democracy" shifted the debate rhetorically from the quantitative claim underlying quotas and affirmative action to a qualitative necessity related to the nature of democracy.

Institutional leverage capacity along with the emphasis on increasing the number of women in decision-making posts could have created the context for sustainable progress toward more gender-balanced societies. Did this in fact take place? Within different contexts, this question has arisen on both sides of the Atlantic. In both the EU and the United States women still form the bulk of those at the bottom of society by income and living standards and they are still a minority in elected assemblies and in the highest positions in governments and large corporations.[4]

In a rapidly changing world, in which diversity and conflicting perspectives are arguably the most efficient way to build consensus, gender equality must be a prerequisite for making good decisions. Still, it will not happen if the bulk of women are left out of the decision-making process. What sort of supplementary leverage capacity do the provisions of the Treaty of Amsterdam provide to advance gender equality in an enlarged European Union? Is the existing institutional framework appropriate to implement these provisions? Which priorities should be addressed, which strategies pursued? These are some of the questions currently floating about on the European equality agenda.

The "human rights" approach to gender equality—implicitly contained in the Treaty of Amsterdam—has already given rise to European initiatives to combat violence against and trafficking in women.[5] This policy area is now developing, but will not be sufficient to maintain economic and social cohesion in a wider Europe, where the rise in inequalities constitute a threat to social and political harmony.[6]

Finally, I wish to stress that the agenda of "mainstreaming gender equality" can be carried forward only if the institutional framework, which has so far on the whole sustained progress toward gender equality, is reconsidered.[7] The fight against discrimination requires commitment at the highest level, time, resources, and a systematic approach in order to detect the sources of inequalities, make them visible, and develop remedies.

From Equal Pay to the Balanced Participation of Women and Men in Decision-Making

Given the awkward circumstances in which the seed of gender equality was sown on the Treaty of Rome, progress has on the whole over the last 40 years been impressive. The European Community has been an active contributor to legal advances made to improve the situation of women in Europe.[8] Based on the legal principle of equal pay for equal work, enshrined in Article 119 of the Treaty of Rome, legislation addressing equal treatment at work and social security has been passed. Realizing that equal opportunities are conditioned upon but not necessarily guaranteed by equality in law, the European Commission also instituted a series of measures through consecutive programs to promote de facto equality. In order to help translate the legal and political commitments of the successive treaties into reality, these programs have lent support to various initiatives, such as setting up networks, stepping up information and communication activities, supporting pilot actions and studies, and identifying and disseminating sound practices.

As we enter a new millennium, the original narrow commitment of the EC member states to equal pay for equal work is being widened to the progressive recognition of equality between women and men as a fundamental principle of democracy for the whole European Union.

Article 119 of the Treaty of Rome generated inter alia the adoption by the Council of Ministers in 1996 of a "recommendation for the balanced participation of women and men in decision-making."[9] The reasons behind this adoption are to be found in the original "European policy making context," which has provided space for challenging and reformulating policies both at the EU and national level. In this context, the short history of the European women's policy shows how many advances have been driven by interactions between institutions and gender-minded actors.

In 1958 "equal pay" became a "European issue," finding its place in the Treaty of Rome for economic reasons, which had little to do with the advancement of women. Examining the compatibility of the six original member states' social policies with economic integration, the Ohlin report expressed confidence that market forces would, as a general rule, progressively reduce the differences in social charges imposed by different member states as such changes were minimal.[10] The report, however, mentioned the issues of women's pay and paid holidays, which might have required a harmonization of legislation. The differences in existing legislation could cause significant distortion of competition among industries. During the negotiations this point was made by the French delegation, which feared the difficulties in convincing a heavily protected industry to accept the progressive dismantling of tariff barriers. The French textile industry, which had to comply with the constitutional requirement of equal pay for women workers, would be appeased if the same requirement applied to its Dutch competitors. Because Article 119 stated that "the member states shall ensure that the principle of equal pay for male and female workers for equal work is applied," it helped to make the treaty acceptable to France as a condition for the fair competition between textile industries.

However, when in May 1960 the governments of the six original member states decided to accelerate the implementation of the common market by engaging earlier than planned in the second phase of tariff dismantling, France, still reluctantly accepting the dismantling of trade barriers, had to remind them about this commitment to a binding provision of the treaty. This was an obligation that had to be fulfilled before moving on to the second phase. At that stage, legislation on equal pay had not been passed in the member states that had not previously had this requirement and none of the governments was ready even to report on progress made. The French government's insistence convinced the Council of Ministers to ask the European Commission at the end of 1960 to produce a program for the implementation of Article 119.

Member states justified their inertia on the subject by stressing the lack of factual information. The "Article 119 Group," composed of statisticians and lawyers from the commission and the member states, compiled a long list of surveys and further research necessary for a scientific approach to pay disparities. As the agreed deadline for passage to the second phase (December 31, 1961) approached, technical difficulties were used to justify a "political" solution: a resolution proposing a staged timetable for equalizing discriminatory wage rates and for removing discriminatory clauses in collective agreements was passed. This resolution was deemed to be sufficient evidence of good faith on the issue of equal pay and convinced the French government to accept the transition to the second stage. Fifteen years later the European Court of Justice admitted that the procedure used then had been "a violation of the Treaty with the complicity of the institutions."[11]

Events between 1961 and 1976 provide the first example of how a setback in political will could be compensated for by activism in institutions, particularly in the European Commission and the European Court of Justice. In the first period, as economic conditions were changing, immigrant workers started to replace member-state women workers in the textile industry, lowering the pressure on the industry to pay equal rates. Equal pay dropped down the political agenda. The Article 119 Group continued to produce reports that revealed a decreasing interest in the Council of Ministers, which in any case was in 1965 facing the worst political crisis in the EEC's history.[12]

From the setback of 1961, it took almost a decade for women and equal pay to reemerge on the European agenda. The two decisive events that provided a fistful of gender-minded actors opportunities to revive the issue were the Herstal equal pay strike and the Sullerot study.

In June 1966, for the first time in history, women workers marched in the streets of Brussels, carrying banners asking for the national implementation of the Treaty of Rome's Article 119. At that time in the Herstal National Arms Company, wages of qualified women machine-tool operators working on three specialist machines were less than those of men sweeping the floors. Charlotte Augustine, trade union representative at Herstal, was the first unionist to discover that Article 119 imposed binding obligations, that had not been transcribed into national law. Not only did the article exert pressure on the Belgian government and on public opinion as the level of discrimination against women in employment was exposed, but it acted as a catalyst for women's rights activists.

Following the strike, Professor Eliane Vogel Polsky, a Belgian professor and practicing lawyer who will forever remain an emblematic figure for European women, initiated the first equal pay case referred to the European Court of Justice, the case of Gabrielle Defrenne. In the judgment of the second Defrenne case (1976), Polsky persuaded the court to recognize the direct application of Article 119 and the "violation" of community law by the member states in 1961.

The Sullerot report, entitled "Women's Employment and its Problems in the Member States of the European Economic Community," prompted renewed institutional attention to women's policy. Written by the French sociologist Evelyne Sullerot on behalf of the European Commission, the study revealed that crucial changes were taking place quite simultaneously across Europe. The increase in longevity and the reduction of the number of pregnancies by surviving children was transforming women's use of time. Their roles and aspirations could no longer be confined to their maternal function. The time devoted to maternity in 1970 represented on average one-seventh of the average life span of a European woman, releasing a new wave of energy to be directed to other activities.

The European Commission, as was expressed then by its Director General of Social Affairs in the European Commission, acknowledged this study as opening the way for prospective thinking in radically new directions. The Treaty of Rome's focus on equality in the labor market, though initially quite limited, symbolically started then to "spill over" into other fields.

In the early seventies, prior to the oil shortage shocks, the European economies were flourishing and had been for a considerable time *("trente glorieuses")*. The EEC was a success story, attractive to non-member states. Its first "enlargement" with three new member states (UK, Ireland, and Denmark) took place in 1973. These simultaneous events and the "second wave of feminism," brought to the governments' attention by the mobilization of women's movements and the first World Conference on Women organized by the United Nations in Mexico (1975), formed the ground on which European institutions promoted the creation of structures and legislation for women's rights. A "Women's Bureau" (later called the Equal Opportunities Unit) within the commission services, assisted by an advisory committee composed of member states' representatives, made up the core group created in the late seventies. Draft directives on equal pay, equal treatment at work and in social security were presented to the Council of Ministers and adopted.[13] In June 1979, the first directly elected European Parliament created an ad hoc committee for women's rights, which was to become permanent in 1984. Finally, the European Court of Justice in April 1976 in its ruling in the second Defrenne case explicitly recognized the principle of equality in its double economic/social objective to be "a founding principle of the EEC," opening the way to spillovers beyond the workplace.

The first "spillover" that could have been symbolically meaningful came in the early eighties inspired by market demands. Business interest in "flexi-working" (that is, part-time work) for the development of the service sector stimulated a need to ease conciliation of family and work demands on women. Was the symbolic barrier between the private and public spheres becoming blurred? Not really. Despite the work done by a European network of experts for ten years (1986–1996) on the question of childcare, and later eldercare, and the rather daring content of a recommendation (a non-binding tool in EU legislation) passed in 1992, the first binding community text (a directive) on the issue of "reconciliation" offered a mild framework for the regulatation of parental leave.[14] While addressing women and men, the text finally adopted in 1997 did not contain provisions likely to induce change in the sharing of tasks within the family. Meanwhile, employment and the containment of unemployment became the member states' first priority.

Two years earlier, a second severe blow had been forced on the European gender equality policy, threatening to neutralize the fight against discrimination. In its Kalanke judgment, the European Court of Justice, which had so far adopted a rather progressive stance in interpreting the European provisions on equality (for instance, in the Defrenne case), condemned the absolute and unconditional priority given to a woman by the administration of the city-state of Bremen. In line with decisions made at the same time in the United States, the European Court of Justice severely limited the scope of "positive action" as an instrument to compensate for indirect discrimination and to promote gender equality. Applauded by the press in the first instance, this judgment evoked strong reactions from the gender-equality actors of member states, the European Parliament, the women's lobby, and the European Commission, which then adopted an interpretative communication. In November 1997, the court partially reestablished the legality of positive action in the Marschall case, which recognized that even when male and female candidates were equally qualified, male candidates tended to be promoted in preference to female candidates, due to prejudices concerning the role and capacities of women in working life. Accordingly, a national rule containing a saving clause would be acceptable if the male candidate was guaranteed an objective assessment, which could override the priority given to the women candidate.

The Maastricht Treaty, for example, added a third paragraph to the EU Treaty's Article 119 on equal pay for equal work aiming to strengthen it. But the text was ambiguous and, for a time, it was feared that the new language would be used to justify protective measures in national legislation that create obstacles to women's labor market participation, for example, allowing governments to pay childcare allowances to employers rather than directly to parents, bans on women assuming night work, etc. Another instance was the Barber case which established that different retirement age for women (60) and for men (65) was discriminatory toward men.[15] The result was that most countries changed their legislation to mandate a single retirement age at 63, a changed that benefited men and hurt women in the name of equality. A small program run directly by the EU Commission, the New Opportunities for Women program, provided two weeks of funding for training child care workers while endorsing professionalization of jobs occupied mainly by women as a main political objective. Such attempts have rarely been deliberate, usually caused either by the actors' fashionable ignorance or the widespread belief that gender equality has been achieved.[16] Does this indicate that the roots of gender inequality have to be exposed in a different way, that public policies have to be reoriented?

In the first part of this chapter I described what have so far been some of the strengths and weaknesses in the European arena for the promotion of gender equality. Its institutional embeddedness and the scrutiny of a network of gender-minded actors have guaranteed its permanence, but its low priority on the European agenda has repeatedly threatened the achievement of its objectives. As one of the main tools available to promote gender equality in the 1980s, the European gender-equality policy was moving onto new ground: the issue of equal participation in decision-making on the one hand and the ambiguous concept of mainstreaming on the other. Does this shift open a window of opportunity for more sustained progress toward the equalization of working and living conditions of women and men in Europe? So far, the objective results on real equality leave much to be desired.

Forty years after the commitment of European governments to ensure the principle of equal pay for male and female workers, statistical evidence reveals that on average in the EU a woman earns one-fourth less than a man does. This pay differential persists beyond what can be explained rationally by segregation and working hours, and European women are disproportionately represented among the unemployed and poor.[17] The promises of a single market and the contraction of public spending linked to the Economic and Monetary Union have left a very bitter taste in the mouths of women, who have been granted the "poisoned gifts" of unemployment and flexible working conditions in the new employment economy.[18] Newly emerging labor market segregations indicate that the gender gap is widening rather than narrowing.[19] Are the new approaches likely to yield fairer results?

Gender Parity:
From a Quantitative Claim to a Qualitative Necessity

Beyond its role as a "guardian of the treaties" and a force behind proposals for new legislation, the European Commission's influence can be measured in this particular area by the intensity of the debate created around equality issues in Europe and the empowerment of actors at the national level. The pluriannual action programs initiated in the 1980s to help translate legislation into reality provided the means to disseminate knowledge, create networks, and stimulate the debate on sexual equality. While the first two programs focused respectively on the implementation of legislation and positive action, the "Third Medium-Term Community Action Program for Equal Opportunities for Women and Men" (1991–1995) opened a new chapter; the "status of women in society" had to be improved in order to reach the objectives set out in the treaty. Both the low participation of women in decision-making and their image in the media were seen as obstacles to equality of women and men in the labor market.

This opened the door for actions to promote the participation of women in decision-making. At that time, the "glass ceiling" had become a buzz-phrase in America. The implied denunciation of structural discrimination (just as affirmative action in the early eighties) was increasingly associated with the dysfunctioning of democracy. Moreover, as a decisive report by a high level group of OECD experts stated in 1991, "effective structural adjustment, including the social transformation needed to achieve economic growth and social cohesion in the 1990s and beyond, depends upon empowering women to play a greater role in shaping structural change. That role implies increased participation in both employment and decision-making structures."[20]

Extending the agenda to the decision-making arena provided European equal opportunity advocates with a breath of fresh air, bringing new dynamism to the policy's promotion. The mainstream European Union agenda itself provided occasions for drawing the attention of European decision-makers to gender equality: the completion of the single market in 1992, which Jacques Delors, then president of the commission, had set as a political objective, was considered a potential threat to women, requiring public authorities' active involvement to transform these threats into "opportunities."[21] In June 1992 the Danish "no" in the referendum on the Treaty of Maastricht provided a clear indication of the opposition of a majority of Danish women to the European project. Shortly afterward, the opening of negotiations for the accession of Sweden, Finland, Norway, and Austria made women less scarce in the corridors of the Council of Ministers and started to give a new standing to women's policy on the European scene.

Served by circumstances, decisive gender equality proponents professionalized their approach: the European Women's Lobby became a more credible channel for women's associations as well as in European institutions. The Women's Rights Committee of the European Parliament, approaching its tenth year of existence, gained a new reputation and began to develop a more offensive approach within the European Commission. While still modest, the resources available to promote gender equality increased significantly, allowing actors to take on new responsibilities under the program.[22]

International events also provided important impulses: preparations for the Fourth World Women's Conference in Beijing called on UN member states to announce publicly their achievements and list what remained to be done at the national level to advance gender equality. Finally, the geopolitical changes set off by the end of communism created new demands on Western democratic regimes. Increasingly in the 1990s, the question of legitimacy came to the forefront of the political agenda. At every level of public decision-making (including the European Union) democratic institutions, processes, and actors came increasingly under scrutiny. Women's absence or scarce presence among those making decisions in the name of all citizens began to be seen as an anomaly. Gender equality in decision-making was slowly becoming a "requirement for democracy."[23]

The European debate over the concept of parity democracy was initiated at the first European Summit of Women in Power, held in Athens in November 1992.[24] This summit had been organized by the new "European network of experts on women in decision-making," created to assist the European Commission with the implementation of the Third Action Program. At the end of the summit, 20 European women in power signed the "Athens Declaration," asserting their commitment to promote the participation of women in decision-making positions. The declaration openly stated that "equality between women and men imposed parity in the representation and administration of Nations," supported the plea for representativeness (based on both the politics of ideas and the politics of presence), pointed out the inefficient waste of women's talents and aspirations, and denounced the "democratic deficit." This declaration, which later gained international recognition, provided those who argued for gender equality in the member states with useful ammunition.[25] Not only was it widely used in practice by the women's movement, but it also brought the debate into national parliaments, receiving a unanimous vote in the Spanish *Congresso de los Disputados* (February 1993) and in the Portuguese Parliament (resolution adopted on March 8, 1993). Theoretically, the five basic arguments supporting the necessity to promote the equal participation of women and men in decision-making arenas—equality, democracy, good use of human resources, needs and interests of women, and the quality of policymaking—were presented as nonexclusive of each other. The declaration offered both common ground for a European debate as well as a possible adaptation to the views prevailing in each national context.

The Athens Declaration marked the beginning of a process now recognized to have been decisive in most member states, spawning an intensive follow-up process across Europe.[26] After the Athens summit and during the implementation of the European Program (1991–1996), the coordinator and the national experts of the network on "women and decision-making" found renewed strength in their European endeavor. Arguments, theories, and practices found a new forum for debate among women associations, political parties, decision-makers, and politicians on the national scene. They were compared and tested during national and European events or campaigns. From the initiative provided by the Athens summit in 1992 to the adoption of a "recommendation for the balanced participation of women and men in decision-making" in 1996, a large number of creative initiatives were implemented.

"Can you imagine a world with 81 percent of Romeos and 19 percent of Juliets" or "why 81 percent of the European Parliament has to shave in the morning" were among the slogans promoted by the network throughout Europe during the 1994 European Parliamentary election campaign. In the resulting legislature the percentage of women increased from 19 percent in the previous parliament to 27 percent. "A positive trend which was unexpected in a parliament with increased powers" would conclude the coordination network structure.[27] A bipartisan, trans-European campaign, "vote for balance between women and men," launched all over Europe by associations and national agencies, emerged at the right time. In all member states a new mobilization had occurred. The members of the network had coordinated and encouraged citizen's initiatives. In the United Kingdom a Eurobus went from precinct to precinct. In Germany, demonstrations were organized to call for gender balance among the proposed party candidates. In France, a petition signed by more than 100,000 famous persons was sent to the heads of the main parties and political institutions. In all the member states, pins, magnets, and posters with the European campaign logo were disseminated. Meetings and debates were organized in Denmark, Italy, and Spain. In Portugal in January 1994—four months before the election—a highly symbolic event was held, a day-long session of a "parity parliament" composed of equal numbers of women and men politicians of all parties gave some idea of the changes that could occur in parliamentary debates.[28]

The European Commission gave the network on Women in Decision-Making the following mandate: "To remove the obstacles to women acceding to decision-making positions and propose strategies to overcome them." Both the commission and the network then developed several activities in pursuit of this mandate: (1) providing easy to use and regularly updated facts and figures on the gender gap in decision-making positions (panoramas, studies, databases); (2) involving women through highly visible events, such as large conferences and symbolic documents: for example, the Declaration of Athens (1992), Charter of Rome (1996), Declaration de Paris (1999), which developed strategies to increase the number of female candidates and elected representatives at local, regional, and national levels, women in professional organizations, in academia (innovative research), and promoting networking; (3) reforming legislation: a recommendation on the balanced participation of women and men in decision-making was adopted in 1996, following the council's resolution of March 1996. A few months later (June 1997), the Amsterdam Treaty enlarged the European mandate on gender equality in a crucial manner.

The experience gained during the campaign created a valuable source of references and inspiration, mobilized women's associations, and helped to create national "machineries."[29] The pressure exerted on national governments by civic actors (associations, parties) and the recommendations and resolutions adopted at the European level created new dynamics on the national scene. In some member states it resulted in changes in electoral laws (Belgium in 1997; Italy in 1998) and state constitutions (Portugal in 1998 and France in 1999). In others the result was renewed commitments and/or more efficient and firm measures to reach a gender balance in decision-making.

Looking back, it seems that one of the consequences of these efforts was the evolution of a debate on women's representation in the public sphere and the new conceptual approach brought about by the concept of parity democracy, marking a shift in the thinking on gender equality policies. From a quantitative claim associated with remedies like affirmative actions and quotas, the debate has increasingly been seen as a qualitative necessity associated with structural change and the rethinking of democracy.

Attempts to move more women into decision-making positions have always implied binding measures (such as affirmative actions, quotas, limits to the number of representatives of the same sex), which have often been unpopular, and resisted by the very actors and organizations dedicated to past struggles for the elimination of inequality.[30] The concept of parity democracy does not remove the need for quotas. In most countries, quotas have proved in the past to be the most effective way to boost the proportion of women in positions of power. But quotas, or affirmative actions, are to be seen as transitional measures, necessary to create a fairer democratic order. Parity democracy brought about a new spirit congruent with the changes taking place in democratic thought.

Low electoral turnouts, disaffection toward the political class, skepticism about the effectiveness of political parties as instruments of the political process and citizens' mistrust of governments, which came in the nineties to the forefront of political attention in Europe, raised a number of fundamental questions concerning the nature of representation itself at a time when society was becoming more interactive. The concept of parity democracy was brought into this context in order to point out the fundamental injustice of women's economic and political marginalization, proposed as a cause of political systems' inefficiencies, and offered as a way out of a crisis. In other words, it proposed a way to perpetuate the status quo but using different faces.

Mainstreaming:
From Equal Opportunities to a Culture of Equality

The debates over the concept of parity democracy since the beginning of the 1990s have become much more ambitious and far-reaching than just proposing a more acceptable way to pursue gender equality policies. Parity introduced the idea that democracy had to be deepened structurally in order to facilitate the equal participation of women and men and, vice versa, equality implied a reconceptualization of democracy. Beyond the "provisional" changes to be introduced in electoral and appointment systems to ensure women's presence on an equal footing with men throughout democratic institutions, the concept of parity democracy is supported by the idea that a gender-shared exercise of power is likely to transform the functioning of democratic systems dramatically. Because there are no existing examples of societies governed according to a gender parity principle, one can only use the available evidence to speculate what would actually change and rely on judgment.[31] One useful approach is to examine elements of the "vision" of some women who have experienced high public office.[32]

At the 1995 conference, "Equality and Democracy: Utopia or Challenge?" organized by the Council of Europe, Cristina Alberdi, the minister for social affairs during Spain's presidency of the European Union in 1995, argued that the object of parity democracy is to "ensure a proper balance between the interests, which no men traditionally represent, and those which men traditionally represent, until such time as it stops making sense to draw that distinction, because women and men both attach equal importance to private life and public life." Among the changes that women should introduce into policy "for making democratic institutions properly equality-conscious," she mentioned, first, measures to ensure equality on the labor market but also the reorganization of community life (caring facilities, changes in working hours, opening hours for shops, public services, etc.) in order to give individuals the chance to balance their productive and reproductive roles properly. "The private sphere needs proper acknowledgement and attention," she cautioned.

Mary Robinson, then president of Ireland, pointed out that a "reallocation of time to create a better balance in the activities of men and women" is likely to be supported by more women in decision-making positions, but that changes would also translate into leadership style. "One of the striking details which remains in my mind from the women's groups and networks I have visited is that women seem to devise instinctively structures which are open, enabling, consultative and flexible," she said.

Vigdis Finnbogadottir, president of Iceland, argued that "women have a slightly different collective angle on values and justice, which will enrich society as a whole." Maria de Lourdes Pintasilgo noted that "parity democracy is not simply one aspect of equality. It goes beyond this issue by offering women and men a unique opportunity to face up to the question of identity as a key aspect of the organization of society. It represents a newly emerging stage of democracy."

Should and can the challenge represented by this new approach be encouraged at European level? The answer to the first question is positive. The equal pay commitment made in the name of the European Economic Community has still not been met, and women continue to be the most skeptical about European Union's benefits.[33] For both political and socioeconomic reasons, gender equality is substantially linked to the future of the European Union. The results of electoral consultations which took place in the nineties in Denmark, France, Sweden, Finland, Norway, and Austria are confirmed by opinion polls: women are unconvinced by what is seen as a "men-in-gray-suits enterprise." More female faces in the decision-making arenas is a necessary step, but it is yet more important to bring into decision-making circles individuals who will introduce different perspectives. The concept of "mainstreaming" gender equality is a theoretical tool for working out a process, in which the decisions made in the name of the people will properly integrate the interests and needs of those at the bottom of the ladder, who face difficulties rarely experienced by "men in gray suits." The answer to the second question—can the EU take up the challenge and how?—is more ambiguous. On the one hand, most politicians in Europe are conscious that too strong a political stance on gender equality might be perceived as potentially discriminatory against men. On the other hand, gender inequalities are still blatant and pose a potential threat to the enlargement of the European Union. Women are (often discreetly) at the forefront of moves to rejuvenate both the language and the practice of democracy (local initiatives often favor solidarity, combat exclusion, and alleviate poverty).[34]

The new provisions on gender equality contained in the Treaty of Amsterdam remain open-ended. The treaty's overall objective is to solidify the ground for monetary union and prepare for enlargement. The member states realize that measures designed to respond to the growing concerns of citizens for human rights and respect for human dignity have to find their place in European constitutional law. Both this concern and the mobilization of the women's constituency within the European Women's Lobby played important roles in raising the profile of women's rights. But can the EU take up the challenge? The new provisions of the treaty offer a renewed framework. A closer look at the four articles of the new treaty shows both minor, ambiguous, and potentially meaningful changes:

1. On the commitment for equal pay, Article 141 gives legislators a wider margin to compare the pay of the potential plaintiff by extending comparability from equal work to work of equal value.
2. On positive action, a new paragraph at the end of the same article, allows for "measures providing specific advantages"(that is, affirmative action) for "the underrepresented sex" (that is, men or women) "with a view to ensuring full equality in practice between men and women in working life."
3. Non-discrimination in general is mentioned in a new Article 13. It enables the Council to take appropriate action to combat discrimination based on sex, racial or ethnic origin, religion or belief, disability, age, or sexual orientation. This clause however has no direct effect (in contrast with Article 12 on Nationality) and requires a simple consultation procedure with the Parliament (no co-decision procedure) and unanimity in the council. These restrictive conditions are likely to make its implementation fairly exceptional.
4. Last but not least, the most potentially significant change for the status of gender equality is contained in the combination of Article 2 (the promotion of equality between men and women is one of the tasks of the Community) and Article 3(2): "in all the activities referred to in this article [21 activities ranging from a common trade policy to environment, education, health protection], the Community shall aim to eliminate inequalities, and to promote equality between men and women."

If decisions concerning economic and monetary union, the promotion of research and technological developments, agriculture, transport or development policies or trade arrangements, to mention just a few of the EU's activities, are to be designed for the ultimate benefit of citizens, then they should also incorporate a gender perspective. Their potential effects on the relative positions of women and men should be identified, analyzed, and taken into account at every stage of the decision-making process. If the treaty's stated aim is "to eliminate inequalities and to promote equality between women and men," then mainstreaming is an important strategy. It can work "to overcome the structural inequalities in the organization of working and family life, which constrain the participation of many women in the labor market and in public life."[35] On the positive side, mainstreaming should increasingly be seen as well as an essential tool for developing proper accountability systems in public policymaking and as such, a prerequisite to the sustainable progress of a democratic order based on legitimacy and the rule of law.

Can the European Union Take Up the Challenge?

The term, "mainstreaming a gender perspective," which first appeared in a European text in the Third Action Program, bears no bad omens.[36] Borrowed from environmental policies, this notion refers to a difficult practice in sectorally segmented public administrations: the incorporation into a policy area of priorities of another policy area that is deemed of superior value. The "administrative" obstacles proved to be more than a threat when the draft communication made to implement this provision of the program was blocked for "inappropriate timing." In 1993, employment, not gender equality, was becoming a priority issue to mainstream in European Community policies. Moreover, conceived in a time of budget restriction, "gender mainstreaming" was either misunderstood or in some member states or regions was assimilated with a dilution of equal opportunity policies and a suppression of positive actions and specific structures.

How and why did the European Union insist on adding this term to the end of every chapter of the Beijing Platform for action? How and why did "gender mainstreaming" soon after become the new strategy to promote gender equality in the Fourth Community Action Program for Equal Opportunities for Women and Men (1996–2000)? Was it intended as a diversion? Was it likely to boost interest in the issue? In an article soon to be published, Maria Stratigaki, when looking into the two central concepts—"the reconciliation of working and family life" and "gender mainstreaming"—through their use in European Community official texts, effectively makes the point that though these concepts were introduced to promote gender equality, they have in fact been misused in favor of other policy interests.[37] Through examples taken in employment and structural funds, she describes the progressive shift to reduce the scope of the policy and justify the suppression of specific actions or programs. How far forward has mainstreaming of gender equality brought the policy as we approach the end of the Fourth Action Program, three years after the treaty was signed and one year after it entered into force in May 1999?

Some formal commitments have been made which may lead to progress in the future. The promotion of equal opportunities for women and men is an integral part of the European employment strategy and member states have started to integrate this new "constraint" into their annual plans.[38] Within the European Commission new structures of attention have been created: a group of commissioners on gender equality now meets three to four times a year and an interservice group is supposed to diffuse a culture of gender equality throughout the commission's services. The commission and the European Parliament have exchanged communications and resolutions maintaining the issue on the agenda.

Still, one has to admit that in the last few years, the most visible extension of concerns for gender equality in the commission's agenda have mostly been made on issues under the control of women commissioners, especially concerning trafficking of women (Anita Gradin), women and science (Edith Cresson) and in regional policy (Monica Wulf-Matthis). Meanwhile, the budget and human resources of the equal opportunities unit, which had so far been the main focus for developing specific actions, was reduced. The appointment in September 1999 of a committed woman commissioner with specific responsibility for gender equality (Anna Diamantopoulou) has put an end to the slow administrative downgrading of the policy.

Such cases seem to suggest that a precondition for implementing a policy of gender mainstreaming is the vested interest of those in decision-making positions. Having women in positions of power is a necessary condition for lessening gender inequality, but it is not sufficient. If those women are isolated and/or have neither the will nor the strength to challenge the dominant values, they will not change the policy-making culture. With a sufficient number of women, change becomes more easily acceptable. Gender parity is about having a sufficient number of women in the driving seat, not because they are women but because they are self-interested proponents of greater gender equality. This concept, which has grown out of years of frustration with the slow pace of progress toward equality, is possibly the best way found so far not to have to wait 475 years to reach equality between women and men.[39] Gender parity and the progressive change of culture necessary for an effective mainstreaming policy are bound to be linked, until the idea that sex equality can improve democracy is generally accepted. What is at stake is nothing more than a deep change in the political culture.

Conclusion

The Treaty of Amsterdam, in force since May 1999, has committed the European Union to treat gender equality as a transnational issue to be taken into account in all community actions. Is this progress? Certainly, the member states' commitment to what can be considered the European

Constitution is of the highest value. Past European experience shows, however, that without initiatives taken by dedicated institutions and stimulation from interested parties, the treaty's provisions would not spontaneously have been translated into reality.

As the role of institutions and public policymakers changes and they are forced to become more accountable to wider constituencies, the way women's rights policy in the European union has been constantly stimulated by stakeholders in the policy may someday be considered a model. Today, however, gender equality is mingled into the questions of "high politics" that haunt the European agenda. Enlargement to eastern and southern Europe, the redesigning of institutions and procedures to accommodate newcomers, and the full transition to the euro remain at the center of political attention.

However, the necessity to create a European Union nearer to the needs of citizens, which inspired the Amsterdam provisions for gender equality, is on the agenda. Will the new political culture of mainstreaming gender equality penetrate the institutions carrying out the European project? As "guardian of the treaties," the European Commission has to provide the impulse, the European judiciary has to demand a stricter enforcement of the rules, and the European Parliament has to keep the debate alive and grant resources to gender equality policies. The question is, then, will the bulk of women, disillusioned by the negative effects of some European decisions and policies on inequalities in general, maintain a sufficient interest and involvement?

The answers to this question will be found in the way the public institutions of both the union and its member states will or will not be able to renew their decision-making elites. More women are needed not only to fill up the targeted quotas, but to transform the culture of organizations, to add to the diversity, to help bridge the gap between public policies and those they are meant to serve.

The way gender equality has developed and the context in which the European integration process has been accelerated in the last ten years point to the weaknesses and fragility of both processes. The fragmentation of the European geopolitical landscape and the "back to the kitchen sink" trend for women are not mythical hypotheses.[40] They are still lingering patterns used by populist leaders to mobilize a predominantly young electorate.[41] The decreasing legitimacy of the traditional political class and the resistance to a new "gender contract" are underlying reasons for a general feeling of insecurity and extreme electoral choices. Unfortunately, the question of gender inequalities may continue for a long time to disrupt the political landscape, and to provide a useful theme of discussion in a transatlantic context.

Notes

1. The treaty entered into force on May 1, 1999, after it was ratified by the member states' parliaments.
2. Agnès Hubert, *L'Europe et les femmes: identités en mouvement* (Rennes: Apogee, 1998).
3. Equivalent to affirmative action in U.S. terms.
4. *Implementing the European employment strategy: The challenges of integrating young people into the labour market, long-term unemployment and equal opportunities* (Luxembourg: Office for Official Publications of the European Communities, 1999) and Francine Blau, "Trends in the Well-Being of American Women," *Journal of Economic Literature* 36 (March 1998): 112–165.
5. The programs STOP and DAPHNE and the zero tolerance to violence campaign were initiated by the European Commission in 1996, that is, before the revision of the treaty, on the initiative of Anita Gradin, the Swedish member of the college of commissioners from 1995 to 1999.
6. Justice and Home Affairs are developing into intergovernmental issues in European Community policy.
7. Article 3, paragraph 2 of the Treaty of Amsterdam.
8. An exception is to be found in Scandinavian countries, where the full participation of women in the labor market was encouraged already at the end of the sixties, as a result of the distance from Third World labor force reserves and the political will of social-democratic governments.
9. 96/694/CE. This "recommendation," a nonbinding instrument in the European legal order, is the first official act of the council of ministers, which deals exclusively with the issue of the participation of women in decision-making processes.
10. In 1955 Bertil Ohlin, former minister of finance in the Swedish government, chaired a group of economists of the International Labour Organisation (ILO) on the social aspects of European economic integration.
11. *Arrêt Defrenne II*, attendu 33, ECJ, (April 1976).
12. Following a disagreement, General de Gaulle decided that France would not attend council meetings.
13. A directive is a piece legislation proposed at the initiative of the European Commission which, once adopted by the council has to be transposed into national legislation and implemented in all the member states. The four directives mentioned here concern equal pay, equal treatment at work, and social security.
14. The recommendation was inspired by a clear gender equality objective: to challenge the traditional distribution of roles.
15. ECJ (1990). Barber, Case 262/88, *ECR* 1990: 1889.
16. "The marketing for gender equality has been so effective that formal equality is now perceived as real and the responsibility for discrimination is transferred from the collectivity to the individual." Quoted from *The Nordic Countries—A Paradise for Women?*, ed. Brit Fougner and Mona Larsen-Asp (Stockholm: Nordic Council of Ministers, 1994).

17. *Eurostat press release* n°4899 (June 8,1999): 11.8 percent of women and 8.6 percent of men were unemployed in 1998 (*Employment in Europe* 1999—a yearly report published by the European Commission, Brussels).
18. Most often the practical translation for the individuals concerned of this attractive concept has been lower and less secure salaries, awkward working hours, and no job security.
19. Margaret Maruani, ed., *Les nouvelles frontieres de l'inegalite: hommes et femmes sur le marche du travail* (Paris: La Decouverte: MAGE, 1998).
20. "Shaping Structural Change: The Role of Women," report by a high level group of experts to the secretary general of OECD (1991).
21. As a result, the New Opportunities for Women (NOW) initiative, providing 400 million ECU over five years to develop projects aimed at improving women's position in the labor market, was set up.
22. Increases were registered in the commission's human resources (10 to 25 in the administrative unit in charge of equal opportunities), but as well in the member states: nine "networks of experts" with a minimum of one member per member state assisted the commission; and in Financial Resources (budget of 5.5 million ECUs in 1991 to 10 million ECUs in 1996) largely granted because the male politician in charge wanted to appear "women friendly" (how apparently adverse conditions can turn positive in the right circumstances).
23. The expression was used in 1995 by the newly appointed president of the commission in his inaugural speech to the European Parliament.
24. The link between gender equality and democracy appears for the first time in an official text of the Council of Europe in 1988 (declaration of the ministers of the Council of Europe). The same organization will later commission a study on parity democracy from a political scientist, Elisabeth Sledziewsky.
25. The declaration inspired similar declarations in Argentina and India; it was translated into all European Community languages, reproduced on a postcard form, and widely distributed by associations.
26. For example, see: Philippe Bataille and Francoise Gaspard, eds., *Comment les femmes changent la politique et pourquoi les hommes résistent* (Paris: La découverte, 1999).
27. Beyond its power over the European budget, the Treaty of Maastricht had granted the European Parliament co-decision power on a number of European policies.
28. A report on this initiative can be found in *Parité-infos* no. 5.
29. Within the UN context, this term refers to the variety of structures set up by the national government to promote gender equality.
30. The ECJ opinion on the "Kalanke case" (October 1995) is an emblematic example.
31. The Swedish government, composed of an equal number of ministers of both sexes, is the nearest approximation to a parity system. But Sweden suffers great inequality in other spheres of power, that is, the economy disqualifies it to stand as an example.

32. Quotations are taken from a conference on "Equality and Democracy: Utopia or Challenge," organized in February 1995 by the Council of Europe. See also *Equality and Democracy: Utopia or Challenge?* Proceedings from a conference organized by the Council of Europe as a contribution to the preparatory process of the United Nations Fourth World Conference on Women (Beijing, September 4–15, 1995); Palais de l'Europe, Strasbourg, February 9–11, 1995 (Strasbourg: Council of Europe Publishing, 1996).
33. See another source of recent data and analysis on the wage gap in "Implementing the European employment strategy, the challenges of integrating young people into the labour market, long term unemployment and equal opportunities," European Commission (March 1999).
34. It is interesting to note that in the public debate over parity democracy in France, journalists not known to be "raving" feminists recognized that women politicians are less likely to commit the sin of using "stiff language."
35. Mary Braithwaite, "Mainstreaming equal opportunities for women and men in structural fund programs and projects," Documents for the European Commission (Brussels, December 1999).
36. "The Commission will ensure that the equality dimension and the particular problems met by women on the labour market are explicitly taken into account in all appropriate community policies and programs."
37. Maria Stratigaki is a former official of the equal opportunities unit, presently associate professor at Pantheion University in Athens and director of the Greek Research Centre on Gender Equality, KETHI.
38. The European Employment Strategy was adopted at the Luxembourg jobs summit in November 1997. Following this summit, in the proposed 1999 employment guidelines the commission has emphasized the need to pursue the integration of equal opportunities for women and men in all aspects of employment policies, notably by guaranteeing active employment market policies for the vocational integration of women, proportional to their rate of unemployment, and by promoting women in the context of entrepreneurship.
39. "On the basis of the current pace of progress, equality between women and men would be reached in 475 years." Quoted from an International Labour Organization document used as a slogan by NGOs during the 1995 Beijing conference.
40. "Panorama," BBC Television (January 24, 2000): the young woman interviewed preferred the financially dependent option to the stress of permanently juggling between work and family commitments.
41. Jörg Haider's supporters are predominantly young, poorly-educated male voters, "feeling threatened by women with education, ambitious and adaptable, and enjoying the support of equal opportunity and other governmental policies." "Commotion in three-quarter time, Sasa Cvijeti," *Central Europe Review* 2, no. 6 (February 14, 2000).

This page intentionally left blank

Chapter Ten

Quotas, Parity, and the
Discursive Dangers of Difference

Hege Skjeie

An unequal distribution of decision-making positions remains a largely shared tradition of liberal democracies.[1] Brief glimpses into gender representation statistics of both national and international decision-making structures reveal institutional practices that have proven difficult to change. But these practices are increasingly being recognized for what they are, problems of democracy. Debates on political representation have multiplied in both national politics and at United Nations, European Union, and Council of Europe conferences and commissions. In many European parties a new set of measures has been introduced to promote access for women to decision-making bodies, ranging from target figures (via quotas) to ticket balancing. In France, the parity movement has obtained an amendment to the French constitution that simply and boldly asserts the equal right of access to decision-making, a principle that in turn is to be applied through detailed regulations of political nomination and election processes.

In this respect, Scandinavian feminism has its own story to tell. In all the Scandinavian countries a strong mobilization to equalize the distribution of decision-making power can generally be described as a common political project of feminism's "second wave." This line of activism consistently criticized party-based political exclusions. Contrary to other versions of European and American feminism of the 1970s, the critique was not associated with normative rejection of participating in the traditional political institutions. Instead, it attacked the practices of democracy and demanded inclusion. In short, men's monopolization of party politics was seen more as a problem for democracy than party politics was seen as problematic for women. Thus, Scandinavian feminism took up its first double project: to explain why and how women's underrepresentation was a problem, and make proposals to overcome it.

One significant example of this feminist integrationist profile can be found in the opening statement of *The Unfinished Democracy: Women in Nordic Politics* (1985):

> As women researchers we are concerned with forms of injustice and inequality based on gender. As political scientists we are concerned with the disbursement of values and benefits which have been set in place via the political system. In both cases we are concerned with power and its just distribution.[2]

Scandinavian feminism should then present an interesting example of the new debates on political exclusions and inclusions. The gradual development of an extensive system of quota policies in my own country, Norway, is particularly pertinent. The way that quota policies came into being here clearly demonstrates the political effectiveness of a rhetoric of difference. Yet, the Norwegian case also provides a warning of the discursive traps that this rhetoric may contain.

Norwegian Quota Policies

Twenty-five years ago the Norwegian government proposed a constitutional amendment that aimed to establish the principle of men's and women's equal representation in decision-making, an approach stunningly similar to that of the more recent *parité* movement. The Socialist Left Party's newly elected leader, Berit Ås, presented a simple yet radical proposal; women should hold at least half the seats in the Norwegian Storting. As combined her newly won seat in Parliament with intensive involvement in the new feminist movement, working as a university professor and writing about "women's culture."[3] In this combination of roles and activities, she epitomized the formula for feminist activism that Norwegian feminists wanted to project in the 1970s. The preferred formula was political criticism plus movement politics aiming to change political institutions equaled change—a formula, I would add, that is nearly identical to the one guiding present-day efforts to change the practices of the institution of liberal democracy.

Unfortunately, at the time in Norway, the proposed constitutional reform proved to be too far ahead of its time and was rejected by a clear majority among all the other parties represented in Parliament. At roughly the same time, the Socialist Left Party and the Liberal Party introduced new rules in their statutes that required parties to have gender-balance (parity) in the internal party organizations and internal elections and in candidate selection for public elections. The Liberal Party was at this time led by a feminist party/movement politician, Eva Kolstad. She was the former leader of the oldest Norwegian women's rights organization with roots back to the struggle for the vote at the turn of the century. Kolstad became the world's first *Ombud* for Equality when she was appointed to the office responsible for administering a new Equality Law passed by Parliament in 1978.

A majority of the parties had acknowledged in the parliamentary debate on constitutional reform the need to act to address the problems of unequal representation, and in their view, the voluntary adoption of parity quotas was the one acceptable solution. The debate over constitutional or otherwise legally binding remedies ended. In 1981, Gro Harlem Brundtland took over as leader of the largest Norwegian political party, the Labour Party, and the party introduced similar quota measures. The party caucus passed the new rules with no controversy whatsoever. In 1986, when Brundtland appointed her second cabinet in 1986, she simply stated that the party's internal quota regulations obviously would apply to the composition of the party's new cabinet. Thus, Norway obtained the first in a series of "women's cabinets," evoking much international wonder and acclaim.

Today, party quotas are a matter of business as usual. Every time a new government is appointed, the least surprising event will be the appointment of at least 40 percent women. The quotas mainly take the form of a minimum representation requirement of 40 percent for each sex. (The mutuality implied by the language is an expression of respect for formal gender neutrality.) Party statutes regulate the nominations and elections of electoral candidates within five of the seven largest Norwegian parties. Only the two parties on the right have rejected internal use of quotas. For the other parties, the rules mean that equal representation no longer is an issue, with the exception of cabinet appointments, in which the governing parties' own rules on quotas do not apply. Nobody has so far dared to challenge the quotas and they have become a newly institutionalized trait of Norwegian party politics.

In a somewhat different institutional setting, particularly in the extensive corporatist political-administrative structure, more legally binding measures have been applied with less hesitation. In Norway, the corporatist system of publicly appointed boards, councils, and commissions prepare major national policy initiatives and/or exercise public authority over specific areas of responsibility delegated to the corporatist system by the state. Recruitment patterns to this particular decision-making system have been the subject of governmental reform since the early 1970s. In 1987, the

Norwegian Law on Equality introduced a minimum 40–60 quota regulation for the gender composition of all publicly appointed boards. It was subsequently proposed that the law be amended to include the composition of the boards of public and private enterprises, in which statistics show that women constitute less than 10 percent of the members. In addition, different forms of quota policies or affirmative action programs already guide both student enrollments and public sector hirings, although clearly with varying degrees of compliance and effectiveness. In many of these cases, quota policies remain highly controversial.

Formal regulations of integration through quotas have clearly been most prominent in Norwegian party politics. In Denmark, Sweden, and Finland quotas have been primarily directed toward political parties' internal representation structure; only the "green" parties and parties to the left have adopted such means. In Denmark quotas had been in operation since the early 1980s but were abolished by both the Social Democratic Party and the Socialist People's Party in 1996. In Sweden, the Social Democratic Party has employed quotas as a major gender equality strategy only since 1993, in Finland only since 1996.[4] In the 1990s women have come closer to equal political representation with men in both parliaments and cabinets in all the Nordic countries. In Nordic parliaments representation rates now vary (roughly) between 35 and 40 percent; in cabinets roughly between 40 and 50 percent. Iceland remains the exception; representation rates remain comparatively low. In both Iceland and Finland, women have been elected to their countries' very top political postings, the presidency. Only Denmark and Sweden still await a similar event, the appointment of a woman as prime minister.

In the absence of legally binding regulations, there is generally speaking no guarantee of an equal sharing of positions of political power. The outcome still depends on the actual nomination practices of individual parties and on the electoral successes of parties with other selection rules. In 80 percent of Norway's regions, the county mayor position is still held by a man. At the last parliamentary election women's representation rates decreased by four percentage points. At the local level of government representation rates have generally remained lower than on the national level. The publicly appointed committee that is presently considering a revision of Norwegian electoral laws has not put these issues on the agenda. Paradoxically, while legally binding measures are considered relevant to the composition of both public and private boards and committees, they are not seen to be equally relevant to the political parties themselves. In Norwegian politics, issues of political representation somehow seem to belong too much to the past. The continued intensity of such debates, for example at the EU level, largely passes unnoticed, while Norway by the mid-1990s again chose not to accept membership.

Thinking about Politics: The Impact of Social Democracy

Feminist scholarship has played an important role in shaping the conditions of Scandinavian integrationist politics. Generally, there have been close ties between parties, movements, and academia, though they were much closer in the 1970s and early 1980s than in the late 1990s. Despite the harsh critiques offered of established institutional practices, it would still be fair to summarize the dominant tendency of feminist scholarship during this period as a strong belief in the transformative possibilities of party-based politics. At present, this is far less of an issue. The discourse on representation has largely moved away from politics and onto other fields, in which questions of access are formulated differently. The feminist scholarship initiated in the early 1970s stressed gender-structured political interests and political integration as a strategy of empowerment. Established political institutions became of great interest to women, whose political aims concerned fundamental redistribution in terms of social policies.

The vision was by no means modest, as Helga Hernes wrote in 1987 in a path-breaking book:

> A women-friendly society would mean a society where justice on the basis of gender would be largely eliminated, where women are able to have a natural relationship to their children, their work and to public life—without an increase in other forms of inequality, such as among groups of women.[5]

Feminist scholarship made a simple claim, namely that states could be non-repressive and thus "friendly" to women. At the time, many feminists viewed the claims as absurd. In order to understand why that was, it is important to consider what it meant—in the radical 1970s—in general to think and act politically within the specific social democratic political culture. In narratives of the Scandinavian democratization processes, social movements always play the leading role. The social democratic ideal of citizenship is "an activist, participatory and egalitarian ideal"—that is, an ideal largely shaped by the waves of social movements in Scandinavian history since the mid-nineteenth century.[6]

The formation of the welfare state has commonly been described as an alliance between the working class and the peasants, who were able to take over the state apparatus through democratic struggle. Whether we look to history, political science, or political sociology, this general description of gradual integration into state structures—of ongoing transformations of state/citizen relationships based on movement politics—remains central to an understanding of the distinct form of a social democratic tradition of governance and participation. Usually, the notion of social democratic citizenship includes the assumption that both perceptions of "the state" and "the individual," of rights and obligations, are shaped by the defining characteristics of movements mobilizing for political control. To create a nation to which the citizen wishes to belong, ideologies of opportunity must be combined with ideologies of identity that pay due respect to what inspired such movements in the first place.

Quite often, such narratives are composed as "grand statements" about historical changes in political regimes. In Norway, a recent reformulation emphasizes two well-known transformations, the political successes of the peasant movement and of the labor movement, but also suggests a third, somewhat controversial change: the replacement of the political impact of the labor movement with that of the women's movement.[7] Out of this nation-building project also emerges the concept of "state feminism," meaning those policies advocating women's political mobilization "from below" combined with integration politics "from above."[8] In other words, state feminism is another example of a movement mobilizing for—and succeeding in gaining—political influence.

Within this general perspective on democratization, political parties are clearly perceived as arenas for "contestation over questions of value" rather than as arenas for "deciding on questions of preferences."[9] Much feminist research in the 1970s thus was inspired by a twofold research agenda, which also contained a double political project. Criticism of existing power structures should, on the one hand, protest the exclusion of women from political institutions. Research on "women's lives" should, on the other hand, as it was capitalized in one of the 1970s' more straightforward political statements: "Seek out women where they participate and create independent values."[10]

Scandinavia possesses a distinct tradition of women forming political networks and alliances across political parties. (Several parties have associated women's organizations attached to the main party organizations.) On issues of gender equality and social politics, different women's branches of political parties have often cooperated with nonparty women's organizations. Drude Dahlerup's study of the new women's movement in Denmark illustrates how Danish feminists shared a pragmatic attitude toward the state, allowing them to cooperate extensively with both national and local political structures.[11] Nevertheless, Dahlerup argues the crucial element in the 1960s radical feminist movement, the Redstocking Movement, was the effort to push feminist issues onto the political agenda and thus change the discursive opportunity structure of political reforms. While the new feminism was an important political force, it had largely *indirect* effects on public policies.

In Norway, a more interventionist feminist project made more direct contributions to political reforms. An early signal of feminist alliances aimed at changing political parties' own recruitment practices was provided through a series of specific campaigns to promote women's representation in both national and local political elections. The 1970s began quickly, when a "women's coup d'état" produced a majority of women members in three large local councils, including that of the Norwegian capital, Oslo. Although these majorities did not survive the next election, they successfully demonstrated the power of coordinated action, paying great attention to maintaining a non-partisan profile, a practice that would prove to be very important. Such campaigns were partial only to women, and then principally on a cross-party basis. Although undoubtedly radical, they could by no means be associated solely with "the Left." Rather, they were prime examples of more general (social) democratic integrative practices, and as such were clearly to be valued as legitimate.

In the struggle for suffrage nearly a century before, "the common concerns of womanhood" had been at the center of the debate. From the 1970s onwards this appeal again became a primary argument for Norwegian integration politics. Arguments that emphasized the political relevance of gendered differences became increasingly important. The main statement of this political rhetoric of difference is indeed familiar: it matters whether it is men or women making political decisions; men and women represent different values, experiences, and priorities; men therefore can make no legitimate claim to represent women. Such statements did not, however, explore the finer points of controversy over what kinds of values, experiences, or priorities were to be held by which groups of women, nor to what kinds of degrees such values, interests, or experiences represented conflicting or complementary positions as compared to those held by men. This was left completely in the open.

A precarious new balance was thus achieved on the central rotational point in normative discussions about women's rights, the famous equality versus difference debate. A new pragmatic continuum on "identities–interests" was rhetorically produced, in which, to use Joan Scott's words, "the terms of exclusion on which discrimination is premised are at once refused and reproduced in demands for inclusion."[12] From being an argument from a position of power—a reason why women should be excluded from politics—this rhetoric of difference became an argument that mobilized counter-power—a reason for inclusion.

In the early 1990s, I compared the major arguments for the political integration of women over the last 30 years in Norway. The comparison showed how the concept of "gender" was transformed from implying "division of labor" to being synonymous with "values" and "interests," and how completely the language was adopted by political elites. The end result of the transformation process emerged in a series of interviews I did with members of both Parliament and cabinet, in which it emerged that hardly anyone thought that gender was irrelevant to the formation of party politics.[13] In Norway, this new rhetoric of difference gradually came to constitute an argumentative basis for quota policies.

In Denmark and Sweden, however, the integration politics was much more based on a rhetoric of gender equality.[14] In this respect, it is interesting to note that in these countries, quota systems never became the same "favored solution" to problems of political exclusion as they did in Norway. The tendency within feminist scholarship in Scandinavia to underscore the possible transformative role of party-based representative politics has obvious parallels in more recent discussions of representation and citizenship in liberal democracies. The new emphasis on a "politics of presence" clearly claims that the issue of representation is an issue of great importance to feminism.[15] Movement-based forms of local activism cannot alone solve the problem of political exclusion. Rather this must combine with an adoption of institutional designs that change the very principles of democratic representation. Iris Marion Young's work is another example of a feminist perspective that focuses upon diversity and tries to formulate a basis for arguing group representation.[16] Both Phillips and Young's analyses mark a shift toward a firmer focus on conditions for women's inclusion in politics in a broad sense. They both seem to develop arguments that rest upon a common perception of the relative autonomy of politics, in many aspects quite similar to the way that Scandinavian feminist scholarship has argued for access to decision-making. Not least are they similar in their common effort to keep issues of "identities-interests" pragmatically open rather than predefined.

Discursive Dangers of "Difference"

We do know that the very notion of "representation" remains controversial. This knowledge comes in part from refreshed knowledge about the problems of categories; any references to "women" is a provocation for some people to ask who "women" are and set off endless debates on whether women have common values, or shared interests or identities. What exactly is to be "represented" by women? Two questions are involved here. From the first question of "who women are," regularly follows the closely related second of "what women have to offer." Women must have a new vision of a better society, and it must be true. Otherwise, what is really the point of having women being present? More and more frequently, however, feminists blandly reject these types of questions outright.

The answer is that women have everything and nothing in particular to represent. The point is not what different women have to represent.

The parity movement in France is another example of new feminist interest in gaining access to established political institutions. This movement has demanded a legal reform that will secure "as many women as men in all elected assemblies, as well as in the advisory cabinets and committees nominated by the executive and legislative branches to participate in decision-making."[17] This demand for parity is quite similar to the legally binding quotas for the composition of corporate bodies in Norway. Yet, the two differ somewhat logically and in their bases of legitimacy. French political parties consider parity to be both the means and the permanent goal, while their Norwegian counterparts probably still regard the quota system as primarily a means to equal representation. In Françoise Gaspard's recent explanations of the principle of parity there is also a marked resistance toward any involvement in debates about either shared interests or common identities. In this respect, the parity movement may well have changed somewhat since the early 1990s.[18] Generally speaking, much seems here to have been done to avoid questions on "the meaning of gender," neither to problematize essentialized differences nor to question how women and men "really are."

In fact, at present, this may well be a wise approach, and not only for reasons of ontology. As a discursive strategy it might be better suited to avoid the whole utility trap of many debates on representation. Liberal political traditions have commonly discussed representation in terms of two main but clearly interrelated principles: "fairness" and "social utility." In debates on fairness the critical question of exclusions/inclusions tends to return to a question of "preferences" versus "prejudices." The preference argument could be seen as a somewhat fresher version of the old "nature" argument. Its main contention is as follows: if more women than men do not want to spend their lives in politics, or if more women than men happen not to meet the required standards for recruitment (whatever these might be), no force should be applied to make it otherwise. Within such a framework any forceful argument for change has to prove prejudice—or, if we like, discrimination. In debates on utility the focus changes somewhat. In a crude simplification, the critical question here would be not so much about preferences versus prejudices, but rather about the necessity, or desirability, of different ranges of contributions to contemplating about "the common good."

The Swedish political scientist, Anna Jonasdottir, has strongly criticized the way that debates on gender difference tend to evolve within a conceptual framework of utility. In her view, utilitarianism continues to place a heavy burden of proof on claims to political and social rights.

Two centuries of political discourse has centered on defining women's role. The discussion has recited what the "good" woman may and ought to bring to public life, the order and stability of the state, to the pleasure of men, or to the transformation of politics. This legacy, Jonasdottir claims, still infuses most public policies on equality: "If we take a look at these equality arguments . . . I guess that the most usual kind still imply a utilitarian view of women."[19] Utility arguments are themselves degrading, and contribute to the continued definition of "woman" as "the other," the sex with some "special interests" or "experiences." The proof still rests with women. But contrary to debates on fairness, in which proof must be presented up front, in debates on utility proof must be presented through practice. If women cannot demonstrate that we do indeed represent something different from what men stand for, the easy conclusion may be that there is in fact no point in our (continued) presence.

The argumentative standard in public discourse, which simply maintains that claims must be justified, cannot easily be ignored. For feminism the paradoxical choice thus tends to linger—that is, the choice between making the effort to prove prejudice and the effort to prove worthiness. The very construct of "representative politics" implies that justifications must be provided. Justifications are a general aspect of representative politics, because these politics all present promises to be fulfilled. It is undoubtedly true that only women's political participation has been argued for in terms of gender difference. Yet, in collective terms women are relative newcomers to positions of political leadership. When focusing on "promises of difference," women have made pragmatic use of a set of well known political strategies.

Now, however, matters seem to be changing. Jonasdottir's analysis of what I call the discursive dangers of difference provides an important warning in both normative and more pragmatic terms. It is of course possible for women to survive on political platforms built on "difference." Visions about "the difference to be made" can be involved in any attempt to gain power. Both have obviously been shown in the Scandinavian experiences arguing for greater representation. Within feminism, however, both seem to have become increasingly irrelevant. In their place, another possibility is becoming noticeable, one that elides the whole contribution question. It simply states the aim of a self-evident right to presence. For instance, in Jonasdottir's claim to "full and equal citizenship," I find a striking resemblance to more recent French claims for parity. Jonasdottir claims that "since the dawn of patriarchy, until its change into its prevailing free and equal form, women have been excluded from equal status with mankind not in any particular aspect, but as such. Thus women have to demand citizenship simply as womankind."[20] In Françoise Gaspard's words,

"Parity in representation is quite simply an application of the principle of equality among the people who make up the human race."[21]

I propose that we interpret both kinds of statements to suggest that the "final struggle" for citizenship should no longer be fought through endless investigations into the balances of preferences to prejudices, nor through boundless justifications underscoring women's contributions to the development of a truly good society. Rather, such claims should now be considered obvious, self-evident rights. We should insist that they simply belong among those other famous declarations of "truths we hold to be self-evident." This would be a huge proposition, considering the arguments we are used to making about representation, but it would undoubtedly provide a clearer opposition to the old discursive instruction regarding controversies about exclusions and inclusions: "Let's talk about this. But let us then talk about it like this!"

Notes

1. Some of the arguments presented here are further elaborated in Hege Skjeie and Birthe Siim, "Scandinavian Feminist Debates on Citizenship," *International Political Science Review* 21 (no. 3), July 2000.
2. Elina Haavio-Mannila, ed., *Unfinished Democracy: Women in Nordic Politics* (Oxford: Pergamon Press, 1985), 1.
3. Berit Ås, "On Female Culture," *Acta Sociologica* 17 (no. 3), 1975.
4. Christina Bergquist, A. Borchorst, A. D. Christensen, N. Raaum, V. Ramnstedt-Silén, and A. Styrkasdottir, eds., *Likestilte demokratier? Kjönn og politik i Norden* (Equal Democracies: Gender and Politics in the Nordic Countries) (Oslo: Universitetsforlaget, 1999).
5. Helga Hernes, *Welfare State and Women Power: Essays in State Feminism* (Oslo: Norwegian University Press, 1987), 15.
6. Hernes, *Welfare State and Women Power*, 139.
7. Rune Slagstad, *De nasjonale strateger* (Oslo: Pax, 1999), 417.
8. Hernes, *Welfare State and Women Power*.
9. Cf. Jürgen Habermas, "Three Normative Models of Democracy," in Sheila Benhabib, ed., *Democracy and Difference: Contesting the Boundaries of the Political* (Princeton: Princeton University Press, 1996), 23.
10. Bjørg Åse Sørensen, "Arbeidskvinner og verdighet" (Working Women's Dignity), in Anne Marie Berg, et al., *I kvinners bilde* (Oslo: Pax forlag, 1977).
11. Drude Dahlerup, *Rødstrømperne. Den danske rødstrømpebevægelses udvikling, nytænkning og gennemslag 1970–1985* (Redstockings. The Danish Women's Liberation Movement 1970–1985. With an English summary) (København: Gyldendal, 1998).
12. Joan W. Scott, "The Conundrum of Equality," (School of Social Science, Institute for Advanced Study, Princeton University), 3.

13. Hege Skjeie, *Den politiske betydningen av kjønn. En studie av norsk topp-politikk* (Political Interpretations of Gender) (Oslo: Institutt for Samfunnsforskning, 1992). In particular, see the chapter, "The Rhetoric of Difference," also published in *Politics and Society,* no. 3 (1990).
14. Bergquist et al., *Likestilte demokratier?*
15. Anne Phillips, *Democracy and Difference* (London: Polity Press, 1993); and idem, *The Politics of Presence* (London: Polity Press, 1995).
16. Iris Young, "The Ideal of Community and the Politics of Difference" in Linda Nicholson, ed., *Feminism/Postmodernism* (London and New York: Routledge, 1990), 300–323 and idem, "Gender as Seriality: Thinking about Women as a Social Collective," *Signs* 19, no. 3 (1994): 713–738.
17. Françoise Gaspard, "Parity, Why Not?" *Differences* 9, no. 2 (1998).
18. Cf. Joyce Outshoorn, "Being Present to Make Difference Visible?" Paper presented to the Annual Meeting of the American Political Science Association (New York, 1994).
19. Anna Jonasdottir, *Love, Power and Political Interests: Towards a Theory of Patriarchy in Contemporary Western Societies* (Ørebro, Sweden: University of Ørebro Press, Ørebro Studies 7, 1991), 190.
20. Jonasdottir, *Love, Power and Political Interests,* 203.
21. Gaspard, "Parity, Why Not?" 97.

Chapter Eleven

Constitutional Reform and Gender Mandates

Jutta Limbach

Editors' note: As the first woman to serve as Chief Justice of the German Constitutional Court and a law professor at the Free University in Berlin, Jutta Limbach has been an important actor in shaping contemporary German law on questions of equality between men and women. Prior to her appointment to Chief Justice in 1994, Justice Limbach served on the commission created to amend the constitution, the Basic Law from 1949, after a series of decision by the Constitutional Court and by the European Court of Justice regarding the constitutionality of affirmative action.

The Constitutional Court has played an important role in defining the importance of basic rights in German jurisprudence. As has been the case elsewhere in Europe in the last decade, the court has assumed increasing importance as arbitrator of conflicts between German and European law and between national law and changing social conditions flowing from unification with the former DDR in 1990, immigration, and the transformation of the family.

In a speech in 1999 at the European University Institute in Florence, Justice Limbach had the following to say about the court's role on questions of basic rights,

> The case law on fundamental rights has not only helped flesh out the Basic Law and let it take root in our body politic. Additionally, this judicial relief has created a sense among the population of not being exposed defenselessly to government measures. And not least, the decisions have sharpened the awareness of both public actors and the citizens that the fundamental rights constitute directly applicable law.[1]

At the brink of the twenty-first century, the overwhelming majority of Europeans agree that men and women ought to be granted equal rights, both in their private life and in pursuing a professional career. However, the picture gets rather blurred when the question arises if men should be forced to yield ground to women in order to promote equal representation in higher-ranking positions.

Imagine one male and one female employee applying for the same leading position, for example, in German public administration. Both being equally capable of the task in question, the woman is preferred in order to increase the number of women, who are still underrepresented in those positions. Her male competitor, not willing to comply, claims that he has suffered discrimination because of his gender. Is he right? What have the European Court of Justice and the German Federal Constitutional Court ruled out concerning this issue?

In its first decades the Federal Constitutional Court interpreted the clause "Men and women shall have equal rights" in the Basic Law, Article 3, section 2, as a prohibition against discrimination. The court ruled, "This constitutional command prohibits in principle and once and for all the legal distinction on the ground of sex."[2] Consequently, the aim of the law was to guarantee formal equality—that is, the creation of a legal order that does not refer to the sex of a person anymore. In accordance with this jurisprudence, civil law—particularly family law—in the Federal Republic of Germany was widely worded in an egalitarian manner.

But in view of the fact that egalitarian law by itself does not ensure the equalization of man and woman in social reality, discussion broke out calling for a more dynamic interpretation of the meaning of equality in the constitution. Today, the attention has turned away from rules that differentiate between man and woman to a new focus on positive (or affirmative) action for women. The central question is whether these measures—for example quotas—are in accordance with the Constitution. Indeed, the Constitutional Court has already ruled in earlier decisions that the function of Article 3, section 2 is also to accomplish the equalization of the sexes in the future.[3] But it was not until a decision concerning pensions in 1981 that the court amended its previous understanding of Article 3, section 2, a compensatory element to the prohibition against discrimination. In this decision the court argued that legislators are allowed to write laws that provide for unequal treatment, if they are motivated by the idea of the social state and aim to provide a compensation of disadvantages stemming from biological differences. In that case, the court ruled, inequal treatment is not discrimination "on the grounds of sex" but a measure that aims at the compensation for inequalities suffered.[4]

The main turnaround in the Court's interpretation of Article 2, section 2 came as a result of a decision in 1981 concerning the prohibition of work at night for women. The case concerned the question whether a law that prohibited women from working at night was in accordance with the anti-discrimination doctrine. In its decision, the court stated,

> The clause "men and women shall have equal rights" does not only intend to abolish all legal rules, which attach advantages or disadvantages to the gender of a person, but also intends to promote equality between the sexes in future. It aims to equalize the reality of social life. Consequently, women need to have the same opportunities in employment relations as men. Traditional understandings and stereotypes concerning the role of women, which lay a stronger burden or other disadvantages on them, may not be fortified by public actions. Factual inequalities, which are typically suffered by women, may in view of the anti-discrimination dictate of Article 2, section 2 be removed by way of positive action.[5]

Henceforth, the anti-discrimination dictate has been interpreted to imply a dynamic, reality-correcting task.

Pursuant to this decision, the Basic Law was amended with a second sentence in Article 3, section 2. It now reads, "The state shall promote the actual implementation of equal rights for women and men and take steps to eliminate disadvantages that now exist." The wording is a compromise. The Social Democrats would have preferred a different wording, which expressively allowed for positive action for women to correct imbalances given existing disadvantages. In view of a compensatory clause of this kind, the strict prohibition against discrimination in Article 3, section 2 would have been partially lifted and the argument of reverse discrimination invalidated. But the ever-present ghost of strict quotas suffocated the readiness of the conservative parties to negotiate from the very beginning. I think, however, that with the formulation of a compromise in Article 2, section 2, an anchor at least is fixed in the Constitution, which obliges the state to work to change the reality of inequity based on the obligation to promote equality.

So far, the Federal Constitutional Court has not had an opportunity—or at least did not find—to comment on concrete positive action for women. The European Court of Justice, however, had to deal with statutes concerning the promotion of equality for women in two German states (*Länder*). Both statutes regarded affirmative action for women in public service. The provisions in question ordered the preferential treatment of women if men and women were equally qualified and if women were underrepresented in the relevant employment category.

In the so-called Kalanke case, the court held that national statutes guaranteeing the preferential hiring (or promotion) of women who held qualifications equal to their male counterparts exceeded the requirements of the European Union's Equal Treatment Directive and therefore constituted impermissible discrimination.[6] The ECJ rules that even though Article 2 (4) of the directive permits national measures that give specific advantage to women, with a view to improving their ability to compete in the labor market and to pursue a career on an equal footing with men, national rules that guarantee women absolute and unconditional priority over men overstep the limits of the provision in the directive.

Two and a half years later, in autumn 1997, the European Court of Justice had the opportunity to develop its requirements for a permissible quota in accordance with the Directive on Equal Treatment. Mr. Marschall, a schoolteacher in North-Rhine Westphalia, had been denied promotion. The reason given was that a woman who had applied for the same job was equally qualified, and since fewer women than men occupied positions of this particular classification, there were "no reasons specific to him, which would tilt the balance of the decision in his favour." The reason given, the so-called saving-clause, made the decisive difference for the court in comparison to the earlier case. In the Kalanke case, the rules under review applied a strictly automatic preference for the women in instances with equal male and female qualifications and female underrepresentation. In the latter case, the rules contained this saving-clause that allowed for a flexible decision-making taking into account all individual aspects of the person involved and the decision at hand.

The court was in this case satisfied that a national rule, which contains such a savings-clause, does not exceed the limits of the directive. Thus, it is clear that European law allows for affirmative action for women by way of a general preference in case of equal qualification and female underrepresentation, as long as there is room for taking individual factors into consideration. The court stressed the importance of a preference for women by stating that:

> Even where males and females are equally qualified, male candidates tend to be promoted in preference to female candidates particularly because of prejudices and stereotypes concerning the role and capacities of women in working life [...]. For these reasons, the mere fact that a male candidate and a female candidate are equally qualified does not mean that they have the same chances.[7]

If a court, consisting of only men, is capable of this kind of acknowledgment, the case of the women and their hopes for full equality stands a good chance at the beginning of the new century.

Notes

1. Jutta Limbach, "The Effects of the Jurisdiction of the German Federal Constitutional Court," *EUI Working Papers Law* no. 99/5 (July 1999), p. 8.
2. BverfG 37, 217 <244>.
3. BVerfG 57, 335 <345f> and the cases cited therein.
4. BVerfG 74, 163 <180>.
5. BVerfG 85, 191 <207>.
6. European Court of Justice, C–450/93, official collection, 95 I-3051.
7. Case 4–409/95, official collection 97, I–6363 <6392> marg. nr. 29.

This page intentionally left blank

Part IV

Cautionary Tales

This page intentionally left blank

Chapter Twelve

The Distinctive Barriers to Gender Equality

Rogers M. Smith

Although the United States is a society that genuinely possesses strongly egalitarian liberal and democratic traditions, both gender and racial (as well as class) inequalities remain stubbornly entrenched.[1] To be sure, great progress has been made, but the most promising paths to overcoming the great inequities that persist are not clear. In this essay, I highlight how racial and gender inequalities have been and are combated by significantly different means in the United States, in order to ask the questions: why these differences? What do they imply concerning how gender inequities should be opposed today and in the future?

I suggest the answers may be found in the distinctive aims and forms of subordination women have experienced within their racial, ethnic, or religious communities, or to say it more succinctly, in the ways patriarchy differs from racial hierarchy. My core claim is that since the end of slavery, at least, American whites have deemed non-whites less essential for accomplishing the forms of economic work whites have chiefly assigned to them than men have deemed women essential for the tasks men have chiefly assigned to them. This distinction means that many American whites have been capable of certain sorts of massive brutality toward blacks—in particular, going beyond what most American men are capable of perpetrating on women. At the same time, however, American male resistance to any large-scale transformation of the most basic gender roles and duties is even more intractable than white resistance to transformations in the racial division of labor.

To me, these facts indicate that Americans need a wide range of governmental initiatives to provide positive and negative incentives, resources, and opportunities for people to adopt domestic and work practices that equitably redistribute the disproportionate burdens women currently bear. Rules promoting enhanced female representation in parties and governments will probably assist enactment of such policies, and that is one of many good reasons to favor them. Yet with great reluctance, I also conclude that the distinctive barriers to gender equality may set limits to how far it can be promoted by governmental actions, vital though they are.

Gender equality ultimately requires men to assume more extensive childcare duties, chiefly for their own children, also for others as childcare professionals. In no other way can women be given greater opportunities to pursue the range of career and life alternatives traditionally available to men, and more, should they wish to do so. But if men are to do childcare even minimally well, they must do it willingly, with a far more affirmative spirit than whites need to have to work alongside or even under blacks in military units, business corporations, schools, or governmental offices.

Thus in this area genuine transformations of basic emotional and moral commitments are also needed. Government programs are only very indirectly effective in promoting such changes. Efforts to guarantee gender parity in representation, such as those currently being debated in Europe, should therefore probably not be pursued in the United States if that means minimizing efforts to spur voluntary transformations in the structures of workplaces and domestic divisions of labor. Again, however, those transformations do need to be fostered and reinforced by appropriate public policies. How far these conclusions hold for societies other than the United States, I leave to others to judge, at least for now.

Some Paradoxical Contrasts

If some or all of these points initially seem implausible or even paradoxical, let me begin laying the ground for them by sketching some related apparent paradoxes. For at least some influential scholars, the very persistence of massive racial and gender inequalities in a society based on the universalistic, democratic, liberal rights principles of the so-called American Creed has seemed paradoxical or anomalous.[2] I have argued that these features of American life seem less strange if we analyze civic and social statuses as the products, not of particular intellectual and moral traditions directly, but of the politics of nation-building or, more broadly, "people-building." In such politics leaders gain support by crafting forms of political community that are responsive to the material interests, cultural traditions, and moral ideals of their core constituencies. The American Revolution was a highly risky nation-building enterprise, and its core constituents were British-descended North American male colonists. Most of them led patriarchal families structured in accordance with English common law, with wives performing the duties assigned them by their ruling husbands; and many also sought to profit from African chattel slavery and the acquisition of the lands of the native tribes. They found doctrines of individual rights and republican self-governance useful to champion their own revolutionary cause against imperial, monarchical Britain. However, they also found doctrines of inherent gender and racial inequalities useful to buttress those key hierarchies in the new nation they strove to build. Hence American political development has been shaped by programs, policies and institutions reflecting often illogical but politically potent combinations of "multiple traditions"—including defenses of individual rights and systems of self-governance but also pervasive systems of gender and racial subordination.[3]

Thus the politics of American nation-building in an environment of inherited gender inequalities and economic pressures for racial subordination may help explain peculiar bedfellows like "American Slavery, American Freedom," as Edmund Morgan famously put it.[4] We might reasonably add, "American Declarations of Independence, American Proclamations of Female Dependence." Yet even if that comparison holds, race and gender hierarchies have differed and still differ in important, rather paradoxical ways that need to be explained.

In the area of race, one pattern is clear from the reprinting of the Declaration of Independence on the first page of William Lloyd Garrison's *Liberator* to Frederick Douglass's 1852 Fourth of July condemnation of white hypocrisy to the 1866 Civil Rights Act and the Fourteenth Amendment's equal protection clause. It continues through the demands for "basic rights" and "justice" advanced by Martin Luther King, Jr. and other leaders of the modern civil rights movement. The chief rhetorical weapon in America's battles for racial progress has been the language of equal rights. Other themes have certainly been sounded, and no rhetorical theme has been enough by itself to produce change. Still, the predominance of universalistic equal rights discourse in the struggles that Americans chose to deem "civil rights" issues—not "black rights" issues—is inarguable.

Equally inarguable, however, is the fact that the victories won with the aid of such principles have not been secure. The revolutionary reliance on the Declaration of Independence helped win blacks the vote in many states after the Revolutionary War, but they lost it in most places in the late antebellum period. They regained it with the aid of the egalitarian Civil War Amendments, but then they were largely disfranchised in the 1890s. The 1965 Voting Rights Act was dramatically successful in overcoming those restrictions. Still, some are deeply disturbed by recent narrow judicial readings of that act, along with the growing practice of life disfranchisement for persons convicted of a wide range of felonies by a criminal justice system that disproportionately punishes blacks. They see evidence that white America is finding new ways to deprive blacks of effective voting power.[5]

In the area of gender, the patterns are quite different. Though calls for equal rights have never been absent and have often played important roles in the initial mobilizing stages of important women's movements, both in the late antebellum era and in the modern civil rights era, those calls have not been the chief instruments of eventual success. The dominant rhetoric has been not "human rights" but the more particularistic language of "women's rights" or, in the nineteenth century, even of "woman's rights," despite the contrary preferences of many antebellum feminists. It is an oft-told story how late nineteenth and early twentieth century women activists turned increasingly to arguments for women's distinctive natures, needs and strengths, and potential contributions to win at last the enfranchisement that eluded women at the end of the Civil War. It was first and foremost as public-spirited mothers and female caregivers, not as equal citizens, that they were to improve civic life through their votes. Less dramatically, the modern women's movement has had more success in winning some distinctive rights for women, such as freedoms to choose abortions and protections against sexual assault and harassment, than it had in trying to get the Equal Rights Amendment enacted.[6]

Yet if measures improving the political, economic, and social condition of women have not been won so predominantly through the rhetoric of universal equal rights, they have on the whole proven more secure than the racial victories thus achieved. Female enfranchisement has never been seriously challenged since its modern enactment. Admittedly, other important reforms, notably including abortion rights, have been much less fully supported by recent legislative measures and judicial decisions. Even so, most basic rights recognized in the modern era, including the right of a woman to choose to have an abortion prior to fetal viability, still seem firmly established. Important recent efforts to increase protections for women such as the 1994 Violence Against Women Act are in judicial jeopardy at this writing, and those are matters of grave concern for gender egalitarians. Still, these are struggles over laws that extend earlier victories, not over measures reversing them.[7] So the paradoxical pattern is this: victories for gender equality are not won by asserting equal rights, yet they tend to be less vulnerable to inegalitarian retrenchments than racial victories that were fought via egalitarian themes.

I perceive another contrast between racial and gender inequalities, albeit one open to legitimate dispute. As many of these modern gender issues indicate, brutal violence toward women that includes rape, other forms of sexual assault and harassment, and physically coerced labor have been all too abundant in U.S. history. It is also true that through much of U.S. history wives and daughters were legally treated for certain important purposes as the property of their husbands and fathers.[8] Even so, my judgment is that the conditions of life of most non-African women in the United States never approached the near-total degradation of chattel slavery at its worst. And within African American communities, slave and free, men did not so overwhelmingly treat women as subhuman property in the manner that chattel slavery did. Many women of color, of course, experienced both forms of oppression, and I do not mean to suggest at all that in law and practice many women did not experience denials of quite fundamental rights and vicious, continuing physical and mental abuse that went unremedied. I do believe the forms of oppression experienced by non-slave women, however, was not either in law or life as pervasively degrading as slavery was. The conditions of all African Americans under Jim Crow and all women prior to twentieth century legal reforms seems to me more comparable, though again, of course, black women suffered from both systems of inequality simultaneously, and poor black women suffered most of all.

It therefore may seem somewhat paradoxical, though it may also seem evidence of the same pattern, that legal and popular support for aid to women now (without explicit reference to race) is clearly greater than support for aid to African Americans (without explicit reference to gender). The Supreme Court treats all gender classifications, including affirmative action programs, with the Craig *v.* Boren formula of "intermediate scrutiny," and it frequently sustains them. At the same time, it is imposing on all racial classifications a more and more stringent version of "strict scrutiny" and increasingly striking them down. Survey data indicate that the same differential treatment is visible in public opinion.[9] If American racial hierarchies have indeed been even more oppressive in some important regards than American patriarchal systems, or even if Jim Crow and gender discrimination were roughly equivalent, some troubling questions arise. Why should efforts to remedy resulting racial inequalities be more constitutionally suspect and politically unpopular than remedies for gender inequalities, in an era when Americans allegedly seek to overcome both these sorts of abusive systems? Does this pattern mean that we are less concerned about gender inequities than racial ones, and should we be?

Thoughts toward an Explanation

Adequate answers to those questions must rest on research that I have not undertaken. But undertaking pertinent research requires us to have some plausible answers in mind, and so I offer some suggestions here. The pithy statement of thesis is that whites think they need blacks less than men think they need women. Hence whites are more likely to hurt blacks and less likely to help them—but whites are also in the end more willing to accept alleviation of the subordination of blacks than men are to accept basic transformations in the distinctive subordination of women.

By "needing" blacks, I mean a reliance on blacks to do the kinds of economic work and to occupy the kinds of social and political roles that they predominantly did under slavery and Jim Crow. I believe American whites crafted systems of white supremacy fundamentally for two reasons: first to obtain cheap, profitable labor, especially for undesirable kinds of work, like picking cotton and doing menial domestic tasks. And second, after practices of racial subordination were widespread, whites also received what W. E. B. Du Bois famously called the "psychological wage" of social recognition that they were members of the "master race."[10] Both these reasons in turn have made whites believe it terribly important that they retain the political power to sustain both economic and social systems of racial hierarchy.

European colonists in North American probably set African-born or African-descended persons to the first sort of work under conditions of chattel slavery because, as Barbara Fields and others have argued, the Africans were most vulnerable to this kind of subjugation. They could not claim the rights at common law British workers could, nor could they flee to native lands as Amerindians could. Indeed some blacks had already been slaves in Africa. But apart from these conditions, there was nothing about Africans or "blacks" that made these massively subordinated statuses peculiarly appropriate to their "race." The European colonists could and did try to enslave others, simply under less favorable conditions and hence with less success.[11] Similarly, under Jim Crow whites sought largely to consign blacks to relatively unskilled labor positions like tenant farmers, crop pickers, baggage carriers, shoeshiners, cooks, cleaners, and maids, but they also employed Mexicans, Chinese, and poorer whites of various ethnicities in such roles. Racial ideology often helped whites to exploit blacks most extensively, but blacks were not essential. Others could be and often were found to fill similar economic functions.[12]

The "psychological wage" of being recognized as part of the "white master race" did, in contrast, depend on the existence of "blacks," or at least non-white "lower races." I believe American history provides abundant evidence that many whites have found the satisfactions of this social recognition sufficiently seductive to override real personal and collective economic and political long-term advantages that could be obtained only by racial reform. Reinforcing the immediate economic benefits whites have often obtained by exploiting black labor, these psychic satisfactions have meant that systems of racial inequality have been very deeply rooted in American life, intractably resistant to reform, and often resilient after eras of partial reform. To maintain them, moreover, whites have often felt it essential to confine political power overwhelmingly to themselves.

Even so, it has always been possible, and it has often been quite attractive, for whites to imagine an America without blacks at all. Then, of course, their racial monopoly of political power would be all the more secure. The powerful support given by leading Americans from Thomas Jefferson through Abraham Lincoln to the "back to Africa" schemes of groups like the American Colonization Society attest clearly to how enticing the notion of "getting shut of the Negro" has been.[13] Its attractiveness suggests the possibility that after doctrines of white supremacy had been established, it may not have been so psychologically necessary to have blacks around in order for whites to continue to tell themselves that they were superior beings. If the work blacks had provided could be obtained from other groups, then getting rid of this inevitably angry and dangerous population might seem politically prudent. And though none of those efforts to purge blacks ever amounted to much, many states north and south did ban the entry of free blacks prior to the Civil War.[14] Since then, all too many whites north and south have wrought homicidal violence on blacks seeking to dwell in their midst. Dreams of racial genocide have been and are scarcely absent from the imaginations of extremist whites in America.

Yet if very few American whites have genuinely required blacks for either economic or psychological purposes, at least since the end of slavery, it follows that whites have not really absolutely needed the maintenance of systems of racial inequality, either. The nonetheless powerful economic and psychological attractions of such systems do mean that changing them is hard and that tendencies to regenerate them are strong, as American history abundantly confirms. That history may also make American whites wary of losing too much political power. Even if they may no longer be so concerned to exploit blacks, they may still fears reprisals. Nonetheless, appeals to principles of equal rights may have had the real if limited influence they have had in American political development in part because in actuality many whites have been able to give up practices of white supremacy without enormous tangible losses. They have had only to be willing to do so, and the willingness can even be fairly grudging, so long as it leads to the right behavior. Blacks with well-paying jobs, political offices, and professional status can probably endure some lingering social prejudices without terrible damage. Hence in regard to racial inequalities, exhortations to live in fuller accordance with universal principles of equal rights, reinforced by governmental programs requiring such conduct, have had some chance to inspire necessary changes.

In contrast, no men in America have ever organized any "back to Venus" or "back to the land of the Amazons" movement trying to get rid of women altogether, nor has male violence toward women ever sought to eliminate the "weaker sex" from the body politic. Men have simply sought to dominate women, and also to construct male-only enclaves—clubs, locker rooms, golf courses, at one time boardrooms and legislative chambers—where they could escape female company for a time. The fact that a "back to Venus" effort seems obviously absurd, whereas both American whites and blacks have passionately endorsed "back to Africa" schemes, strikes me as quite revealing. It suggests that most men cannot imagine doing without women altogether, in the way whites have all too often imagined doing without blacks.

Reasons for this contrast are not hard to find. Until recently, male attempts to do without women would have meant the end of the human species. Though some monastic religious adherents have pursued that course, it has understandably not been a widely popular one. Sexual and emotional satisfactions are, of course, also a major source of the incapacity of men to think about doing without women. Most men love at least some women—their wives or lovers, their mothers, sisters, or daughters.

I suspect, however, that this failure of the imagination also emphatically includes an inability to conceive of how men might manage without women doing the sorts of work that historically women have almost exclusively done. White landowners and factory owners could conceive of substituting Mexicans, Chinese, or European immigrants for black laborers in various settings and often successfully did so. But it is unlikely that many men have ever seriously considered finding ways to induce other men to provide all the care for their children, the food preparation, the cleaning of homes and clothing, and the other domestic work that, along with sexual services, women have provided. It is not that some men cannot be found to do some of that work satisfactorily (leaving sex aside).[15] It is that the cost in terms of money or force to compel enough men to do such work can be expected to be prohibitively high.

Yet we must still ask, why is that? I suspect it is not only, and probably not chiefly, because much of this work is inherently undesirable. It surely also has much to do with the enormous psychological wage men receive from perceiving themselves as "manly," as the dominant gender, as precisely those who do not do such womanly work. I suspect this gender "psychological wage" is more fundamental to most men's psychic well-being than white supremacy is to the psyches of most white racists. It helps constitute their identities in one regard, their sexual orientations, that is arguably more inescapable and basic than their "racial" self-conceptions. It therefore contributes to the fact that the work that women have traditionally done for men seems more irreplaceable to its beneficiaries than the work that blacks have done for whites. It also, I think, deepens the sense of many men that they must hold on to their superior power position in the domestic, economic, and public realms if they are not to lose much of what gives them their senses of identity and purpose.

Note that if a male or female Chinese immigrant or French au pair rather than a black maid does the laundry, the laundry still gets done, and the white employer can still be who he wants to be economically and racially. But if a man nurses the babies and stays home to cook and clean while his wife works, he then lacks an independent income and will probably lack the domestic power position associated with traditional maleness, so he may lose his sense of that identity also. In many respects I think that is no great loss, but lacking a sense of attractive alternatives, many men probably will not agree. Economic exploitation, the psychological benefits of patriarchy, and commitments to maintaining patriarchal power thus seem even more tightly interwoven than the economic and psychological benefits and attendant political arrangements imbricated in American racial hierarchies.

These claims suggest, at least to me, some explanations for the various apparently paradoxical contrasts in race and gender systems of inequality I have rehearsed. Because whites can imagine doing without blacks completely and often have longed to do so, both "back to Africa" movements and violent genocide are imaginable possibilities; but so is accepting genuinely egalitarian change. Still, egalitarian changes remain quite costly, and so efforts to stall or reverse them are predictable. In contrast, most men cannot imagine doing without women completely. They wish neither to transport them all nor to kill them all. But this is true because of men's huge material and psychological dependence on the roles and functions women have traditionally performed, and so most men are even more resistant to full gender equality than to racial equality. It is therefore not surprising that when reforms benefiting women come, they are likely to gain support not so much from universalistic equal rights arguments as from positions promising men that traditional gender roles and divisions of labor will fundamentally continue, despite some real modifications in women's formal status. And insofar as these promises are true and the resulting reforms do not dramatically alter gender roles, materially psychologically, or politically, there will also be less pressure for gender reforms to be halted or reversed than racial ones. Genuine gender equality, however, will be visible only in the far distance if at all.

To put it more concretely, men have shown themselves able to accept voting rights for women, formally equal political and economic opportunities for women, even affirmative action to expand such avenues for women. I think they have done and will do so, however, only so long as none of these measures means that women are abandoning their disproportionate responsibilities to be the primary caregivers for children, the primary maintainers of the household, and the primary sexual companions for men. The victories for women's rights in the modern era have not meaningfully altered any of those roles, at least in the United States. My own impression is that like the protective labor laws of the Progressive era, the modern reforms have sometimes been supported by men in part for reasons that have implicitly expressed and reinforced traditional notions of gender. Some of my fellow male citizens sometimes seem to be endorsing these measures in the same spirit that leads them to send flowers on Mother's Day or sweets on Valentine's Day. More equal formal opportunities are delivered essentially as presents to women, not as respectful acknowledgments of their ultimately equal status. These "gifts" are intended not as means to help America's moms, wives, and lovers become different than they have been. They are offerings to make women happier as they nonetheless remain essentially the same, in all the areas most important to men's psyches and to the traditional gender division of labor. That is why, I believe, that victories for formal equality of rights in regards to gender came comparatively easily, in relation to struggles for racial equality. But that ease is only a product of how much has remained effectively unchallenged. The American public agenda today displays very few serious efforts to transform gender roles in the ways that meaningful gender equality would require. Americans would have to alter dramatically the ways the children are reared, homes are cared for, and careers are pursued so that men and women would do all these things roughly equally. Though some incremental steps in those directions can be discerned and some promising policies have been proposed, few Americans, certainly very few American men, are working actively to make major changes in these regards.

Implications for Representation and Public Policies

One implication of that last observation should at this point be clear. If Americans are committed to universalistic principles of equal rights and to gender equality, then they should work more actively to make major changes in their economic, political, familial, and social systems. Those systems still strongly pressure men and women to embrace quite unequal divisions of labor, with women doing most of the homecare and childcare, in ways that substantially limit women's opportunities. The question is, how to change them?

As noted at the outset, many public policies strike me as promising in this regard. Writing from a firmly universalistic equal rights perspective,

Susan Moller Okin has, for example, suggested a number of changes in the way pay is distributed in households, in parents' legal responsibilities for their children, and in work leave and childcare policies, among other topics. Her proposals all aim to promote more egalitarian sharing of income and child care responsibilities, and though I would not endorse every particular, that enterprise seems to me fundamentally commendable.[16] Many other issues that advocates are putting on the agenda of possible governmental action are valuable as well. Examples include continuing legislative efforts to strengthen, rather than to repeal, the Violence Against Women Act, to fund contraception and abortion services, to support public shelters and assistance for abused and homeless women, and to provide tax incentives for employers to create more flexible work schedules that can accommodate substantial childcare by male as well as female employees. Many more could be listed, and for me, the foregoing analysis of the distinctive barriers to gender equality underscores how important such efforts are.

This paper was occasioned, however, by discussions of efforts in Europe to insure in some way that women are 50 percent of those nominated by European parties and close to 50 percent of those serving in various European parliaments. Would such initiatives be desirable in an American context? There are important things to be said in their behalf. Though female officeholding has grown considerably in the last three decades, it is nowhere near 50 percent throughout the nation. The presence of women in legislative chambers in higher percentages would not guarantee that the sorts of desirable laws I've just listed would all be passed, to be sure. But I think it reasonable to assume that such a transformation in representation would tend to produce a transformation in public policies in those directions, in the right directions.

Nonetheless, I confess to some hesitation about advocating a major push to amend the constitutive rules of American political parties and American legislatures to insure something like 50 percent representation of women. Such efforts would encounter enormous resistance, for all the reasons I've noted. Most men and many women believe that formal legal, political, and economic equality for women has been basically achieved, and in most formal regards this in fact the case. Most men and at least some women are deeply resistant to making really fundamental changes in actual gender roles and practices, for powerful economic and arguably even more powerful psychological reasons; and men will hold firmly to political power to protect those economic and psychological interests. Furthermore, in the current American context such efforts are likely to stir all the many conflicting passions that other forms of "identity politics"—racial, ethnic, religious, and cultural—currently do. Politicians and courts have regularly denounced any notion that proportional group representation is consistent with American principles of individual rights and democratic self-governance.[17] Calls for equal representation by gender are likely to provoke opposition not only from those strongly attached to traditional gender orderings but from all those who fear that their interests are threatened by any moves toward proportional descriptive representation. That constituency seems to include a very great number of Americans.

Nonetheless, equal gender representation is an intrinsically desirable goal, I believe, and it also may well prove instrumentally necessary to get public policies conducive to the kinds of broader gender transformations that I think justice and human well-being require. My concern here is a strategic one. If all or most energies working for egalitarian gender changes do not go toward the end of promoting such representation, it is not likely to be achieved, and it may not be achieved for a long time in any case. But if all or most energies go toward this one cause, many other important and more attainable policy innovations may be abandoned. If so, concentrating on this goal to the degree needed to make it happen, if it can be made to happen at all, may be more costly than beneficial, at least for many years to come.

This thinking is reinforced by the related concern I noted at the outset. If indeed males' psychic investments in the maintenance of traditional gender roles exceeds even whites' investments in the maintenance of traditional racial hierarchies, then it not only follows that resistance to such changes in political representation will be quite passionate. It also is likely that even if state power somehow compelled men to restructure domestic work, childcare, and jobs and careers so that these various sorts of labor were shared more genuinely, many men would respond with resentment and smaller acts of everyday resistance. Such conduct is disturbing enough wherever it occurs, in offices, on factory floors, in classrooms, legislatures, courts, or other locales. Still, as with whites' stubborn refusals to work cooperatively with blacks, men's refusals to work willingly with equally positioned adult women is a problem government may be able to cope with effectively. Abusive behavior can be punished, and employers themselves have incentives to punish workers who shirk, for whatever reason.

But when the task involved is childcare, I grow worried. Requiring men to provide real care and nurturing for children when they bitterly resent doing so may well be a formula for disaster. It is undoubtedly true that many women have been equally frustrated and angry about having such responsibilities imposed on them, and such impositions are, again, what most fundamentally need to change. Yet it is likely that, due to a long history of often unjust yet not ineffective socialization, more women today will still in the end decide to embrace such work and do it well than most men will. And as feminists among others have long argued, how children are raised has much to do with the kinds of men and women they will become, including the gender roles and senses of obligation to others they will accept.

Hence I lean at present to the view that the most pressing task in pursuit of gender equality today is not to expand political representation of women via institutional rule changes. It is instead to begin to alter the structures of material incentives and socialization that lead men to feel they cannot be successful if they attempt to do what they have increasingly asked women to do: combine genuinely substantial domestic work and childcare with work outside the home. As men come to believe that the material and psychic costs of living differently are less than they perceive them to be now, and as they come to recognize the advantages of transformed gender roles to themselves as well as to women, and children, their resistance to change may lessen. And more importantly, their willingness to do the crucial work of childcare, which must be done willingly if it is to be done minimally well at all, may increase. Hence the task of finding ways to alter men's material and psychological investments in traditional gender roles seems to me the most pressing one now.

Again, that task certainly requires many changes that government can impose or encourage through appropriate public policies. And such public policies are indeed more likely if more women are in office, so expanded representation of women is certainly a desirable goal. My skepticism is simply about making institutional rule changes right now the only or primary goal of American gender egalitarians. I believe energy should be devoted instead to lobbying, protesting, and electing candidates (doubtless disproportionately women) who will support specific public policies that will both empower women and give men positive and negative incentives to live differently. Considerable effort should also be devoted to private initiatives within businesses, schools, churches, and civic associations to enable men to combine career and home and childcare more fully, to reward them for doing so, and to punish them for resistance. I do not believe that, either in general or in this particular case, social problems can be best solved by relying chiefly on private initiatives. I do think, however, the special need for willing acceptance of new roles in this area means that here private initiatives, which can to some degree proceed and prepare the ground for public actions, are likely to be especially valuable. I make these recommendations only tentatively, however, and only within the American context which I know best. And I do so not out of a sense that the barriers to gender equality are merely weaker but basically similar versions of the barriers to racial or class equality, and therefore less a cause for public concern. I do so rather out of the belief that the gender barriers are in some important ways distinctive and even more resistant to meaningful change, and that strategies appropriate to their distinctiveness are needed. What those strategies are, however, is a question that I think all gender egalitarians like myself should continue to ponder, much more and perhaps much differently than I have done here.

Notes

1. For documentation of racial and gender inequalities in the United States by scholars who stress American progress in these areas, see Stephan Thernstrom and Abigail Thernstrom, *America in Black and White* (New York: Simon and Schuster, 1997), 18, 34–35, 68, 79–81, 116–117, 157, 178, 184–188, 190–197, 215, 233–235, 538, 581n7.
2. I have canvassed and critiqued such views, including classics like Gunnar Myrdal's *An American Dilemma* and Louis Hartz's *The Liberal Tradition in America,* in various works, especially Rogers M. Smith, *Civic Ideals: Conflicting Visions of Citizenship in U.S. History* (New Haven: Yale University Press, 1997), 12–30.
3. Ibid., 40–114.
4. Edmund S. Morgan, *American Slavery–American Freedom: The Ordeal of Colonial Virginia* (New York: W. W. Norton, 1975).
5. Smith, *Civic Ideals,* 16, 104–106, 215–216, 243, 247, 254, 305, 310–314, 383–385; Philip A. Klinkner with Rogers M. Smith, *The Unsteady March: The Rise and Decline of Racial Equality in America* (Chicago: University of Chicago Press, 1999), 265–266, 341–342, 349; Clyde Haberman, "Filtering Out Taint of Bias from the Law," *New York Times,* Jan. 28, 2000, B1 (citing studies showing that currently 13 percent of American black men are thus disfranchised, that 14 states disfranchise felons for life, and that in states like Alabama and Florida, the disfranchisement rates of black men rises to 30 percent).
6. See e.g., Smith, *Civic Ideals,* 230–235, 314–316, 337–342, 385–390, 453–459; Nancy F. Cott, *The Grounding of Modern Feminism* (New Haven: Yale University Press, 1987); Jane J. Mansbridge, *Why We Lost the ERA* (Chicago: University of Chicago Press, 1986); Deborah L. Rhode, *Justice and Gender* (Cambridge: Harvard University Press, 1989); Linda K. Kerber, *No Constitutional Right to Be Ladies: Women and the Obligations of Citizenship* (New York: Hill and Wang, 1998), esp. 81–124, 283–287.
7. The pertinent abortion decisions, which discuss relevant legislative developments, include Roe *v.* Wade, 410 U.S. 113 (1973); Harris *v.* McRae, 448 U.S. 297 (1980); Planned Parenthood of Southeastern Pennsylvania *v.* Casey, 500 U.S. 833 (1992).
8. Smith, *Civic Ideals,* 185, 234, 457.
9. For Supreme Court treatments of gender and race classifications see e.g., Craig v. Boren, 429 U.S. 190 (1976); Johnson v. Transportation Agency, Santa Clara, California, 480 U.S. 616 (1987); Adarand Constructors v. Pena, 515 U.S. 200 (1995). On public opinion concerning race and gender-based

affirmative action programs, see Dara Z. Strolovitch, "Playing Favorites: Public Attitudes toward Race and Gender-Targeted Anti-Discrimination Policy," *National Women's Studies Association Journal* 10: 27–53 (1998).

10. W. E. B. Du Bois, *Black Reconstruction in America* (New York: Atheneum, 1992 [orig. 1935]), 700–701.
11. Barbara Jeanne Fields, "Slavery, Race and Ideology in the United States of America," *New Left Review* 181: June, 1990, 101–108.
12. See e.g., Matthew Frye Jacobson, *Whiteness of a Different Color: European Immigrants and the Alchemy of Race* (Cambridge: Harvard University Press, 1998), 39–90.
13. Smith, *Civic Ideals,* 104–105, 174, 207–208, 279–280.
14. Ibid., 175–180.
15. I leave sex aside because, though history does provide some examples to suggest that men can get used to obtaining sexual pleasure from men alone, the generalizability of those examples is, to say the least, not self-evident. I view that possibility with overwhelming skepticism, but I may be parochial, and in any case I see no need to decide on it here.
16. Susan Moller Okin, *Justice, Gender, and the Family* (New York: Basic Books, 1989).
17. See, for example, the majority opinions in Adarand Contractors, cited above, and in Shaw v. Reno, Miller *v.* Johnson, 115 S. Ct. 2475 (1995).

This page intentionally left blank

Chapter Thirteen

Representation and the Electoral Interests
of Women and African Americans:
A Convergence at Last?

Carol Swain

Our legislative bodies are not representative of the rich diversity of the United States population. In 1999, there were 37 blacks in the House of Representatives (comprising 8.5 percent of the entire body), 21 Hispanics (4.8 percent), 3 Asian Americans (less than 1.0 percent), 56 women (12.9 percent), and no Native Americans (0 percent). By comparison, a House whose membership was proportional to the U.S. population in 1999 would be 13 percent African American, 12 percent Hispanic, 4 percent Asian-American, 51 percent women, and about 1 percent Native American.[1] Greater percentages of these groups would create a more descriptively representative institution and might increase substantially the influence these groups exert over policy outcomes.[2] However, the House of Representatives is not likely to become more representative of the nation's diversity unless changes are made in the electoral system or in the strategies of party activists and leaders who now exercise considerable control over nomination procedures.

Some scholars and activists have argued that the lack of proportionality in legislative bodies is a reflection of an unfair electoral system. They argue that combining single-member plurality districts with winner-take-all rules works against minority representation. They also attribute low voter turnout, wasted votes, issueless campaigns, and discrimination against women and racial minorities to the existing electoral system.[3] Instead, they propose a switch to some form of proportional representation. These scholars and activists point to a growing number of Western democracies that have taken steps to change their electoral systems along with others that have debated the feasibility of doing so.[4]

Although the subject of proportional representation for federal elections in the United States has barely been on the radar screen despite the efforts of activists, this state of affairs is beginning to change. Spurred by the politics of Western Europe and the advances that women and minorities have made in penetrating legislative bodies, scholars and activists in the United States are increasingly engaged in more robust discussions of the desirability of changing the electoral system from a single-member, winner-take-all system to one of proportional representation. In the forefront of the debate is the Washington-based Center for Voting and Democracy, a public interest group devoted to changing the U.S. electoral system to make it more reflective of the systems used in other democracies. The benefits the center extols include fairer elections, higher turnout, better representation of political and racial minorities, and the elimination of the need for legislative gerrymandering.[5]

However, serious reservations regarding proportional representation are widespread, and some of the most vociferous and effective opposition to proportional representation historically has come from African Americans. In this essay, I discuss a possible convergence of interests between activists for the empowerment of women and racial and ethnic minorities, and I explore some of the tradeoffs associated with different forms of representation.

Proposals to Change the Electoral System

Among the methods most frequently mentioned as offering minority voters the best opportunity to elect candidates of choice is a form of proportional representation known as cumulative voting.[6] This system allows voters to have as many votes as seats to be filled in multimember districts. For example, a state like North Carolina with 12 representatives might opt for 4 multimember districts with 3 seats each. African Americans and other minorities would have the option of spreading their votes across candidates or concentrating them on a single candidate. If a single African American candidate competed against several white candidates in each of the 4 multimember districts, black voters could possibly elect 4 black representatives if they voted cohesively for a single candidate while the white voters split their votes across the other candidates.[7] Blacks have had some success in getting elected in the few places where cumulative voting has been tried as a court ordered remedy for past discrimination.[8]

In recent years, a few African American representatives have been persuaded by this line of reasoning and have therefore introduced bills that would repeal a congressional statute enacted in 1967, which mandated single-member districts for House elections. In 1996, Georgia's Cynthia McKinney (D-GA) introduced the first of several bills that would allow states flexibility as to how they filled their congressional seats by removing the requirement for single-member districts, thus giving states the option of using multimember districts. In 1998, Mel Watts (D-NC) introduced the more recent form of this bill (H.R. 1173) and gathered eleven co-sponsors. In September 1999, congressional hearings on this bill allowed advocates and proponents a rare opportunity to debate the merits of changing the electoral system.[9]

The advocacy of this type of electoral reform represents a new position on the parts of some African American leaders. Voting rights activists worked many years to eliminate multimember districts because they saw them as racially discriminatory devices designed to thwart the intentions of the 1965 Voting Rights Act.[10] Now, after aggressively using the provisions of the Voting Rights Act to strike down multimember districts, some activists have been convinced by changing circumstances that this electoral arrangement can benefit minorities by softening the impact of the loss of majority-black districts.

However, activists were once in conflict over issues of fairness and the desirability of pursuing single-member districts versus multimember districts because the single-member districts that helped elect racial minorities seemingly disadvantaged women.[11] Using a comparative analysis of elections, Wilma Rule and Pippa Norris have shown that countries using multimember districts elect more women legislators than those with single-member districts.[12] Furthermore, they show that the countries with multimember districts and some form of proportional representation elect more women officeholders. Rule and Norris argue that in countries using proportional representation, "political parties have an *incentive* to place women on their respective lists to broaden their appeal. But in single-member districts where only one person is elected, political elites have a *disincentive* to risk backing a woman candidate." Similarly, Richard Matland and Deborah Brown have found that the number of seats per district can greatly reduce the barriers that discourage women from entering legislative races and increase the likelihood that women will win legislative seats. Slating women in multimember districts, they argue, avoids the zero-sum politics of single-member districts, appeases women activists, and avoids the probability that a woman candidate will compete against an establishment male candidate one-on-one.[13]

Now changing circumstances brought about by the invalidation of numerous majority black legislative districts have brought advocates for women and blacks closer together on the subject of multimember districts.

Nevertheless, it will take substantial coalition building to approach the 218 legislative votes needed to repeal the 1967 law mandating single-member districts. Advocates of proportional representation will need to persuade members from both political parties that the current system is unfair. Despite the convergence of interests, I am aware of no white women cosponsors of the Watts and McKinney bills. In fact, African American legislators have not been successful in obtaining unanimous support among Congressional Black Caucus members for their initiatives to change the electoral system. So far, Representative Tom Campbell (R-CA) is the only Republican to testify in support of offering more electoral system options to states.

Why Potential Supporters May Hold Back

A number of reasons may account for the general reluctance to change a system that many people consider to be working. Some legislators who value fair elections may be deterred by fears that the proposed changes to the electoral system could lead to negative unanticipated consequences, which could be hard to resolve. The same electoral changes that could make it easier for women, blacks, and other minorities to win office might do the same for representatives of extremist groups such as the Ku Klux Klan and the Citizens Council—a David Duke, for example, might be assured a seat in the House under a proportional representation system.[14]

Moreover, mixed electoral systems that combine a proportional representation system with cumulative voting are not flawless. They assume polarized voting and a single minority candidate that voters can elect by engaging in strategic voting. Electing a minority candidate, however, becomes far more uncertain if more than one minority candidate competes against several white candidates. The minority vote can be split so that no minority candidate is elected. Moreover, nothing in the system would prevent white Americans from voting strategically to ensure the elections of white candidates. Even if the system worked as anticipated, numerical minorities would still be numerical minorities when they reached the legislature and would still risk being tyrannized by the majority in much the manner that Lani Guinier discussed in her many writings on the subject.[15]

Given occasional discord and instability in countries like Israel and Italy where proportional representation systems reign supreme, any failure to adopt proportional representation for the United States might be a blessing in disguise. In Israel, extremist religious groups have been able to play key and often undesirable roles in the formation of coalition governments. In addition, limited accountability and frequent instability have led Italy to abandon a pure form of proportional representation in favor of a mixed system. There are other approaches that the United States may take. For example, the United States can follow the lead of other Western democracies by experimenting with different electoral systems, and party leaders can make a greater effort to remove financial and other barriers that impede the election of minority candidates.

Why We Need Clarity About Representation

The underlying problem of proportional representation is its heavy focus on numerical descriptive representation without any real discussion of the tradeoffs involved and how efforts to maximize the former can lead to decreases in substantive representation.[16] Descriptive representation refers to the statistical correspondence of particular demographic characteristics in the population—for instance, race, gender, religion, occupation, or age—with those of the representative.[17] For example, women representing women is a form of descriptive representation as is blacks representing blacks and Latinos representing Latinos. Anne Phillips referred to this type of representation as the "politics of presence," which she deeply values along with the importance of the "politics of ideas," which is akin to substantive representation of tangible interests.[18] David Canon refers to these concepts as the "politics of difference" versus the "politics of commonality." The "politics of difference" occurs when a legislator who is descriptively representative of a given group seeks primarily to represent the needs of the racial, ethnic, or gender group of which he or she is member. The "politics of commonality" focuses on the representation of interests that do not require shared descriptive attributes since they are not so unique that someone outside the group cannot identify them and provide adequate representation.[19]

As I have shown in *Black Faces, Black Interests,* substantive representation or the "politics of commonality" does not depend on shared race or gender between the representative and constituency. Its presence can be determined by examining the responsiveness of the representative to the electorate using several different indicators, including committee service, the quality of casework, the racial and ethnic makeup of the staff, languages spoken in district offices, and how and where the representative spends time. Descriptive representation often brings with it substantive representation, but it can also create a false appearance of something that is not actually there. Political party can be more important than the race of the representative when it comes to the maximization of particular types of outcomes.[20]

Although researchers have documented that men and women in state legislatures pursue different priorities on issues affecting women and children, healthcare, discrimination, and sexual harassment, and that women are more likely than men to favor open decision-making, inclusion, and general legislative responsiveness, often these different priorities and outcomes can be explained by the liberal-conservative agendas of the two dominant political parties.[21]

The real tradeoffs of maximizing one form of representation at the expense of another are nontrivial costs that can have a lasting impact on the nature and quality of representation that minorities receive. Although I have argued that aggressively pursuing descriptive representation at the expense of substantive representation can be harmful to the needs and preferences of racial minorities, others seem prepared to accept that tradeoff. Phillips believes that the "politics of ideas"—that is, substantive representation by representatives outside one's group—is inadequate to ensure effective representation of members of politically excluded groups. Expressing the views of many activists, she argues that "contemporary demands for political presence have often risen out of the politics of new social movements.... Women do not want to change their sex, or black people the colour of their skin, as a condition for equal citizenship; nor do they want their differences discounted."[22] Answering the question of whether blacks should be represented by blacks and women by women, Jane Mansbridge gave a qualified yes. While fully recognizing the complexity of minority representation, Mansbridge argued there are some situations involving disadvantaged groups in which constituents may want to be represented by individuals whose backgrounds and experiences mirror those of group members. This desire is particularly true, she argues, in contexts of "group mistrust, uncrystalized interests, a history suggesting inability to rule, and low de facto legitimacy."[23]

Concluding Observations

Mansbridge and Phillips raise legitimate concerns that are especially relevant for enhancing our understanding of the complexity of representation and the values that lead to moral disagreement among scholars who support more diversity in institutional settings. Nevertheless, I am still critical of demands for descriptive representation that seem to come at the expense of greater substantive representation of the articulated interests of a majority of the empowerment seeking subgroups. I believe it is a healthy signal that our Congress is debating alternative electoral systems, even if the debates are mere symbolism. As a nation, we should not be satisfied with a state of affairs in which women, constituting 51 percent of the national population, hold so few positions of power. Nevertheless, we cannot totally absolve women of complicity and blame for this situation. Gender discrimination and the electoral system cannot be the sole cause of the underrepresentation of white women in positions of power and authority. Surely some of what we see is reflective of the personal choices that women have made about how and where they wish to spend their time and their money.

Notes

1. U.S. Bureau of the Census, Internet Release, December 12, 1998.
2. Carol Swain, "Women and Blacks in Congress: 1870–1996," in Lawrence C. Dodd and Bruce Oppenheimer, eds., *Congress Reconsidered,* 6th ed. (Washington, D.C.: Congressional Quarterly Press, 1997): 81–99.
3. See Douglas J. Amy, *Real Choices, New Voices: The Case for Proportional Representation Elections in the United States* (New York: Columbia University Press, 1993).
4. A. Reynolds and B. Reilly, *The International IDEA Handbook of Electoral System Design* (Stockholm, Sweden: Institute for Democracy and Electoral Assistance, 1997).
5. Robert Richie and Steven Hill, *Reflecting All of Us: The Case for Proportional Representation* (Boston: Beacon Press, 1999), and Amy, *Real Choices.*
6. J. Gray, "Winning Fair Representation in At Large Elections: Cumulative Voting and Limited Voting in Alabama Local Elections," pamphlet (Washington, D.C.: Center for Voting and Democracy, 1999); and Lani Guinier, *Tyranny of the Majority: Fundamental Fairness in Representative Democracy* (New York: The Free Press, 1994).
7. The Center for Voting and Democracy has developed a number of such plans to demonstrate to different states how multimember districts could be used to elect members of Congress. For more information, consult the Center's *Electing the People's House* (Washington, D.C.: The Center for Voting and Democracy, 1998).
8. Gray, "Winning Fair Representation."
9. See www.fairvote.org/library/statutes/scvsa99/hearing1.htm
10. Bernard Grofman, Lisa Handley, and Richard G. Niemi, *Minority Representation and the Quest for Voting Equality* (Cambridge: Cambridge University Press, 1992).
11. Wilma Rule, "Why Women Should Be Included in the Voting Rights Act," *National Civic Review* (Fall-Winter 1995): 355–366; and Wilma Rule, "Women, Representation, and Political Rights," in Mark E. Rush, ed., *Voting Rights and Redistricting in the United States* (Westport, CT: Greenwood Press, 1998), 177–93.
12. Wilma Rule and Pippa Norris, "Anglo and Minority Women's Underrepresentation in the Congress: Is the Electoral System the Culprit?" in Wilma Rule and Joseph F. Zimmerman, eds., *United States Electoral Systems: Their Impact on Women and Minorities* (New York: Praeger, 1992).

13. Richard Matland and Deborah Brown, "District Magnitude's Effect on Female Representation in U.S. State Legislatures," *Legislative Studies Quarterly* 16 (November 1992): 469–92.
14. Carol M. Swain, "Racial and Political Minorities in the House of Representatives: What We Can Expect in the Next Century," in Joseph F. Zimmerman and Wilma Rule, eds., *The U.S. House of Representatives: Reform or Rebuild?* (Westport, CT: Praeger Press, 2000).
15. Guinier, *Tyranny of the Majority*.
16. C. Cameron, D. Epstein, and S. O'Halloran, "Do Majority-Minority Districts Maximize Substantive Black Representation in Congress," *The American Political Science Review* (December 1996): 784–812; David T. Canon, *Race, Redistricting, and Representation: The Unintended Consequences of Black Majority Districts* (Chicago: University of Chicago Press, 1999); David Lublin, *The Paradox of Representation: Racial Gerrymandering and Minority Interests in Congress* (Princeton: Princeton University Press, 1997); Carol M. Swain, "The Future of Black Representation," *The American Prospect* (Fall 1995): 78–83; and Swain, "Racial and Political Minorities in the House of Representatives."
17. Hanna F. Pitkin, *The Concept of Representation* (Berkeley: University of California Press, 1967).
18. Anne Phillips, *The Politics of Presence* (New York: Oxford University Press, 1995).
19. Canon, *Race, Redistricting, and Representation*.
20. For more information about the tradeoffs of pursuing descriptive representation over substantive representation, see Swain, "The Future of Black Representation."
21. E. J. Barrett, "The Policy Priorities of African American Women in State Legislatures," *Legislative Studies Quarterly* 20 (May 1995): 223–247; R. Mandel and D. Dodson, "Do Women Officeholders Make A Difference," in Paula Ries and Anne J. Stone, eds., *The American Woman: 1992–93 Status Report* (New York: Norton, 1992); K. Schlozman, N. Burns, and S. Verba, "Gender and Citizen Participation: Is There a Different Voice?" *American Journal of Political Science* 39 (May 1995): 267–293; Sue Thomas, *How Women Legislate* (New York: Oxford University Press, 1994); A. Vega and J. Firestone, "The Effects of Gender on Congressional Behavior and the Substantive Representation of Women," *Legislative Studies Quarterly* 20 (May 1995): 213–222.
22. Phillips, *The Politics of Presence*, 8.
23. Jane Mansbridge, "Should Blacks Represent Blacks and Women Represent Women? A Contingent 'Yes'" *The Journal of Politics* 61 (August 1999):628–657.

Chapter Fourteen

When Women Voted for the Right: Lessons for Today from the Conservative Gender Gap

Jytte Klausen

It is generally assumed today that measures that aim to mobilize women's vote and political participation benefit the Left. While the gender gap in voting generally speaking has favored the Left in the past decade (in some countries for the past two decades), there was a time when the gender gap benefited the right.[1] I wish to make two observations and two tentative conclusions in this chapter based upon my research on the conservative gender gap.

The first observation is that there has been a gender gap in electoral politics as long as we have had survey studies that have allowed us to compare the voting patterns of men and women. (Since men and women are not handed different-colored ballots in the voting both, surveys that ask people how they voted are our only source of information about sociological variations in electoral preferences.) What is new is that the gender gap now helps rather than hurts the Left, which might in part explain why left parties suddenly have become supportive of feminist causes. The second is that political parties only benefit from appealing to the "women's vote" as long as the associated gain is not neutralized by a concomitant loss of men's votes.

The assumption that the Left stands to benefit from women's increased participation may be sound in a short-term perspective, but only because the Left offers a bundle of policies (of which parity may be one) that appeals to women without causing a negative tradeoff among male voters. I will suggest that this was not the case in the past due to the constraints of the male-breadwinner model, which severely limited the Left's capacity to speak to women's interests.

I conclude that we should be careful to distinguish between the short-term and the medium-term (or long-term) effects of equity policies. Parity mandates are long-term commitments, particularly if they are formulated as constitutional or legal requirements, applying to all parties and other public and private actors. If parity rules apply to all political actors, the competitive advantage of using them will be neutralized. In other words, once all parties have (whether by voluntary or compulsory means) accepted parity, elections cannot be won or lost on the number of women put on the ticket anymore. The second conclusion is that at best, parity rules will reform the gender composition of political parties but they are unlikely to change the dynamic of partisan competition beyond the process of the mandates' diffusion across the party system.

I shall begin by describing the role of women's votes in shaping conservative policies and supporting conservative governments in the 1950s and 1960s, and on that basis speculate about the contingencies of "women's interests." I will then suggest some guidelines for how historical evidence may help us think about the political consequences of gender parity mandates, and help us develop strategies for achieving gender equality while minimizing the risk of unintended consequences of the sort associated with what is popularly known as "backlash."

Gender and the Structuration of the Vote

One way to appreciate the importance of gender in shaping politics is to imagine that it does not matter. The most convenient way of conceptualizing a gender-neutral politics is by "sterilizing" voting preferences for the effect of gender. Voting is an expression of basic political values and has the added methodological advantage of being quantifiable. (It is much harder to assign numeric values to other types of political gender gaps, for example, political power or career trajectories.) We may do this by means of what is commonly known as a shift-share analysis; an estimate of the reallocation of votes that would take place if women voted like men.[2] A number of different sources are required to estimate (a) the total number of votes made by women for the main left and conservative parties, and (b) the votes needed to shift government power from one party to another. National election statistics report the number of votes by party and turnout. Survey data provides an estimate the differences in party preference by sex.[3] Multiple steps are involved in the procedure, and a number of assumptions had to be made along the way. Census data provided a basis for estimating the relative share of women by age cohorts, a correction required by the population bias created by high death rates among men during the war years. In postwar elections, the so-called surplus of women was an important demographic factor, particularly in Germany, the United Kingdom, and France, where two wars had reduced the male population. The implication for electoral politics was that any party that successfully mobilized and encapsulated a voting bloc based on "women's interests" had a competitive advantage.

The analysis permits us to calculate the alternative government outcomes that would have been made possible by the reallocation of votes between the major parties in the absence of a gender gap. Table 14.1 below shows the actual and "sterilized" distribution of votes by sex between the Conservative and the Labour party in Great Britain. Table 14.2 provides an estimate of the reallocation of votes between the parties that would have taken place had women voted like men, as well as the likely result in terms of government outcome. The shift-share analysis shows that the gender gap hurt Labour badly in the 1950s and 1960s but that it was not a deciding factor in Labour's political misfortunes during the 1970s and 1980s, the Thatcher years.

Table 14.3 shows how the gender gap contributed to the German Social Democrats' isolation from power in the 1960s and the shift to the left among women beginning in 1972. Table 14.4 lists the actual and "postdicted" number of seats held by each party. The Free Democrats (FDP) are included in the table to illustrate the changes to the calculus of coalition government. The shift-share perspective suggests that had the Social Democrats done something earlier to attract the votes of women, the party might have challenged the Christian Democrats' hold on power already in 1961. In the absence of the conservative gender gap, the Social Democrats may have held government power throughout a decade that instead was thoroughly marked by Christian Democratic hegemony, the years of Konrad Adenauer and Ludwig Erhard.

A few words of caution are necessary. Shift-share analysis involves a number of counterfactual assumptions and can be utilized only as a heuristic device for highlighting the role of gender in postwar politics. A shift-share analysis should not be used to theorize about "roads not taken." It is an aid in conceptualizing a counterfactual assumption—that gender did not matter, as political scientists and political elites claimed—in order to appreciate the role that gender did play. We cannot make any assumptions based on the counterfactual image that the analysis produces, in part because of the uncertainties of the assumptions made, but more importantly because it is based on an "everything else equal" postulate. It is assumed, for example, that men would *not* change their vote if women changed

Table 14.1 British Parliament: Party Preferences by Sex, Actual and Corrected for Gender Gap, 1945–1997 (percentages)

Year	Conservative Party			Labour Party			Labour gender gap gain or loss	Labour voting shares corrected	Conservative voting shares corrected
	Actual Election	Men	Women	Actual Election	Men	Women			
1945	39.8	35.0	43.0	47.8	54.0	45.0	9.0	56.8	30.8
1950	43.5	41.0	45.0	46.1	46.0	43.0	3.0	49.1	40.5
1951	48.0	46.0	54.0	48.8	51.0	42.0	9.0	57.8	39.0
1955	49.7	47.0	55.0	46.4	51.0	42.0	9.0	55.4	40.7
1959	49.4	45.0	51.0	43.8	48.0	43.0	5.0	48.8	44.4
1964	43.4	40.2	43.1	44.1	47.4	46.5	0.9	45.0	42.5
1966	41.9	36.3	40.9	47.9	54.3	50.9	3.4	51.3	38.5
1970	46.4	42.7	48.3	43.0	47.5	42.0	5.5	48.5	40.9
1974	37.9	37.4	38.6	37.1	41.6	39.8	1.8	38.9	36.1
1974	35.8	34.6	37.4	39.2	44.9	40.0	4.9	44.1	30.9
1979	43.9	45.3	48.5	36.9	37.7	37.5	0.2	37.1	43.7
1983	42.4	45.5	44.9	27.6	29.8	27.7	2.1	29.7	40.3
1987	43.4	44.0	44.2	31.7	31.2	30.9	0.3	32.0	43.1
1992	42.3	44.1	47.0	35.2	35.8	32.9	2.9	38.1	39.4
1997									

Sources: Gallup Poll, BES, Butler and Sloman, *British Political Facts.*

Table 14.2 British Electoral Majorities. Actual and Corrected for Gender Gap, 1945–1997 (number of votes)

Year	Conservative Party		Labour Party		Electoral outcome corrected for gender gap[1]	
	Actual outcome	Estimated outcome	Actual outcome	Estimated outcome		
1945	9,988,306	8,908,742	11,995,152	13,074,716	4,165,973	Labour—No change
1950	12,502,567	12,104,569	13,266,592	13,664,590	1,560,021	Labour—No change
1951	13,717,538	12,462,164	13,948,605	15,203,979	2,741,816	Labour—Reversal
1955	13,286,569	12,170,122	12,404,970	13,521,417	1,351,296	Labour—Reversal
1959	13,749,830	13,139,053	12,215,538	12,826,315	(312,738)	Cons.—No change
1964	12,001,396	11,891,544	12,205,814	12,315,666	424,123	Labour—No change
1966	11,418,433	10,974,225	13,064,951	13,509,159	2,534,935	Labour—No change
1970	13,145,123	12,475,259	12,179,341	12,849,205	373,946	Labour—Reversal
1974	11,868,906	11,659,400	11,639,243	11,848,749	189,350	Labour—No change
1974	10,464,817	9,903,420	11,457,079	12,018,476	2,115,056	Labour—No change
1979	13,697,690	13,674,626	11,532,148	11,555,212	(2,119,413)	Cons.—No change
1983	13,012,315	12,834,719	8,456,934	8,634,530	(4,200,190)	Cons.—No change
1987	13,763,066	13,732,977	10,029,778	10,059,867	(3,673,109)	Cons.—No change
1992	14,092,891	13,757,659	11,559,735	11,894,967	(1,862,691)	Cons.—No change
1997						

Notes: [1] Conservative majorities in parentheses. "Postdicted" government outcome in last column.
Sources: Butler and Sloman; BES, Gallup Poll.

Table 14.3 Germany. Party Preferences by Sex. Actual and Corrected for Gender Gap, 1953–1987 (%)

Year	CDU/CSU			SPD			SPD gender gap loss or gain	SPD voting shares corrected	CDU/CSU voting shares corrected
	Total	Men	Women	Total	Men	Women			
1953	43.3	38.9	47.2	29.9	32.5	27.6	-4.9	34.8	38.4
1957	49.3	44.6	53.5	31.9	35.3	28.9	-6.4	38.3	42.9
1961	45.3	40.4	49.6	36.1	39.7	32.9	-6.8	42.9	38.5
1965	47.1	42.1	51.7	39.8	44.0	36.2	-7.8	47.6	39.3
1969	46.0	40.6	50.6	42.8	45.6	40.4	-5.2	48.0	40.8
1972	44.6	43.0	46.0	46.3	46.9	45.7	-1.2	47.5	43.4
1976	48.0	47.2	48.8	43.3	43.6	43.1	-0.5	43.8	47.5
1980	44.0	44.2	43.7	43.5	43.1	43.9	0.8	42.7	44.8
1983	48.5	47.7	49.2	38.9	38.4	39.4	1.0	37.9	49.5
1987	43.8	42.5	45.1	38.1	38.5	37.8	-0.7	38.8	43.1

Source: Gerhard A. Ritter and Merith Niehuss. 1987. *Wahlen in der Bundesrepublik Deutschlands. Bundestags-un Landstagswhalen, 1946–1987.* München: C.H. Beck Verlag. Various tables.

Table 14.4 Federal Republic of Germany. Distribution of Seats in the Bundestag by Party, Actual and Corrected for Gender Gap, 1953–1987

	(1) Est. SPD average mandate gain/loss	(2) Actual SPD mandates	(3) SPD corrected mandates	(4) Actual FDP mandates	(5) FDP and SPD coalition potential	(6) Actual CDU/CSU mandates	(7) Corrected CDU/CSU mandates
1953	16	151	167	48	215	243	227
1957	21	169	190	41	231	270	249
1961	22	190	212	67	279	242	220
1965	25	202	227	49	276	245	220
1969	17	224	241	30	271	242	225
1972	3	230	233	41	274	225	222
1976	1	214	215	39	254	243	242
1980	−2	218	216	53	269	226	228
1983	−3	193	190	34	224	244	247
1987	2	186	188	46	234	223	221

Source: Gerhard A. Ritter and Merith Niehuss. 1987. *Wahlen in der Bundesrepublik Deutschlands. Bundestags-un Landstagswhalen, 1946–1987.* München: C.H. Beck Verlag. Various tables.

theirs. Only the major parties contending for government power are included in the analysis. In the case of the Federal Republic, the shift-share analysis "redistributes" female votes only to the Social Democrats and not to the other government partner, the Free Democrats, for reasons of parsimony. In this case, the "postdiction" of government outcomes is particularly uncertain because the composition of governments cannot be surmised directly from electoral losses or gains. (As rule, German governments have been coalition governments, and election outcomes are not the only deciding variable in government formation.)

The result of the shift-share analysis is to illustrate how much the Right, in both countries, benefited from the gender gap for most of the postwar period. It is axiomatic today that the gender gap favors the Left, but viewed in a medium-term perspective going back to the postwar years (as long back as reliable survey data can be obtained), the Right has benefited the most from political differences between men and women. The analysis also illustrates the truism that elections are lost and won on marginal votes. In the 1951 British parliamentary election, Labour lost to the Conservative Party by 230,000 votes out of a total of 34.5 million votes. This was an important election. Had Labour won, the party would have been allowed to carry on the reform agenda set by Clement Attlee's 1945 government.[4] And had women voted like men, Labour would have won the election with an estimated 2.7 million votes. In the peculiarly counterfactual political world depicted in the tables, aside from a Conservative win in 1959, Labour would have governed from 1945 to the dawn of the Thatcher era in 1979. In actuality, the Conservative Party controlled the government from 1951 to 1964 and from 1970 to 1974.

Because of difference in the electoral system, the calculations have to be modified in the German case. In addition to the actual and "corrected" number of seats held by the two main parties, the SPD and the CDU/CSU, Table 14.2 includes the number of seats held by the perennial coalition partner, the Free Democrats.[5] By 1961, the number of seats held by the SPD and the FDP combined (column 5) exceeds the "corrected" number of seats held by the CDU (column 7). This suggests that had the SPD not suffered from a conservative gender gap, the Christian Democrats' postwar stronghold on government power might have come to an earlier end. In actuality, the SPD and the CDU joined in a "grand coalition" government in 1966 and in 1969 the SPD and FDP formed a government together for the first time. Table 14.2 starts with the 1953 election due to the lack of reliable survey data from the 1949 election, which was narrowly won by the CDU. One survey suggests, however, that the SPD suffered a negative gender gap of about 12 to 13 percent in the 1949 and 1953 elections.[6] It appears likely that in the absence of a conservative gender gap, the SPD would have won the 1949 election. In the 1970s, the gender gap did not affect government outcomes, and by the 1980s, the SPD was its beneficiary.

The British Labour Party was even more handicapped by its failure to appeal to women voters. Leaving out the 1964 election, when men and women's voting preferences converged, the Labour Party suffered an average loss among women of about 12 percent from 1945 to 1974. Germany and Great Britain may be extreme cases but they are not exceptional. In the United States, women were more loyal to the Republicans in the 1948, 1952, and 1954 elections, and may well have provided the margin of victory to Dwight Eisenhower in 1952. In France, Italy, and in the Nordic countries, women provided significant, and sometimes critical, electoral margins for conservative parties.

The tables also show that the conservative gender gap evaporated in the 1970s. What they do not show is that the shift took the form of a generational switch. Older women continued to vote conservative, while a new generation of women voters turned to the left. By the 1980s, the contours of a left-wing gender gap emerged. A decade later, open electoral competition over the "women's vote"—a.k.a. the "soccer moms" or "Worcester woman"—was a favorite topic for pollsters and pundits.[7] For reasons of theory, it is of interest also that the German Social Democrats benefited from the new gender gap at an earlier time than the British Labour Party. One explanation could be that the transformation of women's lives that produced the shift from the right to the left proceeded earlier in Germany than in Britain, but this was hardly the case. The demographic changes associated with the shift in voting patterns was if anything more advanced in Britain than in Germany. The likely explanation is instead that other variables—party strategies, policy issues invoked in appeals to voters—play an essential role in crystallizing and mobilizing gender gaps.

I have stressed the contingency and variability of the gender gap, yet it is also the case that the recent shift to the left was a generalized phenomenon across advanced industrial nations. Women helped elect Bill Clinton, Tony Blair, and Gerhard Schroeder in elections in the 1990s. In the 1992 election pitting Clinton against Bush, women voted for the Democratic candidate by a margin of 11 percent, and the gender gap suddenly became a popular term in the vocabulary of political observers and entrepreneurs. In the 1996 U.S. presidential election, when the gender gap was particularly large, 54 percent of women preferred Bill Clinton while 38 percent voted for Bob Dole.[8] (The gender gap concept implies a singularity of focus, which sometimes exaggerates the importance of gender difference. We should not lose sight of the fact that the majority of women vote like men, and vice versa.)

Two puzzles remain. First, why did women, as a group, once vote to the right of men while they now vote to the left? Second, why did left parties allow the gender gap to persist when it prevented the Left from capturing government power? There are common answers to both questions, and they are almost certainly wrong. The first is that women voted for the Right because they voted on emotions (or "values") rather than interests. The second is that the Left did not know any better. In my view, women voted for the Right because they voted their interests, and the Left knew that winning women's votes was critically importance for capturing the government but was unable to address the problem.

The Left, the Right, and the Political Scientist: Explaining Women's Political Personae

Political scientists assumed that women voted to the right of men because they were moralists or unsophisticated voters, but also expected that eventually women would "catch up" with men and begin to exhibit behaviors comparable to those exhibited by men. That is, the gender gap would fade as women adapted to the model set by men. As it turned out, gender has retained a more stubborn role in party competition.

It is difficult not to be shocked by the sexism implied by the theories put forward at the time to explain the observed difference in voting patterns between men and women. The authors of the first major U.S. voting behavior study, *The Voter Decides* (1954), Angus Campbell, Gerald Gurin, and Warren E. Miller, briefly concerned themselves with what at the time was called "sex" differences in voting behavior. (We will today frequently prefer to use the term gender where sex was used in the past. Still, sex is often the more correct term since statistical records inevitably recognize biological sex rather than gender.) Noting that women's turnout rates were not significantly different from those of men, they dismissed the issue by declaring that sex was not important. Women were found to have low levels of interest (and knowledge) in politics. The authors were relieved to find that women turned to the men in their lives for guidance as to how to vote, and were able to conclude that the low levels of interest among women made little difference for the functioning of the political system.[9]

A notable hardening rook place in political science's view of women in the years that followed. A study from 1964, *The American Voter,* took a significantly dimmer view of women's political involvement and concluded that "sex roles" prevented women from using their rights to full advantage. On that question the authors had this to say,

Decades after the first successes of the suffragettes many wives wish to refer our interviewers to their husbands as being the person in the family who pays attention to politics. Or the woman may say in so many words: "I don't know anything about politics—I thought that business was for men, anyway."[10]

Women were described as "politically unsophisticated" and considered a source of political "fluidity" (a code word for volatility, a dreaded condition). Yet, they found "no reason to believe that women as *women* [emphasis in original] are differently attracted to one of the political parties." The evolution of highly gendered political personae attributed to the sexes was evident in the following description of the political role of "wives."

The wife who votes but otherwise pays little attention to politics not only tends to leave the sifting of information to her husband but abides by his ultimate decision about the direction of the vote as well. The information that she brings to bear on "her" [emphasis in original] choice is indeed fragmentary, because it is secondhand. Since the partisan decision is anchored not in these fragments but in the fuller political explanation of the husband, it may have greater stability over a period of time than we would otherwise suspect. The independent woman, on the other hand, may well fill in a set of political concepts more parallel in quality to those employed by men.[11]

Comparative election studies confirmed the findings of the Michigan studies. As Gabriel Almond and Sidney Verba put it in their immensely important book, *The Civic Culture,* published in 1963,

Wherever the consequences of women's suffrage have been studied, it would appear that women differ from men in their political behavior only in being somewhat more frequently apathetic, emotional, parochial, conservative, and sensitive to the personality, emotional, and esthetic aspects of political life and electoral campaigns.[12]

In a book aptly titled *Political Man,* Seymour Martin Lipset similarly complained, "in practically every country for which we have data (except perhaps the United States), women tend to support the conservative parties more than men do." But he too concluded that the evidence did not support the position that women voted differently than men because they had different interests, since "the parties, which are backed by women, cannot be considered as representing women's interests against those of men." His conclusion was that women voted based on "values" rather than interests.[13]

Political science only reflected conventional wisdom among political elites, particularly on the left where the trade unionist perspective often precluded a clear-headed view of why women did not support the Left. In the post-1945 political context, it was often the Right that took the lead in the mobilization of women in support of "women's interests" policies. The French case is particularly interesting because it illustrates how the Left's position on class often awarded the Right a window of opportunity to affirm women's legitimate political role and encapsulate their votes. On April 21, 1944, the *Comite Francais de Liberation Nationale,* the French government-in-exile headed by Charles de Gaulle, issued a proclamation that awarded women the right to vote. De Gaulle affirmed the decision upon his arrival in Paris four months later, and French women voted for the first time in the municipal elections in April and May 1945. The 1944 proclamation was issued in a context of overall constitutional reform. Strong pressures existed on the French in exile to conform to a template for postwar reconstruction created by the Allied powers expressed in documents such as the Atlantic Charter. But the proclamation was also an effective intervention in domestic politics, in which the CFLN was otherwise disadvantaged by its location in exile.

A January 1944 draft constitution issued by the collaborationist Vichy government granted partial suffrage for to women. A rival left-wing organization composed of domestic resistance groups, the *Conseil National de la Resistance,* dropped the ball on women's suffrage by issuing a charter in March 1944 in which the organization simply asked that "universal" suffrage be reinstated without specifying that the term from now on would include women. The French Socialist Party had championed women's suffrage prior to the war, but the Communist trade union confederation, CGT, opposed its inclusion in the 1944 charter.[14]

Like political scientists, the Left was inclined to believe that women were more inclined to vote for the Right because they were politically backward. Unless women were wage earners and union members—which they mostly were not because of ever-deepening labor market segregation—the Left offered women only the position of auxiliary army in the class struggle. The European Left—from the Communist parties to the centrist Social Democrats—continued to regard what was known as the "woman question" as a diversionary issue and a matter of concern to bourgeois women only. The Second International's axiomatic belief that "women's emancipation" would—and should—follow the emancipation of the working class segued neatly into unquestioned support for the post-1945 male-breadwinner model of full employment and welfare state policies calibrated to sustain female domesticity.

When a few German feminists argued strenuously for more attention to women's equality and women's rights in the post-1945 reconstruction process, Annedore Leber, a high-ranking member of the SPD, articulated the feelings of the majority when she said, "It is no good now to talk too much about women's rights, women's movement, women's parties, and women's lists."[15] Again, it was the CDU that appealed directly to women voters by advocating protective policies tied to family and domesticity, while the SPD focused on supporting trade unionism.[16]

In 1959, after finally confronting the party's declining electoral prospects, the SPD passed a new party program aiming to gain ground with middle-class and female voters whose support for the CDU had estranged the party from power for a decade. Old socialist ideas about the "socialization" of the family were abandoned as the SPD instead tried to beat the Christian Democrats by promising even more support for the family.[17] The new program affirmed that the family was a fundamental unit of society—"Die Familie ist als ursprügliche Einheit eine grundform der Gesellschaft"—and declared motherly love to be essential to the raising of children.[18] The party also committed itself to social and economic policies in support of the family and declared as a matter of principle that no mother with school-age children or younger should be forced for economic reasons to go to work. With "need" out of the picture—even if only in principle—no justification existed for public support for childcare either. Legal equality between men and women was embraced on the condition that "women's special psychological and biological character" be taken into consideration.[19]

The British Labour Party was similarly caught in the bind created by the primacy of the male-breadwinner policies. The party could not compete with the Conservatives' appeal to women voters as long as women's interests were defined in terms of domesticity. In 1959, Hugh Gaitskell asked the party simultaneously to drop its demand for public ownership—stated in Clause IV of the party constitution—and to do more to attract the vote of women.[20] Biographers have spent many pages on the battle over Clause IV but one looks in vain for discussions of Gaitskell's attempt to get the party to address the "woman problem."[21] Gaitskell's appeal to the party to reconsider how Labour might do better with women voters elicited the following comment from one regional party officer,

> The impact of prosperity is nowhere more deeply felt than in the home, and home to the housewife, irrespective of whether she goes out to work or merely remains at home, is the focal point of her life. Consequently, she is very susceptible to [Conservative] propaganda. [. . .] Her life is one in which a new house, a family car, a television, an electric washer, cooker, and perhaps even a "frig," predominate. If she does not already possess all these things then she aspires to do so as quickly as possible, and the "telly" is a daily reminder that life is not complete without them.[22]

The statement is immensely suggestive of the constraints imposed upon the party by the male-breadwinner appeal and consumerist economic development strategy. Only women's reentry into the workforce in the 1970s, when the twin scourges of high wage inflation and super-tight labor markets broke down the resistance to the mobilization what was regarded as the "reserve" labor force, opened upon for a reconceptualization of women's political personae in non-familialist terms. And even then, it took two decades for the question of equality to arrive at the doorstep of political parties.

Reexamining the Past: A New Perspective on the Conservative Gender Gap

Did women vote for the Right because of "values" or because of "interests"? Do they vote for the Left today because of "values" or "interests"? The answer matters both for ontological reasons and for practical reasons. The dominance of behavioralist assumptions within political science helped sustain the fallacy that women's conservatism and underrepresentation were "natural." William H. Riker, a proponent of the rational choice approach to the study of politics, has argued that "the will to win" explains why minorities make strategic use of procedures and institutional norms to prevail over opponents. "The political world selects for people who want to win politically," he concludes, "that is, those who do not win are more likely than others to lose and thus to be excluded from political decisions."[23]

An alternative explanation that takes women's political responses as a dependent variable rather than a product of nature focus on what we might call the interaction effect between policy and politics.[24] The male-breadwinner consensus and protective labor market policies cordoned women off from well-paying jobs and professional careers. In the absence of access to paid employment, the Left's package of policies appealing to wage-earner interests represented a positive choice for women who responded on class terms mediated by their husband's occupational status. The primacy of the male-breadwinner model in policy was matched in organizational theory by the elevated status within left-wing parties of the trade unions and party rules and traditions that awarded the unions automatic representation on party tickets and within party organizations.

Another test is to examine how each explanation may account for the reversal of the gender gap from right to left. In either perspective, shifting party alignments loom large, albeit for different reasons. If women vote on "values," the shift can be explained because the Left today represents "caring" values, while the new Right represents neoliberal values, hostile to the preservation of family and community. Alternatively, the policy-begets-its-own-politics explanation would stress that because women's occupational status now converges in many significant regards with men's (albeit not with respect to lifetime income), women are now included under the protective umbrella of labor market policies designed to eliminate risk. Conversely, the Right's continued emphasis on familialism and on providing benefits directly to family services has become a liability, implying as it does that women's role is in the home rather than in the labor market.

Value divergence between the sexes remains in either case an important causal variable in shaping voting preferences, but the partisan advantage shifted due to the collapse of the single-breadwinner wage. In other words, women are still more supportive of generous social policies (and the taxes to pay for them) than men are, but the preferred mode of delivery has changed. Because of their increased labor market participation and the new weakness of the family, women now have a direct interest in attaching the provision of services to labor market institutions and public authorities.

In short, we are still unable to decide between "values" and "interests" because the two remain intertwined in ways that only the most abstract social science reasoning can take apart. On a few scores, the "values" argument is obviously weakened. The rapid recent increase of women in public office, although more in some countries than in others, suggests that any explanation that assumes that women are "naturally" disinclined to assume political power is fatally flawed. It is, it may be added, not just rational choice explanation of the "will to win" type but also feminist theory stressing the "essentialist" differences between men and women that stands up poorly to the test of time.

On the other hand, there is also evidence that women have little patience with certain aspect of political life as it has been practiced. (The research is necessarily still based on spotty evidence, but one of the effects of more women in politics appears to be shorter meetings and other differences in the management of political decision-making. It may also be the case that women are more willing then men to retire from politics and at an earlier age.) Again, it is the case that irrespective of the basic causes of the transformation of political role of gender, its political significance—and magnitude and timing—is elicited and reproduced by the rules and institutions that set the boundaries for the process of representation and interest articulation.

Although this may seem to be good news for advocates of gender mandates, it may also be bad news. Parity mandates may help mobilize women as actors in the political process, but ultimately voters vote for bundles of policies and few voters will put the sex of their representative over the policies they espouse. As women's life experiences become increasingly more diverse and women's presence in politics ubiquitous, we should expect not only increased partisan competition over women's votes but also more offerings of what "women's interests" may be.

The Political Role of Gender and The Prospects for Equality: Some Cautious (and Cautionary) Conclusions

Viewed in a medium-term historical perspective, the parity movement heralds both a small and a big revolution. The small revolution is the policies it proposes. The big revolution is that it exists and has been successful. Gender has played an important role in politics since women received the right to vote, and even before that. The difference is that the role is no longer a covert one. The parity movement is an expression of the collective impatience of a generation of women with the ability of political systems to change. Parity mandates are a "quick fix" measure to achieve an old promise of political equality. The movement proposes a singular but highly effective view of what equality implies; parity means equal access.[25] The question is: by what means?

It is difficult not to be impatient, but impatience is not sufficient grounds for deciding on strategy. Although we tend to think of women's suffrage as old hat, the larger story here is the recent origins of any pretense to equality, or for that matter, liberal democracy itself. Suffrage for women came only in 1944 in France and 1946 in Italy, in 1948 in Belgium, and 1971 in Switzerland. All citizens—men and women—over the age of 20 were enfranchised by the Weimar Constitution in 1919, but no democratic elections took place in Germany between 1933 and 1947. Nor did they in Italy between 1924 and 1946, in Austria from the *Anschluss* to the German Reich in 1934 to its collapse in 1945. Spanish women voted briefly in the early 1930s, but civil war and then fascism eliminated the opportunity to engage in electoral democracy until 1976. Portugal and Greece likewise suffered from halted political development.

The postwar "Golden Age" welfare state produced many social policies that were beneficial to women, but it was not helpful on questions of access to political power. In some countries, more women were actually elected to national office in the first postwar elections than for the next five to six decades. Thirty-five women were elected to the French National Assembly in 1947, in the first national election in which women were permitted to vote. The number of women elected subsequently continued to decline until the 1986 election, when it once again rose to match the postwar level.[26] The unhappy equilibrium was broken only recently by proactive measures to increase the recruitment of women to political office.

The tenacity and extent of women's numerical underrepresentation constitute sufficient evidence, in my view, to conclude that women will not be present in the political system in equal measure unless the rules of political transaction are changed. The question then arises: which rules must be changed and how much changed? I find it difficult to answer that question without speculating about the consequences of different types of rules. In my view, the Kantian position implied in John Rawls' concept of "the original position" presents a safe starting point. In Rawls's view, we should try to imagine ourselves in the opposite position of our current one when we try to design rules for how to deal with conflicting claims to justice.[27] For feminists impatient to end women's underrepresentation in the exercise of political power (at least the kind of legitimate power for which you get elected), this might mean that we as women try to imagine what would happen if men were the underrepresented group and the rules suddenly benefited them. Could we live with the rules in that case? A left-wing party about to adopt new legislation imposing parity mandates on society in general should consider if it could live with the rules were women again to vote disproportionately for the Right.

Rawls's test may be more than good political theory; it may also prove to be a good prudential precaution against self-inflicted political wounds. Indeed, as is already clear, the Left is not alone in reaching for women as a means for reinvigorating party appeals. The German Christian Democrats' selection of an unseasoned East German woman, Angela Merkel, to succeed Helmut Kohl as party leader after the discovery of Kohl's secret bank account containing illegal party contributions, is a recent example of how the Right can make instrumental use of the new political feminism.

At the various junctures, at which a male-dominated political system has been faced with an irrepressible demand for new steps toward women's political equality, two common sources of opposition have emerged. The first has been an often quite personal fear of displacement from positions of power on the part of male office holders. The second has been fears of political displacement. In other words, parties have tended to support reforms only when they saw partisan benefits to the reform in question. On balance, reforms have happened when the latter weighed more heavily on the minds of decision-makers than the former. In the contemporary situation, left-wing parties have been more inclined to adopt party rules mandating women's presence on electoral tickets and in party leadership position and inevitably have done so in a context of platform adjustment with the aim of capturing new voters. Reforms of this sort tend to spread over time through the process of partisan adjustment and competition.

Therein lies the irony. Once all the major parties have adopted women-friendly rules, there will be more women in politics but no partisan gain to be derived from more reform and the reform movement may dissipate. The constitutional strategy pursued by the French parity movement effectively shortcuts the process by imposing parity mandates on all parties. The unanticipated consequences may be to neutralize the partisan implications of parity, which may not be the best thing to do if the aim is to politicize the role of gender in politics and elicit substantive party commitments. On the other hand, it may be what we want, if the aim is simply to get more women in politics and then go on with the business of fighting over policy. In either case, what applied to earlier reform movements probably applies also to the parity movement: success may well be the movement's worst enemy.

Notes

1. The term "gender gap" can refer to any difference in group means between men and women, for example, mean income or mean life expectancy. In this paper, it is used to refer to the difference between men's and women's share of the vote for the Left and the Right—that is, if GG stands for gender gap and MV for men's vote and WV for women's vote, then:

$$GG = MV_{left} - WV_{left}.$$

   A negative integer denotes a conservative gender gap, a positive a left-wing gap.
2. Shift-share analysis is mostly used to study long-term sectoral change in industry or labor markets; for an application, see Helzi Noponen, Ann R. Markusen, and Karen Driessen, "Trade and American Cities: Who Has the Comparative Advantage?" *Economic Development Quarterly* 11, n. 1 (Feb. 1997): 67–87.
3. As is always the case when survey data is used, multiple sources of bias exist and the data has to be interpreted with caution. Voting preferences are based on self-reporting, and surveys predict actual election outcomes with variable success depending on the quality of the survey or the nature of the election in question. The mean error compared to actual election results varies from survey to survey in the range of 0.5 to 2 percent.
4. Labour won the election in terms of the distribution of the popular vote, but the Conservative Party won by 27 seats.
5. The FDP's political fortunes would also have changed had the party appealed to male and female voters in equal measure, and in an interactive model, the party should have been included in the reallocation of votes derived from the neutralization of the gender gap. In view of other uncertainties deriving from the constraint of the data and assumptions used in the calculation, which in any case make it impossible to "postdict" government outcomes with completely accuracy, no such reallocation was done.

6. The Social Bases of West German Politics (ICPSR no. 7104), July–August 1953. My calculations. Since election returns do not distinguish between women's votes and those of men, all information about group differences in political preferences comes from survey data.
7. Andrew Kohut, "A Gender War at the Ballot Box," *New York Times*, February 8, 2000, A23.
8. http://www.cawp.rutgers.edu/Facts.html
9. Angus Campbell, Gerald Gurin, and Warren E. Miller, *The Voter Decides* (Evanston, IL: Row, Paterson, 1954), 154–155, 206.
10. Angus Campbell, Philip Converse, Warren E. Miller, and Donald E. Stokes, *The American Voter* (New York: Wiley and Sons, 1964), 255.
11. *The American Voter*, 260.
12. Gabriel Almond and Sidney Verba, *The Civic Culture* (Princeton: Princeton University Press, 1963), 388.
13. Lipset, *Political Man*, 31 and 221.
14. The Popular Front government headed by Léon Blum introduced a bill to grant women voting rights, which passed the National Assembly on July 16, 1936. The bill died in the Senate. On the CGT's role, see Maurice Larkin, *France Since the Popular Front: Government and People, 1936–1986* (New York: Oxford University Press, 1988), 137. The suffrage struggle is chronicled in Steven C. Hause, *Women's Suffrage and Social Politics in the French Third Republic* (Princeton: Princeton University Press, 1984).
15. Renate Genth et al. *Frauenpolitik und politische Wirken von Frauen im Berlin der Nachkriegszeit 1945–1949* (Berlin: Trafo Verlag, 1996), 128. "Nicht gut mutet in dieser Stunde das viele Gerede von Frauenrechten, Frauenbewegung, Frauenparteien, und Frauenlisten an." See also Robert G. Moeller, *Protecting Motherhood. Women and the Family in the Politics of Postwar Germany* (Berkeley: University of California Press, 1993).
16. The 1949 constitution for the Federal Republic included a clause that affirmed the equality of men and women, but the Civil Code preserved the legal subordination of wives to husbands until 1958.
17. Renate Genth et al., *Frauenpolitik und politische Wirken von Frauen im Berlin der Nachkriegszeit*, 124.
18. SPD, *Jahrbuch 1960/1961*, 467.
19. SPD, *Jahrbuch 1960/1962*, 413. The revisions coincided with important changes in the legal position of married women after the 1957 *Gleichberectigunggesetz* and a series of court decisions revising the 1900 Civil Code's paternalist legal framework. For a discussion, see Christine von Oertzen, "Women, Work, and the State: Lobbying for Part-Time Work and 'Practical Equality' in the West German Civil Service, 1958–1969," in Rolf Torstendahl, ed., *State Policy and Gender System in the Two German States and Sweden, 1945–1989* (Uppsala Historiska institutionen, Uppsala universitet, 1999).
20. *The Report of the Fifty-Eighth Annual Conference of the Labour Party* (London: 1959), 107.

21. Both Brian Brivati and Phillip M. Williams fail to mention the women voter issue; see Brivati, *Hugh Gaitskell* (London: Richard Cohen Books, 1996); and Williams, *Hugh Gaitskell: A Political Biography* (London: Jonathan Cape, 1979).
22. Yorkshire Regional Office of the Labour Party, "Report on Women's Organization for Consideration at a Special Meeting of Women's Advisory Councils with the Chief Woman Officer on 13th, 14th, and 15th January, 1960," cited in Steven Fielding, ed., *The Labour Party: "Socialism" and Society Since 1951* (Manchester: Manchester University Press, 1997), 62–63.
23. William H. Riker "The Heresthetics of Constitution-Making: The Presidency in 1787, with Comments on Determinism and Rational Choice." 1983 Presidential Address, American Political Science Association, *American Political Science Review* 78, n. 2 (March 1984), 15.
24. The concept has much in common with the more complex theory of institutional causation forwarded by Paul Pierson, "When Effect Becomes Cause: Policy Feedback and Political Change," *World Politics* 54 (July1991): 595–628.
25. Merriam-Webster's Collegiate Dictionary, tenth ed.
26. Jean Pascal, *Les femmes deputes de 1945 a 1988* (Paris: published by author, 1990), various tables.
27. John Rawls, *A Theory of Justice* (Cambridge, MA: Belknap Press of Harvard University Press, 1971).

Contributors

ANNA COOTE is Director of the Public Health Programme at the King's Fund, London. She was formerly Deputy Director of the Institute for Public Policy Research, a London-based, left-of-center think-tank. From June 1997 to July 1998 she was consultant to the new Labour Government's Minister for Women and Secretary of State for Social Security. She has previously been current affairs editor for Channel Four TV and deputy editor of the *New Statesman*. She is the author (with Polly Pattullo) of *Power and Prejudice: Women and Politics* (London: Weidenfeld and Nicolson, 1990).

FRANÇOISE GASPARD is professor of sociology and political science at l'Ecole des Hautes Etudes en Sciences Sociales, Paris. In 1999, she was visiting scholar at University of California, Berkeley. She received degrees in history from the Sorbonne and in political science from l'Institut d'Etudes Politiques de Paris in 1968. She has been a consultant to the Council of Europe on gender equality issues and, since 1998, the French representative to the UN Commission on the Condition of Women. She is author of *A Small City in France* [in French, *Petite ville en France*] (Cambridge, MA: Harvard University Press, 1995) and (with Farhad Khosrokhavar), *Le foulard et la Republique* (Paris: Decouverte, 1995). In 1992, she wrote the book that started the parity movement (with Claude Servan-Schreiber and Anne Le Gall), *Au pouvoir, citoyennes! Liberté, egalité, parité* (Paris: Seuil, 1992).

ISABELLE GIRAUD is a doctoral candidate in political science at the Université de Montréal. Her thesis is an analysis of the feminization of elected assemblies in France, Germany, and Guebec, *La restructuration des régimes de représentation politiques des femmes en France, en Allemagne et au Québec des années 1980–90*.

AGNÈS HUBERT was born in Algeria and spent her childhood in the Far East and Africa. She studied economics and political science at the Université Pantheon-Sorbonne in Paris. In 1998–1999, she was a European

Union Fellow at the Fletcher School of Law and Diplomacy. She started her career as a journalist and joined the European Commission in 1981, where she has been involved in North-South dialogue, communication policy and gender issues. In 1992, she became Head of the Equal Opportunities Unit, and in 1996 she joined the Forward Studies Unit, a group of advisors to the President of the European Commission on future challenges. She is author of *L'Europe et les femmes: identités en mouvement* (Paris: Apogée, 1988) and co-author (with Bénédicte Caremier) of *Democracy and Information Society in Europe* (Paris: Ed. Apogée/Kogan Page, 2000.)

JANE JENSON is professor of political science and director of the Université de Montréal/McGill University Institute of European Studies. She has been the director of the Family Network of Canadian Policy Research Networks since June 1999. She is editor of *Lien social et politiques–RIAC,* a franco-Quebec social policy journal. Her most recent book (with Mariette Sineau) is *Qui doit garder le jeune enfant? Les représentations du travail des mères dans L'Europe en crise* (Paris: LGDJ, 1998). A substantial revised version will appear as *Who Cares? Women's Work, Child Care and Welfare State Redesign* (Toronto: University of Toronto Press, 2000).

JYTTE KLAUSEN is associate professor of comparative politics at Brandeis University and a research affiliate at The Center for European Studies at Harvard University. She is the author of *War and Welfare: Europe and the United States, 1945 to the Present* (New York: St. Martin's Press, 1998) and co-editor (with Louise A. Tilly) of *European Integration in a Social and Historical Perspective: 1850 to the Present* (Lanham, MD: Rowman & Littlefield Publishers, 1997). She is currently working on a book about the conservative gender gap in Western Europe and the United States in the 1950s and 1960s.

CHRISTIANE LEMKE is professor of political science at the University of Hannover, Germany. She received her Habilitation in 1989 at the Freie Universität Berlin. She was the Director of the Institute of Political Science at the International Women's University 2000. She is the author of *Die Ursachen des Umbruchs. Politische Sozialisation in der ehemaligen DDR* (Opladen: Westdeutscher Verlag, 1991) and editor (with Gary Marks) of *The Crisis of Socialism in Europe* (Durham: Duke University Press, 1992) and (with Virginia Penrose and Uta Ruppert), *Frauenbewegung und Frauenpolitik in Osteuropa* (Frankfurt: Campus Verlag, 1996). Her most recent book is *Internationale Beziehungen. Grundkonzepte, Theorien und Problemfelder* (Munich/Vienna: Oldenbourg Verlag, 2000). Forthcoming (with K. Braun, G. Fuchs, and K. Töns) is *Feministische Perspektiven der Politikwissenschaft* (Oldenbug Verlag Munich/Vienna).

JUTTA LIMBACH was appointed Chief Justice of the German Constitutional Court in 1994 and has been a professor in the law faculty at the Freie Universität Berlin since 1971. She has been a member of the SPD (*Sozialdemokratische Partei Deutschlands*) since 1962. She served on the Justice Committee in the Berlin Senate in 1989–1994. Between 1992 and 1993, she was a member of a joint constitutional commission appointed by both houses of the German national legislature to propose changes to the Constitution on questions related to the equality between men and women. She has written extensively about German constitutional history and gender equality law, most recently (with Roman Herzog and Dieter Grimm) *Die deutschen Verfassungen: Reproduktion der Verfassungsoriginale von 1849, 1871, 1919 sowie des Grundgesetzes von 1949* (Munchen: Beck, 1999) and (with Marion Eckertz-Hofer) *Frauenrechte im Grundgesetz des geeinten Deutschland. Diskussion in der Gemeinsamen Verfassungskommission von Bundestag und Bundesrat und der Bundesratskommission. Verfassungsreform Dokumentation* (Baden-Baden: Nomos, 1993).

CHARLES S. MAIER is Krupp Foundation Professor of European Studies at Harvard University and Director of the Center for European Studies. He is the author of *Dissolution: The Crisis of Communism and the End of East Germany* (Princeton: Princeton University Press, 1997); *The Unmasterable Past: History, Holocaust, and German National Identity* (Cambridge, MA: Harvard University Press, 1988); *In Search of Stability: Explorations in Historical Political Economy* (Cambridge: Cambridge University Press, 1987); *Recasting Bourgeois Europe: Stabilization in France, Germany, and Italy in the Decade after World War I* (Princeton: Princeton University Press, 1975, 1988); as well as editor of several collaborative volumes, among them: *The Marshall Plan and Germany: West German Development within the Framework of the European Recovery Program* (New York: St. Martin's Press, 1991), *Changing Boundaries of the Political: Essays on the Evolving Balance between the State and Society, Public and Private in Europe* (Cambridge: Cambridge University Press, 1987), and *The Politics of Inflation and Economic Stagnation: Theoretical Approaches and International Case Studies* (Washington, D.C.: Brookings Institution, 1985). He is currently collaborating on a world history of the twentieth century and writing a book tentatively entitled "The Passing of the Territorial Age (1860–2000)," which examines transformations of territoriality and their impact on domestic and international politics.

JANE MANSBRIDGE is the Adams Professor of Political Leadership and Democratic Values at the John F. Kennedy School of Government at Harvard University, where she is the Faculty Chair of the Women and Public Policy Program. She is author of *Beyond Adversary Democracy* (New York: Basic

Books, 1980; Chicago: University of Chicago Press, 1983); *Why We Lost the ERA* (Chicago: University of Chicago Press, 1986); and editor of *Beyond Self-Interest* (Chicago: University of Chicago Press, 1990) and, with Susan Moller Okin, *Feminism,* 2 vols. (Cheltenham, Glos.: Edward Elgar, l994). Her current research includes work on representation, trust, and deliberation, as well as *Oppositional Consciousness,* edited with Aldon Morris, and *Everyday Feminism,* on how non-activists affect social movements.

PIPPA NORRIS is Associate Director (research) at the Shorenstein Center on the Press, Politics, and Public Policy and Lecturer at the John F. Kennedy School of Government, Harvard University. She has published two dozen books on comparative gender politics, elections and voting behavior, and political communications, among them *Electoral Change in Britain Since 1945* (Oxford: Blackwell, 1997) and (with Joni Lovenduski) *Political Recruitment: Gender, Race, and Class in the British Parliament* (Cambridge: Cambridge University Press, 1995). Her most recent book is *A Virtuous Circle: Political Communications in Post-Industrial Societies* (Cambridge: Cambridge University Press, 2000).

CLAUS OFFE is professor of political science at Humboldt-Universität zu Berlin. He has been visiting professor at University of California, Berkeley; The New School for Social Research, New York; and Harvard University. He studied sociology, economics and philosophy in Cologne and at the Freie Universität Berlin. He is the author of *Disorganized Capitalism: Contemporary Transformations of Work and Politics* (Cambridge, MA: MIT Press, 1985) and *Contradictions of the Welfare State* (Cambridge, MA: MIT Press, 1984), and (with Jon Elster and Ulrich K. Preuss), *Institutional Design in Post-Communist Societies: Rebuilding the Ship at Sea* (New York: Cambridge University Press, 1998).

HEGE SKJEIE is associate professor of political science at the University of Oslo, Norway. She received her doctorate in 1992 from the University of Oslo. In 1984–1997, she was a Researcher at the Institute for Social Research funded by the Norwegian Research Council. She is currently a member of the Norwegian Power Study Commission (1998–2003). She has written extensively in Norwegian on gender equality issues, most recently *Vanens makt. Arbeiderpartiet som regjeringsparti* (Oslo: Ad Notam, 1999). She has published articles in *New Left Review* and *Politics and Society.*

ROGERS M. SMITH is the Alfred Cowles Professor of Government at Yale University and co-director of the Center for the Study of Race, Inequality, and Politics. He is the author of *Liberalism and American Constitutional*

Law (Cambridge, MA: Harvard University Press, 1985) and co-author (with Peter H. Schuck) of *Citizenship Without Consent: Illegal Aliens in the American Polity* (New Haven: Yale University Press, 1985). His most recent book (with Philip A. Klinkner) is *The Unsteady March: The Rise and Decline of Racial Equality in America* (with Philip A. Klinkner) (Chicago: University of Chicago Press, 1999).

CAROL M. SWAIN is professor of political science and law at Vanderbilt University Law School. Until 1999, she was an associate professor at The Woodrow Wilson School of Public Policy at Princeton University. She is the author of *Black Faces, Black Interests: The Representation of African Americans in Congress* (Cambridge, MA: Harvard University. Press, 1993, 1995) and editor of *Race Versus Class: The New Affirmative Action Debate* (Lanham: University Press of America, 1996). Her current book-in-progress is tentatively titled *Demographic Changes, Racial Preferences, and the Rise of White Nationalism.*

This page intentionally left blank

Index

abortion, 56, 57, 58, 79, 137, 188, 195, 198n.7
affirmative action, 89–108, 144; anti-essentialist argument, 19–33; European adoption of, 8–14, 71; in Germany, 13, 71, 127, 132, 134–38, 177–80; male reverse discrimination claims, 127, 132, 178, 179–80; as reparations, 7; in United States, 4, 9–10, 14, 15, 189, *See also* positive discrimination strategies; quotas
African Americans, 21–22, 24, 28, 29, 185–94, 187, 201–7
aggregative representation, 25–27
Alberdi, Cristina, 152
all-women shortlists, 13, 62, 89, 91, 95–98, 101–8, 113
Almond, Gabriel, 219
anti-essentialism, 19, 29–33, 49
Argentina, 89, 94
Ås, Berit, 166
Athens conference (1992), 60, 71, 75–76, 152, 153–54
at-large districts, 30
Australia, 94
Austria, 151, 156, 220

Badinter, Élisabeth, 63
Balladur, Édouard, 78
Bangladesh, 93
Barber case (1990), 149, 161n.15
Bard, Christine, 75
Basic Law (Germany), 8, 71, 126–27, 177–80

Beijing Platform, 158
Belgium, 147, 154, 220
Bergmann, Christine, 132
Blair, Tony, 13, 96, 103, 105, 107, 111, 113, 114, 116, 117, 118, 217
Brazil, 94
Brundtland, Gro Harlem, 167
Burke, Edmund, 6

Campbell, Angus, 218
Campbell, Tom, 204
Canadian Charter of Rights and Freedoms (1982), 71
Canadian Royal Commission on Electoral Reform, 31
Center for Voting and Democracy, 202, 207n.7
Charte des droits et des libertés (Quebec; 1975), 71
Charter of Fundamental Rights (EU), 7–8
Charter of Rome (1996), 71, 153–54
child care, 114–15, 129, 148, 149–50, 194, 196–97
Chirac, Jacques, 58, 61, 78, 81, 82, 83
Chombeau, Christiane, 75
Christiam Democratic Union (Germany), 99, 125, 133, 134, 135; appeal to women voter, 221, 225; gender voting gap analysis, 211, 214, 215, 216
Christianity, 116
Christian Social Union (Germany), 133, 214, 215, 216

citizenship, 41, 56, 123; social democratic ideal of, 169, 170; women's right to, 174–75
civil liberties: definition of, 41–42; fundamental, 177–80; German constitutional protections, 127, 129
civil rights movement (U.S.), 9, 187, 188
Common Market. *See* European Economic Community; European Union
communism: collapse in East Europe, 58, 152; view of "women's emancipation," 220
Communist parties, 78, 82, 94
communitarians, 64
conflict resolution, 43–54
Congressional Black Caucus (U.S.), 24, 204
conservatism. *See* Right
Conservative Party (G.B.), 98, 101, 105, 106, 115–16; appeal for women voters, 221; gender voting gap analysis, 211, 212, 213, 216
Constitution, French, 8, 10, 55, 62–65, 69, 70, 72, 82–83, 165
Constitution, German. *See* Basic Law
contraceptives, 56, 57, 79, 195
Council of Europe, 58–59; "Equality and Democracy" conference, 155
Council of Ministers, 145–46, 148, 151
Craig *v.* Boren (1976), 189, 189n.9
Cresson, Édith, 76, 159

Dahlerup, Drude, 170
Declaration de Paris (1999), 153–54
Declaration of Athens (1992), 60, 71, 152, 153–54
Declaration of Independence (1776; U.S.) U.S., 187
Déclaration universelle des droit de la femme (de Gouges), 74
Defrenne, Gabrielle, 147, 148
Defrenne I and II cases, 147, 148, 149, 161n.11
de Gaulle, Charles, 220

Délégation aux droits des femmes et à l'égalitéentre les hommes et les femmes (1999), 69–70
deliberative representation, 20–25, 26–27, 59
Delors, Jacques, 151
Democratic Party (U.S.), 117, 217
Denmark, 126, 148, 151, 153, 156, 172; political party internal quotas, 168; women's movement, 170
descriptive representation, 19–33, 196; bias patterns in, 27–29; criticism of, 206–7; definition of, 205; essentialist pitfalls in, 29–33; substantive proportional, 205–6
Diamantopoulou, Anna, 159
difference: discursive dangers of, 174–75; egalitarian feminist arguments against, 62; equality vs., 171; German cultural outlook and, 127, 131; parity supporters and, 80, 172; political process and, 48–49; problems of legislated parity in face of, 53–54; representation claims and, 5–16, 62, 107, 171, 173–75
discrimination: American racial, 22, 185–94; European Union prohibitions, 8, 131; problems in gender remedies, 53–54; statistical vs. social, 46–47, *See also* equality mandates; positive discrimination strategies; reverse discrimination
division of labor, 53–54, 123, 129–30, 136; EU directives, 149; male dependence on, 193–94, 196
Durand, Marguerite, 74

EEC. *See* European Economic Community
electoral systems: cumulative, 30, 202; mixed, 204–5; multimember, 94, 202, 203, 204; proportional, 4, 6, 10, 25–27, 30–33, 69–70, 75,

81–82, 94–98, 136, 201–6; single-member, 201–4
Equality Law (Norway; 1978), 167, 168
equality mandates: egalitarian vs. difference feminists on, 62, 80; European, 9, 10, 11, 60, 63, 70–71; European Court of Justice and, 131–32; French Left belief in, 64 (*see also* French parity movement); German Basic Law, 126–31, 177–80; parity as, 60; short-term vs. longer-term effects, 210; Third Way opportunity commitment vs., 114–15; voluntary vs. constitutional, 10, *See also* gender equality; parity
Equal Opportunities Unit (EC), 71, 148
equal opportunity, 71, 131, 145, 148, 151, 158–59
Equal Opportunity Law (Germany; 1990, 1994), 131, 132
equal pay for equal work, 57, 59, 118, 119, 131, 143, 145–50, 156, 157
equal rights: British feminist "old left" defenders and, 112; French historical feminist claims, 74–75; three types of, 41–43; in U.S. history, 187–89, *See also* gender equality; civil liberties
Equal Rights Amendment (ERA, U.S.), 9, 15, 71, 188
Eritrea, 93
Esping-Andersen, Gfsta, 130
essentialism, 19, 29–33, 49, 62
European Commission, 8, 59, 147, 149, 159, 160; Athens conference, 60, 71, 75–76, 152; Equal Opportunities Unit, 71, 145, 148; gender parity campaign, 150, 152–55; Sullerot report, 147–48
European Court of Justice, 8, 10, 14, 126, 131–32, 177, 178, 179–80; Barber case (1990), 149; Defrenne I and II cases, 147, 148, 149, 161n.11; Kalanke Case, 132, 149, 162n.31, 180, 181n.7; Marschall case, 132, 149, 180, 181n.7; women's inclusion in German army ruling, 132, 139n.11
European Economic Community, 143, 146, 147, 148, 156, *See also* European Commision
European Network of Women in Decision-Making, 71
European Parliament, 76, 148, 149, 160; women commissioners' agendas, 159; women's increased representation, 153; Women's Rights Committee, 151
European Program (1991–1996), 152
European Union, 116, 152, 168; Charter of Fundamental Rights, 7–8; Equal Treatment Directive, 180; report on equality, 132; women's policy development, 143–60, *See also under* gender equality
European Women's Lobby, 151, 157

Fabian Pamphlet, 112, 114, 119
family-friendly policies, 112–16, 221; as appeal to women voters, 221; egalitarian responsibility-sharing and, 195
family law, 56; German reforms, 128–31, 137
family wage. *See* male bread-winner model
Federal Constitutional Court (Germany), 13, 14–15, 126, 177, 178
feminism: as ahead of popular opinion, 118; anti-quota arguments, 59–60, 137; British advocacy groups, 103; difference, 5–6; difference vs. egalitarian, 62; essentialism in, 29; in France, 55, 57, 58, 59, 72, 74–75, 77; in Germany, 128, 131, 132, 135, 137,

220, 225; liberal democracies and, 4–5; New Labor "Worcester Woman" vs., 116–17; New Labour politics and, 111–20; in Scandinavia, 165–67, 169–72; second wave, 148, 165; turn toward parity by, 13; in United States, 188
Finland, 126, 151, 156, 168
Finnbogadottir, Vigdis, 156
flex-work schedules, 148, 195
Fourth Community Action Program for Equal Opportunities for Men and Women (1996–2000), 158
Fraisse, Geneviève, 70, 71, 73–74, 81
France, 13, 55–65, 89, 153, 156, 217; "exceptionalism," 73–76, 85–86n.11; historical equality claims, 55–56, 60, 74–75; late date of woman suffrage, 17n.11, 220, 224; parity movement. *See* French parity movement; political modernization, 81–84; politics, 13, 58–64, 71–84; textile industry equal pay compliance, 146, 147; women cabinet appointees, 78–79; women in legislative seats, 82, 125, 224; women's current autonomy, 56–57; women voters' party preferences, 220
Free Democratic Party (Germany), 133, 134; gender voting gap analysis, 211, 214, 215, 216
French parity movement, 4, 15, 55–65, 69–84, 163n.34; as affecting all parties, 226; argument for, 32, 62, 173; background, 55–58; birth of, 58–62, 154; classic work of, 73–74; constitutional mandate, 8, 10, 55, 62–65, 69–70, 72, 82–83, 165; critics of, 9, 32, 62–64, 65, 69–71; definition of parity, 80–81; enacted legislation, 64–65; limited ambitions of, 71–84; Norwegian aims vs., 173

French Revolution, 5–6, 62, 73–74

Gaitskell, Hugh, 221
Gambetta, Léon, 64
Gaspard, Françoise, 10, 15, 55–65, 70, 81, 173, 174–75
gender, 28–29, 40; French social relationship changes, 57–58; German traditional outlook, 123–24, 125, 128–29, 136, 220–21; male vs. female boundary crossing, 40; Norwegian concept transformation, 171–72; rights access, 41–42, 45–54; studies of voter-preference gap, 218–24; unity of interests fallacy, 49; value divergence and, 223; vote structuration and, 210–18; women's conservative voting bias, 209–26
gender differences. *See* difference
gender equality: British family policy and, 116; debate on difference vs., 171; as EU objective, 7–8, 9, 10, 14, 59–60, 70–71, 143, 148–60; human rights approach to, 145; liberalism's failure to achieve, 10–11; mainstreaming of, 145, 156, 157–58; male reasons to resist, 93–94, 193–97; parity as compatibile with, 60, 144; policy options, 91–93; Treaty of Amsterdam upgrading, 143, 145, 156–57, 159–60; women's gains in three categories of rights, 41, *See also specific countries*
gender impact statements, 9
gender neutrality, 10, 11, 13, 167, 210; vs. gender-specific language, 13
Germany, 123–38, 177–80, 224; affirmative action plan, 13, 71, 127, 132, 134–38, 177–80; competition for women voters, 135; gender voting gap analysis, 211, 214, 215, 216–17; law and

equal rights, 126–32 (*see also* Basic Law); patriarchal tradition in, 123–24, 125, 128–29, 136, 220–21; political party quotas, 94, 98, 135–38, 51; proactive equality provisions, 8, 10, 15, 95; women in government, 126, 135–38; women in legislative seats, 124, 125, 128, 135–38
glass ceiling, 151
Gouges, Olympe de, 62, 74
Gradin, Anita, 159, 161n.5
Great Britain, 89–108, 148, 153; all-women short lists, 13, 62, 89, 91, 95–98, 101–8, 113; consequences of gender quotas, 103–6; gender equality moves, 8, 10, 125; gender voting gap analysis, 211, 212, 213, 216, 217; Third Way politics, 13, 111–20; women in government posts, 96, 105, 113; women in legislative seats, 91, 102, 103–6, 125
Greater London Assembly, 96, 107
Greece, 60, 89, 220
Green Party (Germany), 78, 82, 98, 135; first quotas introduced by, 134; strict gender parity in, 51, 77
group rights, 46–47
Guigou, Elisabeth, 74
Guinier, Lani, 3–4, 204

Haider, Jörg, 163n.41
Hernes, Helga, 169
Herstal equal pay strike, 147
House of Commons (G.B.), 91, 96, 105, 106–7, 113, 119
House of Representatives (U.S.)., 11, 201, 203–4
Hubert, Agnés, 15
human rights, 145

Iceland, 168
identity politics, 195
incumbency, 12, 60–61
India, 89, 93, 94

International Convention on the Elimination of Discrimination Against Women (1979), 65
Ireland, 148
Israel, 204
Italy, 98–99, 153, 154, 204–5, 217, 220

Japan, 89, 98
Jonasdottir, Anna, 173–74
Jospin, Lionel, 13, 61–62, 63, 72, 81–83
Juppé, Alain, 78–79

Kalanke case (1995), 132, 149, 162n.31, 180, 181n.6
Kinnock, Neil, 112
Kohl, Helmut, 125, 225
Kolstad, Eva, 167

labor law: Germany, 131–32, 179; protective of women, 179, *See also* equal pay for equal work
labor market: British women participants, 112, 125; EU gender equality measures, 143–60; French women participants, 56, 57, 58; German women participants, 129, 130; national differences, 53; preferential hiring rulings, 132, 149, 180–81; prowomen measures, 195; Scandinavian women participants, 161n.8; and women's voting preferences, 222, 223, *See also* division of labor
Labour Party (G.B.), 15, 82; all-women shortlists, 13, 62, 89, 95, 102–8, 113; appeal for women voter support, 221; gender voting gap analysis, 211, 212, 213, 216, 217; landslide victory, 95–96, 103, 105; male insider elite, 118–19; National Executive Council, 101–2; quota acceptance in, 96–98, 106, 113; Third Way, 13,

111–20; twinned constituencies, 96, 107, 113
Labour Party (Norway), 94, 167
Labour Women's Network, 103
Leber, Annedore, 220–21
Leclerc, Christine, 85–86n.11
Left: equality ideology, 64, 112; and French women's representation, 59, 62, 72; new agenda, 12–14, 15, 62, 72 (*see also* Third Way); and openness to German equity, 135, 137; and "woman question," 220; women voters seen as benefiting, 209–10, 216, 217, 222, 225, *See also specific parties*
Le Gall, Anne, 15
Liberal Democrats (G.B.), 98, 105–6
liberalism: "crisis of representation" and, 80; demands for representative quotas and, 4; parity's compatibility with, 10–11; representation principles of, 173; three families of rights, 41–43, *See also* neoliberalism
Liberal Party (Norway), 167
Limbach, Jutta, 14–15, 177–80
list voting. *See* party lists

Maastricht Treaty, 116, 149, 151
male bread-winner model, 123, 128, 129, 130, 210, 220, 221, 222, 223
Manifesto for Parity (1996), 76
Manifesto of 577 (1993), 76
Mansbridge, Jane, 12, 15, 19–33, 206
marital rape, 129
marriage: French rate decline, 57; German women's status in, 128–29, 136; spousal voting patterns, 219, *See also* male bread-winner model
Marschall case (1997), 132, 149, 180, 181n.7
Mattinson, Deborah, 119–20
Mégret, Catherine, 79
Merkel, Angela, 225

Mexico, 94
Mill, John Stuart, 6, 7, 11
Miller, Warren E., 218
Ministry of Women (G.B.), 107
minority group representation, 94, 201–7
Mitterrand, François, 72
motherhood: French patterns, 56, 57; German patterns, 127, 129, 130–31, 136; woman's total lifespan and, 148, *See also* childcare
Mowlam, Mo, 105
multimember districts, 94, 202, 203, 204
Muse de la Raison. La démocratie exclusive et la différence des sexes (Fraisse), 73–74

National Assembly (France), 15, 61, 69–70, 81–82, 84, 85–86n.11, 224
neoliberalism, 72, 76, 84, 115–16, 222–23
Netherlands, 125, 126, 146
New Labour. *See* Third Way
New Opportunities for Women program, 149
New Zealand, 89, 94
Nordic countries. *See* Scandinavia
Norway, 89, 94, 95, 98, 126, 151, 156, 168; quota policies, 166–68, 170–73

Ohlin, Bertil/Ohlin report, 146
Okin, Susan Moller, 195

parental leave, 53, 116, 129, 149
parity, 5–15; alternatives to, 53–54; British women politicians and, 119–20; concept implications, 155, 173, 224–26; consequences of, 10–12; "crisis of representation" and, 77–78, 80; criticisms of, 11–12, 50–54, 62–64; in decision-making as well as politics, 71; definitional

differences, 80–81, 85n.2; as demonstratable redress, 65; distinctive "female" pattern and, 48; as equality, 60; in European context, 7–10, 65, 80–81, 144–60; 50 percent aim, 32, 33, 46, 76, 134, 166, 195; as illustrating fundamental injustice, 154–55; legal intervention effects, 39–54, 126–31; long-term neutralization of, 210; mainstreaming and, 155–59; as new politics symbol, 72, 112–13; partisan dynamics and, 210; partisan neutralization by, 226; in party lists, 61–62; prospects for, 224–26; as qualitative, 144, 150, 152–55; quota implications in, 10, 154; quotas dististinguished from, 60, 85n.2, 154; republicanism and, 76; in Swedish government, 126, 162n.31; U.S. feasibility issue, 195–98; women as "everywhere" argument, 32; women's arguments against, 50–51; women's objectives for, 155–56; women's support for, 50, 51–52, 60, *See also* French parity movement

party lists: all-women shortlists, 13, 62, 89, 91, 95, 102–8, 113; alternation by sex, 70, 78, 94; French parity plan, 61–62, 64–65, 69, 81–84; German women's position on, 136–37; legal quotas in, 94–95, 101–2; rank and order determination, 94; selective descriptive representation in, 30–31

Party of Democratic Socialism (Germany), 133, 134, 135

Phillips, Anne, 172, 205, 206

Pintasilgo, Maria de Lourdes, 156

political correctness, 116, 117

political elite, 5, 61; political tactics and, 47–48; women's exclusion from inner-circle of, 136, 137; young New Labour male insiders, 118–19

political parties. *See* Left; party lists; Right; *specific parties*

political rights: definition of, 42–43; French historical equality claims, 74–75

Polsky, Eliane Vogel, 147

Portugal, 152, 153, 154, 220

positive discrimination strategies, 89–108; European Court of Justice rulings, 149, 177, 179–80; lessons of British case study, 107–8, 113–14; opposed as compulsory quotas, 106; political culture and, 96–98; quotas targets and, 93; reasons for adopting, 95–96, *See also* affirmative action; parity; quotas

proportional representation, 4, 6, 10; aggregative, 25–27; essentialist implications of, 30–31; as favoring women, 136; French historical calls for, 75; French Socialist Party and, 81–82; party lists makeup, 30–31, 69–70, 94–98; underlying problem of, 205–6; U.S. arguments for and against, 201–5

quotas: ad hoc alternatives to, 31–33; affirmative action policies and, 91; consequences of, 103–6; criticized as essentializing, 30; distinctive "female" pattern and, 48; European Court of Justice rulings, 132, 149, 179–80; German, 132, 134–38, 178–79; as one-time term limit on male incumbents, 12; parity distinguished from, 60, 85n.2, 154; party culture and organization and, 96–103; in party lists, 94, 94–95, 101–2; political parties and, 4, 59–60, 62, 86, 95, 113; as positive discrimination strategies, 93–108; Scandinavian,

11, 12, 165–76; as social planning, 12–14; as step toward parity, 62, 78, 82; U.S. vs. European views on, 3–4, 8–9; women's criticisms of, 50–51, 60, 96–97, 137

radical feminism, 128, 170
Rawls, John, 225
redistricting, 30, 62
reparations, 7
representation, 19–33, 196; American women and African Americans, 203–7; areas of male displacement, 12; biases, 27–29; controversial aspects of, 172–75; "crisis" debate, 77–78, 80; of differences, 80; distinctive "female" profile in, 48–49; forms for specific gender rights, 46–54; liberal principles of, 173; mirror view of, 26, 27–29; parity and, 5–15, 65; quotas and, 3, 4–5, 31–33; surrogate vs. descriptive, 6, 22; universalist principles and, 49–50; women's de jure/de facto progress, 41; worldwide by women (1999), 108n.2, *See also* electoral systems
Republican Party (U.S.), 217
retirement age differences, 149
reverse discrimination, 127, 132, 178, 179–80; all-women shortlists as, 13, 103
Right: French politics, 58, 72; hostility to parity, 83; postwar gender voting gap supporting, 209–26, *See also specific parties*
Robinson, Mary, 155–56
Rocard, Michel, 78
Roe v. Wade (1973), 198n.7

Sapiro, Virginia, 28
Scandinavia, 8, 165–75, 217; feminist scholarship, 169–72; political networks and alliances, 170; political party quotas, 11, 12, 165–76; social democracy, 169–72; women in government, 123, 125, 126, 168; women in legislative seats, 11, 105, 125, 168; women's full labor-market participation, 161n.8, *See also specific countries*
Schröder, Gerhard, 125, 217
Scott, Joan Wallach, 5, 62
Scottish National and Plaid Cymru, 98, 106
Scottish Parliament, 96, 107, 113
Selbert, Elisabeth, 126
service sector, 148
Sevan-Schreiber, Claude, 15
Sex Discrimination Action (G.B.), 13, 103
Sineau, Mariette, 69
single-member districts, 201–4
Slovenia, 94
Smith, John, 103, 112
"soccer moms," 217
social democracy, 169–72
Social Democratic Party (Denmark), 168
Social Democratic Party (Germany), 51, 94, 98, 125, 133, 134, 135, 136, 137, 179, 220, 221; gender gap in voting pattern, 211, 214, 215, 216–17
Social Democratic Party (Sweden), 168
Socialist Left Party (Norway), 166, 167
Socialist Party (France), 72, 81–84; *Asemblée des femmes,* 78; gender parity lists, 61–62, 81, 82, 83–84; quotas, 59, 62, 78
Socialist People's Party (Denmark), 168
social rights: definition of, 42; Third Way policies and, 114–15; women's defense of, 223; women's gains in, 41, 53
South Africa, 89, 94
Spain, 152, 153, 155, 220

Stratigaki, Maria, 158
strict scrutiny, 19
student loan foregiveness, 31–32
substantive representation, 205
suffrage, 17n.11, 224; African American, 187, 206; American women, 188; conservative gender gap in, 209–26; feminism and, 118; French women's rights, 17n.11, 75, 220; as political right, 42; vs. yielding actual representation, 6, 61
Sullerot, Evelyne (Sullerot report), 147–48
Supreme Court, U.S., 189, 198nn.7, 9; Craig v. Boren (1976), 189, 189n.9; Roe v. Wade, 198n.7
surrogate representation, 22–23
Sweden, 98, 125, 151, 156, 172; parity in government, 126, 162n.31; political party internal quotas, 168
Switzerland, 17n.11, 220

Taiwan, 93, 94
Tanzania, 93
Thatcher, Margaret, 111, 115, 211
Third Action Program, 132, 151, 158
Third Way, 13, 111–20
"tic-tac" lists, 70, 78, 94
trade unions, 12, 103, 112, 147
transatlanticism, 9–10
Treaty of Amsterdam (1997), 7, 70–71, 154; Article 3 (2), 161n.7; four articles of, 157; gender equality benefits, 143, 145, 156–57, 159–60
Treaty of Maastricht, 116, 149, 151
Treaty of Rome (1957), 59; Article 119, 71, 143, 145–47, 148, 149
twinned constituencies, 96, 107, 113

Uganda, 93
unemployment, 131, 150
United States: affirmation action status, 4, 9–10, 15; deliberative representation, 22, 23, 24; descriptive representation, 28; electoral reform proposals, 201–7; equal rights language, 187; ERA failure, 9, 15, 71; paradoxical inequalities, 185–98; party quota unfeasibility, 101, 186, 195–98; racial vs. gender inequality comparison, 186–94; resistance to quotas, 4; voting behavior study, 217, 218–19; women national legislative seat-holders, 11
universalist principles, 49–50
utilitarianism, 173–74

Veil, Simone, 75–76, 80
Verba, Sidney, 219
Viennot, Éliane, 62, 75
Violence Against Women Act (1994; U.S.), 188, 195
virtual representation, 6
voting patterns, 210–18; values vs. interests in, 223
voting rights. *See* suffrage
Voting Rights Act (U.S.; 1965), 187

wage gap: Belgian women's strike, 147; in Britain, 119; in European Union, 150; in France, 57; in Germany, 130–31, 132, *See also* equal pay for equal work
welfare state, 130–31, 169–70, 224
welfare-to-work program, 114
Welsh Assembly, 96, 107, 113
winner-take-all rules, 201, 202
"Worcester Woman," profile of, 116–17
World Conference on Women (Beijing; 1995), 152, 158
World Conference on Women (Mexico; 1975), 148
Wulf-Matthis, Monica, 159

Young, Iris Marion, 172

GPSR Compliance
The European Union's (EU) General Product Safety Regulation (GPSR) is a set of rules that requires consumer products to be safe and our obligations to ensure this.

If you have any concerns about our products, you can contact us on

ProductSafety@springernature.com

In case Publisher is established outside the EU, the EU authorized representative is:

Springer Nature Customer Service Center GmbH
Europaplatz 3
69115 Heidelberg, Germany

www.ingramcontent.com/pod-product-compliance
Lightning Source LLC
LaVergne TN
LVHW011813060526
838200LV00053B/3764